MACMILLAN/McGRAW-HILL
Language Arts

Contributor

Time Magazine

Macmillan
McGraw-Hill

Published by Macmillan/McGraw-Hill, of McGraw-Hill Education, a division of The McGraw-Hill Companies, Inc., Two Penn Plaza, New York, New York 10121.

Printed in the United States of America

ISBN 0-02-245558-2/2

5 6 7 8 9 (RMN) 13 12 11 10

MACMILLAN/McGRAW-HILL
Language Arts

AUTHORS

Jan E. Hasbrouck

Donna Lubcker

Sharon O'Neal

William H. Teale

Josefina V. Tinajero

Karen D. Wood

Macmillan
McGraw-Hill

Sentences and Personal Narrative

Theme: A New Day

 **Grammar**  *Spiral Review Every Day*

Sentences

Build Skills

McGraw-Hill School Division

Writing

Personal Narrative

Review and Assess

Nouns and Descriptive Writing

Theme: *Person to Person*

 **Grammar**  *Spiral Review Every Day*

Nouns

Build Skills

McGraw-Hill School Division

UNIT 3

Verbs and Explanatory Writing

Theme: *Share with Us*

 Grammar *Spiral Review Every Day*

Verbs

Build Skills

McGraw-Hill School Division

Writing

Explanatory Writing

Review and Assess

TIME
FOR KIDS

UNIT **4**

Verbs and Writing That Compares

Theme: *What Do You Know?*

Grammar  Spiral Review Every Day

Verbs

Build Skills

McGraw-Hill School Division

x

Writing

Writing That Compares

Writing Process

Present Your Writing That Compares

Review and Assess

UNIT 5

Pronouns and Expository Writing

Theme: *Ready...Plan...Go!*

Grammar Spiral Review Every Day

McGraw-Hill School Division

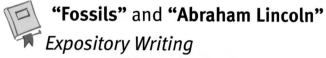

Adjectives, Adverbs, and Writing a Story

Theme: New Directions

McGraw-Hill School Division

Writing

A Story

Review and Assess

Sentences and Personal Narrative

In this unit you will learn about sentences. You will also learn how to write a story about you.

Social Studies Link *People enjoy telling stories about their lives. This writer is telling us about her childhood.*

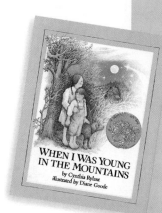

When I was young in the mountains, we pumped pails of water from the well at the bottom of the hill, and heated the water to fill round tin tubs for our baths.

from ***When I Was Young in the Mountains***
by Cynthia Rylant

Thinking Like a Writer

Personal Narrative A personal narrative tells a story about the writer's own life.

- How do you think Cynthia Rylant feels about her childhood?

Sentences Every sentence has a subject that tells who or what does something.

QUICK WRITE Write the words that tell who does something in each sentence.

1

Thinking Like a Writer

Personal Narrative After you read the passage on page 1, write what you think Cynthia Rylant feels about her childhood.

_____

_____

_____

_____

_____

_____

_____

QUICK WRITE Write the words that tell who does something in each sentence in the passage.

_____

_____

_____

_____

_____

Sentences

---RULES---

- A sentence tells a complete thought.

  My new puppy jumped out of the box.

- A group of words that does not tell a complete thought is not a sentence.

  My new puppy.

- A sentence names the person or thing you are talking about. It also tells what happened.

  My new puppy | jumped out of the box.

  ↑   ↑

  what   what happened

THINK AND WRITE

Sentences
What makes a group of words a sentence? Write the answer in your journal.

Guided Practice

Tell if each group of words is a sentence.

1. We see four kittens. _____

2. Two little rabbits. _____

3. My sister wants a turtle. _____

4. Some goldfish. _____

5. The snake is sleeping. _____

2

Handbook
page 432

Extra
Practice
page 58

REVIEW THE RULES

- A sentence tells a complete thought.

- A group of words that does not tell a complete thought is not a sentence.

More Practice

A. Write only the complete sentences.

6. The puppy licks my face.

7. Maria likes the kitten.

8. A loud squawk.

9. Inside the cage.

10. Alex names the bird Tweet.

B. Spiral Review **Add words to each group to make a complete sentence. Write the sentences.**

11. The white mice. _____ .

12. The tan puppy. _____ .

13. The hamster. _____ .

14. The little kittens. _____ .

15. The big dog. _____ .

Writing Activity Sentences

Write three sentences about a pet you would like.

APPLY GRAMMAR: Is each sentence complete?

Science Link

Statements and Questions

RULES

- Every sentence begins with a capital letter.
- A **statement** is a sentence that tells something. It ends with a period.

    The girls are going to school.

- A **question** is a sentence that asks something. It ends with a question mark.

    Are the girls going to school?

- What kind of sentence is each?

    We live in the city. ⟶ *statement*
    Do you live in the city? ⟶ *question*

THINK AND WRITE

Sentences
In your journal write how a statement and a question are different.

Guided Practice

Read each sentence. Tell if it is a statement or a question.

1. Where is your new neighborhood? _____

2. We moved to the city. _____

3. Do you live in a house? _____

4. I live in an apartment. _____

5. I hope I meet new friends. _____

REVIEW THE RULES

- A **statement** is a sentence that tells something. It ends with a period.

- A **question** is a sentence that asks something. It ends with a question mark.

More Practice

A. Underline each statement. Circle each question.

6. Why did your family move?

7. Mom got a new job.

8. Will you visit my new neighborhood?

9. A nice family lives next door.

10. I made two new friends.

B. Spiral Review Circle each complete sentence.

11. Can we visit next week?

12. My dad will drive us.

13. Your new address.

14. We like the city.

15. Are the buildings tall?

Handbook
page 432

Extra Practice
page 59

Writing Activity   Note

Write a friend a note about a building you saw.

APPLY GRAMMAR: Circle each end mark.

Commands and Exclamations

RULES

- A **command** is a sentence that tells someone to do something. A command ends with a period.

    Come to the zoo with us.

- An **exclamation** is a sentence that shows strong feeling. An exclamation ends with an exclamation mark.

    What a funny monkey I saw!

- What kind of sentence is each?

    Read the sign. ⟶ *command*
    That is a huge sign! ⟶ *exclamation*

**THINK
AND WRITE**

Sentences
How is a command different from an exclamation? Write the answer in your journal.

Guided Practice

Tell if each sentence is a command or an exclamation.

1. Bring your camera along. _____

2. I am so excited! _____

3. Let me take your picture. _____

4. How big that elephant is! _____

5. Look for the baby gorilla. _____

6

- A **command** tells someone to do something.

- An **exclamation** shows strong feeling.

More Practice

A. Write C after each command. Write E after each exclamation.

6. Look at my map. _____

7. Help me find the lions. _____

8. What a long snake! _____

9. Take a picture of the tiger. _____

10. This zoo is great! _____

Handbook
page 432

Extra Practice page 60

B. Spiral Review Add the correct end mark to each sentence. Then write S for statement, Q for question, C for command, or E for exclamation.

11. The seals like to swim____ _____

12. Is the giraffe tall____ _____

13. Come see the brown bear____ _____

14. Where is the kangaroo____ _____

15. How big the zoo is____ _____

Writing Activity   Message

Write a message to a zoo worker.
APPLY GRAMMAR: Use an exclamation mark.

Sentence Punctuation

RULES

- • Begin every sentence with a capital letter.

- • A statement ends with a period.

- • A question ends with a question mark.

- • A command ends with a period.

- • An exclamation ends with an exclamation mark.

Handbook
pages 432, 451

Extra
Practice
page 61

Practice

A. **Begin and end each sentence correctly.**

1. tell me about the party_____

2. what a great party it was_____

3. we had so much fun_____

4. did you see the gifts_____

5. tara gave Steve a book_____

B. Spiral Review **Write each sentence correctly on a piece of paper. Then write** *statement, question, command,* **or** *exclamation.*

6. we played some party games _____

7. how many games do you know _____

8. teach me a new game _____

9. there were so many balloons _____

10. did you get a balloon _____

Sentences
Does reading
a sentence out
loud help you
choose the right
end mark? Write
your answer in
your journal.

REVIEW

Sentences

REVIEW THE RULES

- A sentence tells a complete thought.
  A sentence always begins with a capital letter.

- A statement tells something.

- A question asks something.

- A command tells or asks someone to do something.

- An exclamation shows strong feeling.

QUICK WRITE

Sentences

Does using different kinds of sentences help your writing? How? Write your ideas.

Practice

A. **Write what kind of sentence each group of words is.**

1. My family planted a garden. _____

2. What fun we all had! _____

3. How do you plant seeds? _____

4. Come and see our sunflowers. _____

5. Take a walk in our garden. _____

B. **Challenge** **Rewrite the paragraph using the correct end marks.**

6.–10. A garden needs care? There are seeds to plant. What seeds do you have! help us pull out weeds. What a hard job.

_____

_____

_____

Subjects in Sentences

RULES

- The subject of a sentence tells who or what does something.

  The jet sits on the runway.

- Look at who this sentence is telling about.

  <u>*Gail*</u> *goes to the airport.*

  ↑

  subject

THINK AND WRITE

Sentences

Why is the subject an important part of a sentence? Write the answer in your journal.

Guided Practice

Name the subject in each sentence.

1. Many people fill the airport. _____

2. The airport is a busy place. _____

3. Airplanes are coming and going. _____

4. Gail sees a big jet. _____

5. A pilot walks to the plane. _____

Handbook
page 433

Extra Practice
page 62

REVIEW THE RULES

• The **subject** of a sentence tells who or what does something.

More Practice

A. **Underline the subject in each sentence.**

6. The airport is near the city.

7. Mom drives to the airport.

8. A man checks our tickets.

9. The plane will take off soon.

10. My whole family likes to fly.

B. **Spiral Review** **Underline each complete sentence. Circle each subject.**

11. That airplane is huge!

12. Workers check the plane.

13. One worker looks at the wings.

14. The big suitcases.

15. Many people fly on the jet.

Writing Activity   A Journal Entry

Write a journal entry about a place you would like to visit. Remember to begin each sentence in a different way.
APPLY GRAMMAR: Underline each subject.

Predicates in Sentences

RULES

- The **predicate** in a sentence tells what the subject does or what it is.

   The park is large.

- What do the people do in this sentence?

   People jog in the park.

   ↑
   predicate

Guided Practice

Name the predicate in each sentence.

1. The park is nice and clean.

_____

2. People use the park each day.

_____

3. Emma walks her dog.

_____

4. Two children play ball.

_____

5. The park closes at night.

_____

THINK AND WRITE

Sentences

Why do sentences need subjects and predicates? Write the answer in your journal.

• The **predicate** tells what the subject does or is.

More Practice

A. Underline the predicate in each sentence.

6. A child sits on the grass.

7. The park bench is full.

8. We run to the duck pond.

9. Ben feeds some birds.

10. Two squirrels run up a tree.

Handbook
page 433

Extra Practice
page 63

B. **Spiral Review** Circle the subject in each sentence. Underline the predicate.

11. Everyone likes the park.

12. Some children play tag.

13. Two boys fly kites.

14. A woman sells peanuts.

15. Many people ride their bikes.

McGraw-Hill School Division

Writing Activity **A Poem**

Write a poem about a park or the outdoors.
APPLY GRAMMAR: Underline each predicate.

Combining Sentences

— RULES —

- You can put two sentences together if they have the same predicate.

- Use the word *and* to join the sentences.

  Rosa ran fast. Mike ran fast.

  Rosa and Mike ran fast.

- See which words in the two sentences are the same. See which words can be put together with *and*.

  Rosa saw a parade.   Mike saw a parade.

  Rosa and Mike saw a parade.

THINK AND WRITE

Sentences
Why do writers combine sentences? Write the answer in your journal.

Guided Practice

Use *and* to join each pair of sentences.

1. Boys marched. Girls marched.

2. Horns blew. Whistles blew.

3. Dave clapped. Lisa clapped.

4. Flags flew. Banners flew.

5. Drums played. Flutes played.

REVIEW THE RULES

- You can join two sentences if they have the same predicate.

- Use the word *and* to join the sentences.

More Practice

A. Use the word *and* to join each pair of sentences. Write the new sentence on a piece of paper.

6. Elephants marched. Horses marched.

7. Men sang. Women sang.

8. Clowns passed by. Floats passed by.

9. Fran laughed. Jake laughed.

10. Sally cheered. Roger cheered.

B. **Spiral Review** Add the correct end mark to each sentence. Circle the subject.

11. A clown sang and danced____

12. Dad and I took pictures____

13. I never laughed so hard before____

14. We clapped and shouted____

15. That clown was so funny____

Handbook
page 433

Extra
Practice
page 64

Writing Activity A Paragraph

Write a paragraph about a class event.
APPLY GRAMMAR: Use *and* to join sentences.

McGraw-Hill School Division

Commas in a Series

Grammar

RULES

• Use **commas** to separate three or more words in a series or group.

Billy, Lee, and I visited the farm.

Practice

A. Add commas where they belong in each group of words.

1. cat dog and pony

2. Lucy Sam and Roy

3. horses cows and goats

4. hens chicks and roosters

5. house barn and shed

B. **Spiral Review** Circle the subject in each sentence. Underline the predicate.

6. The cows and sheep eat grass.

7. The farmer picks lots of corn.

8. The baskets are really full!

9. Tom, Len, and I rake the hay.

10. The farm is a great place!

Handbook
page 452

Extra Practice
page 65

THiNK AND WRITE

Sentences
How do commas in a series help make the sentence clear? Write your answer.

Sentences

REVIEW THE **RULES**

- The subject of a sentence tells who or what does something.

- The predicate tells what the subject does or is.

- Use and to join two sentences that have the same predicate.

- Use commas to separate words in a series.

Handbook
page 433

Sentences
What do you know about sentences? Write your ideas in your journal.

Practice

A. **Circle each subject. Underline each predicate. Add commas to separate words in a series.**

1. Uncle Ty made sandwiches.

2. Aunt Lu cut up a watermelon.

3. Ashley mixed the lemonade.

4. Bees ants and flies may come, too!

5. Sam Al and Jo got a basket.

B. **Challenge** **Use and to combine each pair of sentences. Write the new sentence on a piece of paper.**

6. Todd brought fruit. Lee brought fruit.

7. Adam ate salad. Mia ate salad.

8. Mom cooked outside. Dad cooked outside.

9. Grandma had fun. Grandpa had fun.

10. Sam carried the bag. Al carried the bag.

McGraw-Hill School Division

Common Errors with Incomplete Sentences

A sentence must tell a complete thought. Sometimes writers make a mistake.

Common Errors	Examples	Corrected Sentences
The sentence is missing a predicate.	My turtle.	My turtle lives in a pond.
The sentence is missing a subject.	Swam away.	The ducks swam away.

REVIEW THE RULES

SENTENCES

- Every sentence has a subject and a predicate.

- Remember, every sentence begins with a capital letter and ends with a punctuation mark.

THINK AND WRITE

Sentences
How do you know if a sentence is not complete? Write the answer in your journal.

Practice

Circle each group of words that is a complete sentence.

1. The children.

2. We saw two goats

3. Ran quickly.

4. The goats ate grass.

5. My dog barked at them.

Troubleshooter, pages 420–421

Mechanics and Spelling

Directions

Read the paragraph and decide which type of mistake appears in each underlined part. Choose the correct answer.

Sample

See if every sentence begins with a capital letter.

Is this a statement or a question? Make sure the end mark is correct.

Mama bird sat on the eggs in the nest. <u>she</u>
(1)
<u>kept them very warm</u>. Soon the eggs began to
crack. <u>Out popped baby birds</u>? They opened
(2)
their mouths wide. <u>Mama bird heard their crys</u>.
(3)
Baby birds are very hungry!

Check all the underlined words for mistakes in spelling.

1 ○ Spelling
   ○ Capitalization
   ○ Punctuation

2 ○ Spelling
   ○ Capitalization
   ○ Punctuation

3 ○ Spelling
   ○ Capitalization
   ○ Punctuation

Test Tip
Read the underlined parts slowly and carefully.

TIME Writer's Notebook
FOR KIDS

RESEARCH

RESEARCH When I do research and read a word I don't know, I look it up in the **dictionary**. The dictionary helps me explain new words to my readers. The more research I do, the more words I learn. In this photo essay, I wrote about Michael Jordan's decision to retire. Do you know what <u>retire</u> means?

COMPOSITION SKILLS

WRITING WELL When I write, I use **paragraphs** to help put together my thoughts. In this photo essay, each paragraph tells something different about Michael Jordan.

VOCABULARY SKILLS

USING WORDS Words like <u>first</u>, <u>middle</u>, and <u>last</u> are **time-order words**. They tell about the order in which things happen. Time-order words help my readers keep track of the events I'm writing about.

Read Now!

Find out more about Michael Jordan. As you read, write down the important information in each paragraph.

TIME FOR KIDS Writer's Notebook

COMPOSITION SKILLS

WRITING WELL Write down the important information in each paragraph of the photo essay about Michael Jordan.

_____

_____

_____

_____

_____

_____

_____

_____

_____

_____

_____

_____

Michael Jordan

A great athlete says good-bye to basketball.

Game Over!

Michael Jordan is one of the greatest basketball players of all time. Jordan led his team, the Chicago Bulls, to six world championships. He was one of the highest scorers in basketball history.

In 1993, Jordan first decided to retire. But he changed his mind and returned to the Bulls. Then in 1999, Jordan quit a second time. He said, "I'm just going to enjoy life. I'm going to do some of the things I've never done before."

What's next for Jordan? He wants to spend time with his family. He wants to watch his kids play one-on-one basketball.

Everyone knows Michael Jordan's big smile.

inter NET CONNECTION Go to www.mhschool.com/language-arts for more information on the topic.

John Biever/Sports Illustrated

Jordan won two gold medals at the Olympic Games. He won the first in 1984. He won the second in 1992.

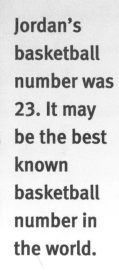

Jordan's basketball number was 23. It may be the best known basketball number in the world.

Write Now!

Everyone is good at something. Michael Jordan was very good at playing basketball. Think about something that you are good at. Write to tell about it.

The Dictionary

A **dictionary** is a book that tells what words mean. The words the dictionary tells about are called **entry words**. All the entry words are in ABC order.

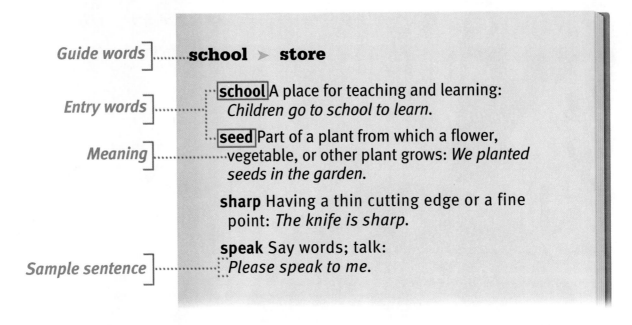

Guide words .... **school** ▷ **store**

Entry words ....
school A place for teaching and learning: *Children go to school to learn.*

Meaning ....
seed Part of a plant from which a flower, vegetable, or other plant grows: *We planted seeds in the garden.*

sharp Having a thin cutting edge or a fine point: *The knife is sharp.*

speak Say words; talk: *Please speak to me.*

Sample sentence ....

Each dictionary page has two **guide words** at the top. The guide word on the *left* tells what the first word on the page is. The guide word on the *right* tells the last word on the page.

Some words have a **sample sentence**. It shows how the word is used.

Practice

A. **Use the dictionary page on page 24 to answer. Write your answers on a piece of paper.**

1. Name the two guide words on the page.

2. Which guide word shows the *first* word?

3. Which guide word shows the *last* word?

4. What does the word *school* mean?

5. Which word comes after the word *seed*?

B. **Complete each sentence with a word or words from the box.**

> dictionary   guide word   sample sentence
>
> entry words   ABC order

6. The _____ tells the meanings of many words.

7. The dictionary gives meanings for the _____ .

8. The entry words are listed in _____ .

9. The first _____ tells the first entry word on the page.

10. The _____ shows how to use the entry word.

inter NET
CONNECTION

Go to
www.mhschool.
com/language-arts

for more information on using the dictionary.

Writing Activity Use a Dictionary

Use the dictionary on pages 480–495 to write the guide words on the same page as *butterfly*. Write the meaning of *butterfly*.

Vocabulary: Time-Order Words

DEFINITION

Time-order words show the order in which things happen.

Time-Order Words and Phrases		
first	after	yesterday
next	before	today
then	now	tomorrow
finally	soon	long ago

Look at the blue time-order words and phrases in this paragraph.

Today our class took a trip to the zoo. *First* we looked at animals in the reptile house. *Next* we went outside to see the bears and big cats. *Then* we stopped to eat lunch. *After* lunch, we went into the bird house. *Last of all*, we stopped at the gift shop.

McGraw-Hill School Division

Practice

A. **Circle time-order words in each sentence.**

1. Yesterday we talked about the zoo.

2. Today we visited the zoo.

3. We had questions before our trip.

4. After our trip, we knew the answers.

5. We will write about the trip tomorrow.

B. **Write *1*, *2*, *3*, *4*, and *5* to show the correct order.**

6. Finally we drove to the zoo. _____

7. Next we sat down in our seats. _____

8. Then the driver started the bus. _____

9. First we got on the bus. _____

10. Soon the driver climbed in. _____

C. **Grammar Link** **Complete each sentence with a word from the box. Use capital letters correctly.**

long ago	then	now	soon	last month

11. _____ zoo animals lived in cages.

12. _____ they live in open spaces.

13. _____ the zoo added more animals.

14. I want to go to the zoo _____.

15. _____ I can see the new panda.

Writing Activity   Sentences

Write about a school event. Use time-order words.
APPLY GRAMMAR: Be sure to use correct punctuation.

Composition: Paragraphs

Good writers put their ideas in paragraphs to make their writing clearer.

> **GUIDELINES**
>
> - A **paragraph** is a group of sentences that all tell about **one idea.**
>
> - The first sentence of a paragraph is indented or moved in.

Look at how the first sentence is indented in this paragraph. Notice that all the sentences tell about one idea.

THINK AND WRITE

Paragraphs
How does putting writing in paragraphs make it easier to understand?

The paragraph is indented.

All the sentences tell about watching a major league ball game.

Watching a major league ball game is a lot of fun. Dad took me to one last week. First, we found our seats in the stadium. Then the game began. We cheered as our team came out on the field. Later, Dad bought us peanuts to eat. At the end of the game, I was very happy. Our team won!

McGraw-Hill School Division

Practice

A. **Write *yes* if the sentence belongs in a paragraph about soccer. Write *no* if it does not.**

1. We played soccer last week. _____

2. I scored a goal in the game. _____

3. Baseball is a lot of fun. _____

4. My team won the soccer game. _____

5. I bought a new baseball. _____

B. **Write a beginning sentence for a paragraph about each topic.**

6. My Favorite Game _____

_____

7. Fun on the Playground _____

_____

8. Sports on Television _____

_____

9. Famous Athletes _____

_____

10. Exercise Is Good for You _____

_____

C. **Grammar Link** **11.–15. Read each sentence you just wrote. Add another sentence that tells more about the topic.**

Writing Activity A Paragraph

Write a paragraph about a game you play with your friends. Indent the paragraph.

APPLY GRAMMAR: Make sure each sentence has a subject and predicate.

29

Better Sentences

Directions

Read the paragraph. Some parts are underlined. The underlined parts may be one of the following:

- Incomplete sentences
- Correctly written sentences that should be combined

Choose the best way to write each underlined part.

Check to see if two short sentences can be combined to make one sentence.

Look out for a group of words that does not tell a complete thought.

Sample

Dogs are not just pets. <u>Many dogs work</u>.
(1)
<u>Many dogs help people</u>. There are seeing-eye dogs who help people who are blind. There are dogs who pull sleds over ice and snow. Some dogs work on farms and help round up sheep. <u>Help catch criminals</u>. Dogs can be good workers
(2)
as well as special friends.

1 ○ Many dogs work many help people.

○ Many dogs and many people help.

○ Many dogs work and help people.

2 ○ Police dogs help catch criminals.

○ Help catch criminals for them.

○ Dogs to help catch criminals.

McGraw-Hill School Division

Vocabulary and Comprehension

Directions

Read the paragraph. Then read each question that follows the paragraph. Choose the best answer to each question.

Sample

I remember the day I learned to ride a bike. I was afraid of falling, but my big sister held onto me. She ran along beside me. I loved the wind against my face. I wanted to go faster. So I pushed my legs harder and forgot about my sister. The next thing I knew, I was riding all by myself! I was very proud. The only problem was that I didn't know how to stop. Underline{Finally}, I had to fall off the bike to make it stop. Ouch!

Some words help you understand the order of when things happen.

1 How did the writer feel about learning to ride a bike?

○ sad

○ bored

○ proud

2 The word <u>finally</u> in the story means—

○ in the end

○ at the start

○ before long

Seeing Like a Writer

Pictures can give you ideas for your writing. Pretend you are in one of these pictures. Look at the details. How would you feel? What would you say about your experience?

Carnival Time in Willow Bend by Jane Wooster Scott.

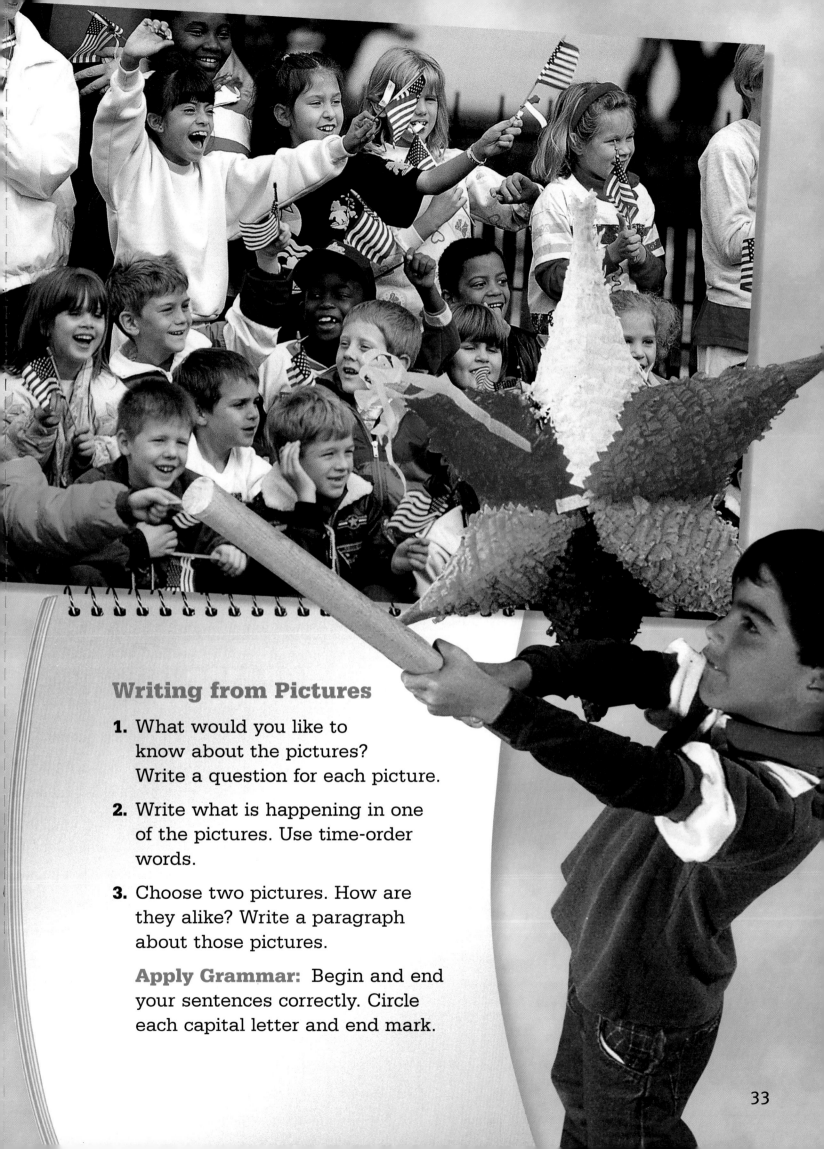

Writing from Pictures

1. What would you like to know about the pictures? Write a question for each picture.

2. Write what is happening in one of the pictures. Use time-order words.

3. Choose two pictures. How are they alike? Write a paragraph about those pictures.

Apply Grammar: Begin and end your sentences correctly. Circle each capital letter and end mark.

Personal Narrative

A personal narrative can be a story about you. When you write a personal narrative, you tell what you did and how you felt.

Learning from Writers

Read these personal narratives. Notice how the authors begin and end their stories.

THINK AND WRITE

Purpose
Why do you think these authors wrote these stories?

The Relatives Came

It was in the summer of the year when the relatives came. They came up from Virginia. They left when their grapes were nearly purple enough to pick, but not quite. The relatives stayed for weeks and weeks. They helped us tend the garden and they fixed any broken things they could find. They ate up all our strawberries and melons, then promised we could eat up all their grapes and peaches when we came to Virginia. But none of us thought about Virginia much. We were so busy hugging and eating and breathing together.

— Cynthia Rylant from *The Relatives Came*

The Skunk Family

Once there was a skunk family that lived near my house. At first, I thought they were cute. But one night as we were driving home, a skunk ran in front of our car.

A few nights later, my dad, my dog Jerome, and I were taking a walk. I saw a skunk. It sprayed Jerome. The smell was so bad that it made my eyes and nose burn. The next night the skunk sprayed Jerome again. Now I know the skunk family isn't cute at all.

— Chris Barnes

PRACTICE and APPLY

Thinking Like a Reader

1. How does the author of "The Relatives Came" feel about her relatives?

2. What events took place in "The Skunk Family"? When did they happen?

Thinking Like a Writer

3. What happens at the end of the first story?

4. What time-order words did you find in the second story?

5. **Reading Across Texts** Both personal narratives are about families. How are the two stories different?

Features of a Personal Narrative

DEFINITIONS AND FEATURES

A **personal narrative** tells about something that happened to you. A good personal narrative does these things:

▶ It tells a story from **personal experience.**

▶ It has a good **beginning** and **ending.**

▶ It uses **time-order words** to show that things happened in a certain order.

▶ Personal Experience

Reread "The Relatives Came" on page 34. Notice the words *our* and *we* in this sentence from the story. They tell us that it is about the author's own life.

> They ate up all our strawberries and melons, then promised we could eat up all their grapes and peaches when we came to Virginia.

▶ Good Beginning

See how the beginning of "The Relatives Came" catches our attention?

> It was in the summer of the year when the relatives came.

▶ Good Ending

"The Relatives Came" ends with these sentences. They tell us how the author felt. It is a good way to end the personal narrative.

> But none of us thought about Virginia much. We were so busy hugging and eating and breathing together.

▶ Time-Order Words

Time-order words help a reader understand the order in which things happen. What time-order word do you see in this sentence?

> They left when their grapes were nearly purple enough to pick, but not quite.

The author uses the time-order word *when*.

Features	Examples

PRACTICE and APPLY

Create a Personal Narrative Chart

1. List the features of a personal narrative.
2. Reread "The Skunk Family" on page 35.
3. Write how the author used each feature.

Writing PROCESS

Prewrite

When you write a personal narrative, you tell a true story about your life.

Purpose and Audience

The **purpose** of something is why you do it. The purpose of writing a personal narrative is to share something you did. The people who read your personal narrative are your **audience**.

Choose a Topic

Begin by **brainstorming.** Think of different things that have happened to you. Choose one. Then **explore ideas and list your ideas.**

THINK AND WRITE

Audience

How can you make your writing more interesting to others?

Here is how I explored my ideas.

A Picnic

got up early

drove to lake

sat under tree

ate lunch

played catch

nice to be with family

fed dog

McGraw-Hill School Division

Organize • Sequence

A personal narrative tells about things in order. You can use a chart to help organize your writing. You may not need all your ideas.

PREWRITE

DRAFT

REVISE

PROOFREAD

PUBLISH

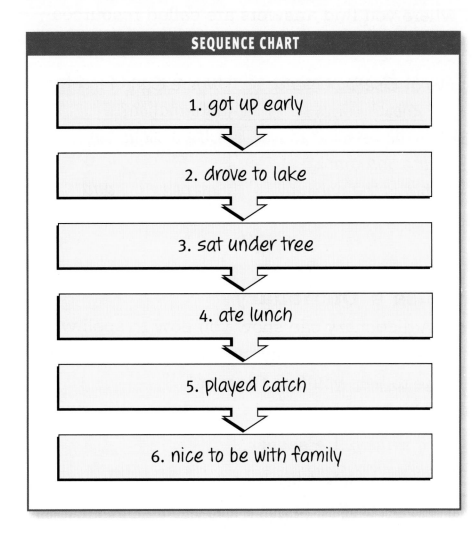

SEQUENCE CHART

1. got up early
2. drove to lake
3. sat under tree
4. ate lunch
5. played catch
6. nice to be with family

Checklist ✓
Prewriting

- ☐ Do you know your purpose and your audience?
- ☐ Did you choose a topic and explore it?
- ☐ Did you organize ideas in a chart?
- ☐ Do you need to do any research?

PRACTICE and APPLY

Plan Your Own Personal Narrative

1. Think about your purpose and audience.
2. Brainstorm ideas for a topic.
3. Choose a topic and explore ideas.
4. Organize your ideas.

Writing PROCESS

Prewrite • Research and Inquiry

▶ Writer's Resources

Do you need more information? You can do research to find it. First, make a list of questions. The books and other materials where you find answers are called resources.

What Else Do I Need to Know?	Where Can I Find the Information?
How do I spell what we ate and drank?	Use a dictionary.
What is the name of the lake?	Interview my dad.

▶ Use a Dictionary

A dictionary can show you how to spell words correctly. Use the guide words at the top of each page to help you find the word.

These are guide words

sandwich ▶ saucer

The first guide word is the first word on the page.

sandwich A sandwich is food made of two pieces of bread with something between them.

The second guide word is the last word on the page.

sandy Something sandy contains or looks like sand.

▶ Conduct an Interview

An interview is two people talking. One person asks questions and the other person answers. You can do an interview by phone, by e-mail, in a letter, or in person.

▶ Use Your Research

Put the new things you learned in your chart. This writer got more details from a dictionary and from interviewing her dad. How did her chart change?

Handbook
page 454

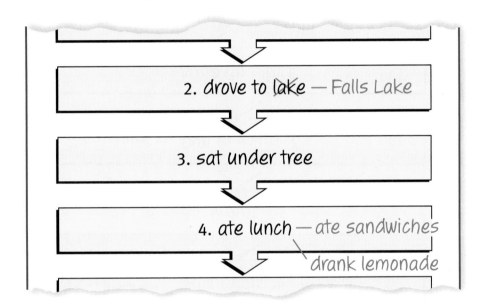

2. drove to lake — Falls Lake

3. sat under tree

4. ate lunch — ate sandwiches
drank lemonade

PRACTICE and APPLY

Review Your Plan

1. Look at your chart.

2. Make a list of questions you have.

3. Decide on resources that will help you.

4. Add new information to your chart.

Checklist ✓

Research and Inquiry

☐ Did you list your questions?

☐ Did you find helpful resources?

☐ Did you take notes?

Draft

Writing PROCESS

Before you start your personal narrative, look at the chart you made. Think about a main idea for the story. The details should tell about this main idea.

Main idea for paragraph:

It was a special day.

✓ Checklist

Drafting

☐ **Did you think about your purpose and audience?**

☐ **Did you include details to make your ideas clear?**

☐ **Did you include a good beginning and ending?**

SEQUENCE CHART

1. got up early
2. drove to ~~lake~~ — Falls Lake
3. sat under tree
4. ate lunch — ate sandwiches / drank lemonade
5. played catch
6. nice to be with family

Write detail sentences to tell about the main idea.

McGraw-Hill School Division

Here is a good first draft. The writer stated a main idea. Then she added details. Her draft has a beginning and an ending.

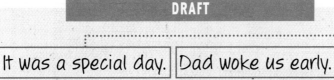

DRAFT

It was a special day. Dad woke us early.

We drove to Falls Lake. We sat under a

tree. Dad unpacked a picnic lunch.

We ate sandwiches. We drank lemonade.

After lunch, we played catch in a grassy

field. It wus nice to be with my family.

— Main idea of paragraph

— Narrative has a good beginning.

— Details add interest.

— Narrative has a good ending.

PRACTICE and APPLY

Draft Your Own Personal Narrative

1. Review your prewriting chart.

2. State a main idea.

3. Add detail sentences.

4. Include a good beginning and a good ending.

TECHNOLOGY

Don't worry about making your first draft perfect. Type your ideas first. You can use the spellchecker program later to find spelling or typing errors.

43

Revise

Elaborate

You can elaborate to make your writing even better. Add feelings and details. They will help you build a clear picture.

found a shady spot under a big

We sat under a tree.

TIME-ORDER WORDS

first	after
next	before
then	later
last	finally

Word Choice

Remember to use time-order words to tell about events in order. What time-order words were added to the revised draft?

TiP!

Conferencing for the Reader

☐ Read your partner's writing. Give some suggestions.

☐ Are all the parts of a personal narrative included in your partner's writing?
  • personal experience
  • interesting beginning and ending
  • time-order words

☐ Make sure to point out what's good about the writing.

Better Sentences

Look over your draft. Read your sentences aloud. Are there too many short sentences?

Look at how this writer joined two short sentences to make one longer one. Think about your partner's suggestions as you revise. See how this writer revised her story.

PREWRITE

DRAFT

REVISE

PROOFREAD

PUBLISH

REVISE

A Surprise Picnic

First,
It was a special day. Dad woke us early.
Next,
We drove to Falls Lake. ~~We sat under a~~ Then
found a shady spot under a big
tree. Dad unpacked a picnic lunch.
                              and
We ate sandwiches. ~~We~~ drank lemonade.

After lunch, we played catch in a grassy
I had fun
field. It wus nice to be with my family.

PRACTICE and APPLY

Revise Your Own Personal Narrative

1. Read your draft to yourself.

2. Share your draft with a partner.

3. Elaborate to make your writing better.

4. **Grammar** Combine short sentences.

Checklist ✓

Revising

☐ Does your writing keep your purpose and your audience in mind?

☐ Did you include details and feelings?

☐ Did you use time-order words?

☐ Does your story have an interesting beginning and ending?

☐ Did you add a title that makes a reader want to read the story?

Writing PROCESS

Proofread

Proofread your personal narrative after you revise it. Look for a different kind of mistake each time.

STRATEGIES FOR PROOFREADING

- **Reread your writing several times.**

- **Check for complete sentences.**

- **Check for correct capital letters and end marks.**

- **Check for correct spelling.** Start with the last word and read backward.

Spelling

Add *-es* to words ending in *x, z, s, sh,* or *ch* to form plurals. *(sandwich = sandwiches)*

REVIEW THE RULES

GRAMMAR

- A sentence tells a complete thought with a subject and a predicate.

MECHANICS

- Begin a sentence with a capital letter.

- End a statement with a period.

- End a question with a question mark.

- End a command with a period.

- End an exclamation with an exclamation mark.

Look at the proofreading corrections made on the draft below. What does the symbol ⊙ mean? Why is this correction needed?

PROOFREAD

A Surprise Picnic

First,
⌗ It was a special day. Dad woke us early.
Next,   Then
We drove to Falls Lake. We sat under a
found a shady spot under a big
tree. Dad unpacked a picnic lunch.
                and
We ate sandwiches. We drank lemonade.

After lunch, we played catch in a grassy
I had fun⊙ was
field. It was nice to be with my family.

PRACTICE and APPLY

Proofread Your Own Personal Narrative

1. Fix spelling mistakes.

2. Check capital letters and end marks.

3. Fix incomplete sentences.

4. Indent paragraphs.

Checklist ✓
Proofreading

☐ Did you spell all words correctly?

☐ Did you use capital letters and end marks correctly?

☐ Are all sentences complete?

☐ Did you indent the paragraph?

PROOFREADING MARKS

⌗ new paragraph

∧ add

℘ take out

≡ Make a capital letter.

/ Make a small letter.

ⓢⓟ Check the spelling.

⊙ Add a period.

47

Publish

Good writers look at their writing one last time before they publish it. A checklist helps.

✓ **Self-Check** Personal Narrative

- ☐ Did I keep my audience in mind?
- ☐ Did I remember my purpose?
- ☐ Did I write a main idea sentence?
- ☐ Did I write a good beginning and a good ending?
- ☐ Did I use time-order words?
- ☐ Did I add a good title?
- ☐ Did I use capital letters and end marks correctly?
- ☐ Did I proofread and fix all mistakes?

Read "A Surprise Picnic" on the next page. Talk about it with a partner. Would you change anything in it? Why?

A Surprise Picnic

by Sarah Brown

It was a special day. First, Dad woke us early. Next, we drove to Falls Lake. Then we found a shady spot under a big tree. Dad unpacked a picnic lunch. We ate sandwiches and drank lemonade. After lunch, we played catch in a grassy field. I had fun. It was nice to be with my family.

PREWRITE

DRAFT

REVISE

PROOFREAD

PUBLISH

PRACTICE and APPLY

Plan Your Own Personal Narrative

1. Check your revised draft one last time.

2. Make a neat, final copy.

3. Place your writing in a scrapbook.

TECHNOLOGY

Try different kinds of fonts for your title. Use a font that is large enough to stand out.

49

Present Your Personal Narrative

You need to plan before you present your personal narrative.

STEP 1

How to Tell Your Story

Strategies for Speaking Your purpose is to share your experiences with others as clearly as possible.

- Write the main event on a note card to help you remember.
- Make important points stand out by using body movements.
- Look at your audience. Smile.
- Speak so that everyone can hear you.

Multimedia Ideas

You might want to play music. Find music that goes with your topic. Play it softly.

STEP 2

How to Show Your Story

Suggestions for Illustration

You can make your personal narrative more interesting with pictures.

- Show a scrapbook or a poster.
- Use souvenirs and drawings.
- Show a map of where things happened. Remember to label it.

STEP 3

How to Share Your Story

Strategies for Rehearsing Practice your presentation before you give it.

- Watch yourself in a mirror.
- Have a partner listen and give ideas.
- Rehearse in front of a small group.

Viewing Strategies

- Look carefully at each of the pictures and objects the speaker shows you.
- Read all the labels on the pictures.
- Look for details in the pictures.

PRACTICE and APPLY

Plan Your Own Personal Narrative

1. Make notes to help you remember.
2. Speak clearly and with feeling.
3. Show interesting pictures or objects.
4. Practice your personal narrative.

Writing Tests

A writing test shows you a prompt to read and asks you to write something. A prompt gives you an idea and tells you what kind of writing to do. Look for key words and phrases that help you know what to write about and how to do your writing.

Look for words that tell if the purpose is to entertain or inform.

Check to see if the prompt tells who the audience is.

Look for words that tell what kind of writing this is.

> **Prompt**
>
> The first day of school can be a fun time.
> Write a story telling about how you felt or what you did on your first day at school.

How to Read a Prompt

Purpose Look back at the prompt. Find the words that tell you the purpose of the writing. The words "a fun time" and "write a story" tell you that your purpose will be to entertain.

Audience Sometimes a prompt will tell you who the audience is. If it does not, think of your teacher as your audience.

Personal Narrative When you are asked to write about something that happened to you, you are writing a personal narrative. The words "how you felt and what you did" tell you that you should write about your own experiences and feelings.

McGraw-Hill School Division

How to Write to a Prompt

Here are some tips to remember when you are given a prompt for a writing test.

Before Writing **Content/Ideas**	• Think about your writing purpose. • Remember who your audience is. • Make a list of things to tell in your story.
During Writing **Organization/ Paragraph Structure**	• Start with a good beginning. • In a personal narrative, use time-order words to show order. • Give your writing a good ending.
After Writing **Grammar/Usage**	• Proofread your work. • Start each sentence with a capital letter. • Use correct end marks.

Apply What You Learned

When you read a prompt on a writing test, always look for words that tell you what to write about. Look for the purpose and audience.

> **Prompt**
>
> Learning how to do something new can be fun or it can be difficult.
> Write a story telling about learning to do something and how you felt.

Name _____

Grammar and Writing Review

pages 2–3
Sentences

A. Underline each group of words that is a sentence.

1. Our new school is almost ready.

2. Into the empty building.

3. The desks, chairs, and tables.

pages 4–9
Four Kinds of Sentences

B. Add the correct end mark to each sentence. Write *S* for *statement*, *Q* for *question*, *E* for *exclamation*, or *C* for *command*.

4. Have you met the neighbor's children___   ___

5. Tell me about them___   ___

6. How nice they are___   ___

pages 10–15
Subjects and Predicates

C. Use *and* to join each pair of sentences. Write the new sentence on a piece of paper. Then draw a line between the subject and predicate.

7. Amy went bike riding. I went bike riding.

8. Ted came with us. Carl came with us.

9. My friends had fun. I had fun.

pages 8–9, 16
Mechanics and Usage

D. Write each sentence correctly on a piece of paper.

10. how I miss you

11. are you coming to to visit soon

12. we will eat pizza fruit and ice cream

pages 26–27

Vocabulary: Time-Order Words

E. Write 1, 2, 3, 4, and 5 to show the correct order for these sentences. The time-order words will help you.

13. Then, we ate lunch. _____

14. This morning, Grandma came to visit. _____

15. Tomorrow, we will go to the park. _____

16. First, we helped her unpack. _____

17. After lunch, we looked at pictures. _____

pages 28–29

Composition: Paragraphs

F. Think about a paragraph for each title. On a piece of paper, write a beginning sentence for each.

18. Winter Fun   **20.** The Neighborhood Park

19. Our New House

Proofreading a Personal Narrative

pages 46–47

G. 21.–25. Use proofreading marks to correct 5 mistakes in capitalization, punctuation, grammar, and spelling. Then write the paragraph correctly on a piece of paper.

Last Friday our class had a party First,

we ate sandwichs. Next, played games.

Then, we talked and listened to music.

what a great time everyone had

Save this page until you finish Unit 1.

55

Project File

A Book Review

A **book review** tells what a book is about.
It also tells what the writer thinks of it.

Ruby the Copycat

by Peggy Rathmann

Ruby is the new girl in Miss Hart's class.
Ruby is also a copycat. On Monday, when Angela wears a red bow in her hair, Ruby comes back from lunch with a red bow in her hair. On Tuesday, Angela wears a sweater with flowers on it. When Ruby comes back from lunch, she is wearing a sweater with flowers on it! What do you think happens on Wednesday, Thursday, and Friday? What do you think Miss Hart does when Ruby copies her?

I read Ruby the Copycat with my mom. We had fun guessing what Ruby would do next. I also liked the way Miss Hart helps Ruby to feel special in her own way. This is a book you will really enjoy.

Book title Comes at the beginning.

Author's name Follows the title.

A strong beginning grabs the reader's interest.

Main characters are introduced right away.

Story events Choose a part of the story to share. Don't give away the whole plot, though.

Opinion Tell what you liked and didn't like about the book.

56

Write a book review Write about a book you enjoyed. Was it funny, scary, sad, or exciting? Where did the story take place? Who were the main characters? What happened in the book?

Tell your friends about the book. Look at the model to make sure you include all the parts.

TIME FOR KIDS

PROJECT 2

A Personal Narrative

Michael Jordan played basketball very well. Imagine that you are a famous player like Michael Jordan.

A Famous Player Write a personal narrative about being a great player of a popular sport. Tell how you play your game.

Name _____

Grammar

Sentences

A. **Write S for each group of words that is a sentence.**

1. Pam has a surprise. _____

2. Her cat had six kittens. _____

3. A few days old. _____

4. Are sleeping in a basket. _____

5. Lulu sleeps, too. _____

6. Takes care of her kittens. _____

7. The kittens are so tiny. _____

8. Cannot see yet. _____

9. The kittens wake up. _____

10. Six kittens are hungry. _____

B. **Circle only the sentences.**

11. Want a kitten.

12. The gray kitten is cute.

13. Fluffy likes to.

14. The kittens are very small.

15. I visit the kittens every day.

McGraw-Hill School Division

 Save this page until you finish Unit 1.

Statements and Questions

A. Write *statement* or *question* for each sentence.

1. Have you ever moved to a new home? _____

2. We moved from the city. _____

3. Now we live in a town. _____

4. Do you have new friends? _____

5. Do you like your new neighbors? _____

6. What is your new school like? _____

7. I miss my friends in the city. _____

8. When do you move? _____

9. The movers will come tomorrow. _____

10. All our things are in boxes. _____

B. Underline each statement. Circle each question.

11. Is the van here?

12. The apartment is empty.

13. Can you take my bag?

14. Who has the dog?

15. It is time to say goodbye.

Grammar

Commands and Exclamations

A. Write *command* next to each sentence that gives an order. Write *exclamation* next to each sentence that shows strong feeling.

1. Help me build a treehouse. _____

2. I love treehouses! _____

3. I can't wait! _____

4. Check over the plans. _____

5. Make a list. _____

6. Come to the store with me. _____

7. These nuts and bolts are big! _____

8. Help me with the paint. _____

9. This store has everything! _____

10. My treehouse is great! _____

B. Circle the end mark in each sentence. Then write **C** after each command. Write **E** after each exclamation.

11. Welcome to Maria's treehouse! _____

12. What a great treehouse! _____

13. Be careful on the ladder. _____

14. Climb to the top of the treehouse. _____

15. How high up we are! _____

McGraw-Hill School Division

Sentence Punctuation

A. Write the underlined words that should have a capital letter. Add the correct end mark.

1. caterpillars turn into butterflies___ _____

2. how beautiful the butterfly is___ _____

3. where did the butterfly go___ _____

4. butterflies like flowers___ _____

5. do you see the butterfly now___ _____

6. this butterfly has yellow wings___ _____

7. what kind of butterfly is it___ _____

8. read a book about butterflies___ _____

9. butterflies come in all sizes and colors___ _____

10. a butterfly would make a neat pet___ _____

B. Write each sentence correctly.

11. here is a story about moths.

   _____

12. this is such an interesting story

   _____

13. how are moths like butterflies

   _____

14. go find a gray moth

   _____

15. i found a huge moth

   _____

Subjects in Sentences

A. Circle each sentence in which the subject is underlined.

1. <u>Tim</u> visits the museum.

2. He <u>rides the subway</u>.

3. The subway <u>is fast</u>.

4. <u>The museum</u> is in the city.

5. <u>People</u> visit the museum every day.

6. Children <u>like the dinosaurs</u>.

7. <u>The dinosaur hall</u> is their favorite room.

8. The teacher <u>leads the class</u>.

9. A museum guide <u>answers questions</u>.

10. <u>Everyone</u> asks about T-Rex.

B. Underline the subject in each sentence.

11. The dinosaur hall is busy.

12. Students also like the sea life hall.

13. The blue whale is the biggest kind of whale.

14. Visitors stop and look up at the exhibit.

15. Museums are really great!

Predicates in Sentences

A. Circle the sentences that have a line under the predicate.

1. Our home <u>is at the beach</u>.

2. <u>Many families</u> come to the beach.

3. <u>People</u> jog along the water.

4. A boy <u>runs after his dog</u>.

5. The children <u>build a sand castle</u>.

6. <u>Gulls</u> dive for fish.

7. A girl <u>picks up shells</u>.

8. <u>Lifeguards</u> watch the swimmers.

9. <u>Many boats</u> go out to sea.

10. Six children <u>play tag</u>.

B. Underline the predicate in each sentence.

11. We jump over the waves.

12. My brother wades in the water.

13. A lifeguard calls to a swimmer.

14. My sister finds a shell.

15. My cousin looks for starfish.

Combining Sentences

Use *and* to join each set of sentences. Write the new sentence.

1. The boys are ready. The girls are ready.

_____

2. Carla made a sign. Ana made a sign.

_____

3. Don put up posters. Tony put up posters.

_____

4. Yolanda sent invitations. Wes sent invitations.

_____

5. The singers practiced. The dancers practiced.

_____

6. Luis sang. Lee sang.

_____

7. Tina danced. Pedro danced.

_____

8. Ben played drums. Nikki played drums.

_____

9. Allen hummed. Nel hummed.

_____

10. Juan clapped. Rita clapped.

_____

Commas in a Series

A. **Add commas where they belong.**

1. Mom Dad and I

2. clothes shoes and books

3. cars trucks and buses

4. bags suitcases and gifts

5. washer dryer and TV

6. windows doors and garage

7. dog cat and bird

8. Thursday Friday and Saturday

9. apples oranges and pears

10. pencils pens and crayons

B. **Add commas where they belong.**

11. We drove past cities towns and farms.

12. We crossed plains hills and deserts.

13. The minutes hours and days flew by.

14. I bought gifts postcards and stamps.

15. I took pictures of Grandma Mom and Dad.

Nouns and Descriptive Writing

In this unit you will learn about nouns. You will also learn how to describe things in your writing.

🔍 **Science Link**   *Jamaica and Berto are building a sand castle. Can you picture it?*

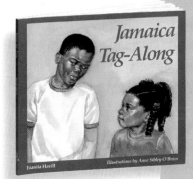

Jamaica sat down in the sand and began to dig. She made a big pile with the wet sand from underneath. She scooped sand from the mound to form a wall.

"Berto help," said the little boy. He sprinkled dry sand on the walls.

"Don't," said Jamaica. "You'll just mess it up."

〜 from ***Jamaica Tag-Along*** by Juanita Havill

Thinking Like a Writer

Descriptive Writing
Descriptive writing tells what a person, place, or thing is like.

• What details help you picture the sand castle?

Nouns The author used nouns that name people, places, and things.

⏰ **QUICK WRITE** Write the nouns you find in the passage.

Thinking Like a Writer

Descriptive Writing After you read the passage on page 67, write the details that help you picture the sand castle.

_____

_____

_____

_____

_____

_____

_____

QUICK WRITE Write the nouns that tell about things in the passage.

_____

_____

_____

_____

_____

Nouns

> **RULES**
>
> • A **noun** is a word that names a person, place, or thing.
>
>   *My dog brings a bone into the house.*
>
> • Look at the nouns in the sentence below.
>
>   *My dad makes soup in the kitchen.*
>   ↑   ↑   ↑
>   *person   thing   place*

THINK AND WRITE

Nouns
Look around the room. Write the names of five nouns you see.

Guided Practice

Name the noun in each sentence.

1. The soup is warm. _____

2. The pot looks big. _____

3. My brother stirs. _____

4. My sister is hungry. _____

5. Our dog sits up and begs. _____

REVIEW THE RULES

- A **noun** names a person, place, or thing.

More Practice

A. **Circle the noun in each sentence.**

6. The yard is sunny.

7. My dad loves to cook!

8. The food is ready.

9. The chicken smells good.

10. The corn looks fresh.

Handbook
page 434

Extra Practice page 128

B. **Spiral Review** Write *statement*, *question*, or *exclamation*. **Then write each sentence on a piece of paper with the correct end mark.**

16. This restaurant is fun _____

17. Is our table ready _____

18. My friends are so happy _____

19. The food comes at last _____

20. Does the lunch taste good _____

Writing Activity   Paragraph

Write a paragraph about what the people in your home like to eat. Include interesting details.
APPLY GRAMMAR: Circle each noun.

More About Nouns

RULES

- A **noun** can name a person, a place, or a thing.

  The children ride the bus to the park.

- Look at what each noun in the sentence above names.

Person	Place	Thing
children	park	bus

Guided Practice

Name the nouns in each sentence. Tell if each noun names a person, a place, or a thing.

1. Our teacher has a backpack.

_____

2. The driver is ready.

_____

3. The bus goes down the street.

_____

4. The children are happy.

_____

5. The city is so noisy!

_____

THINK AND WRITE

Nouns
How can you tell if a word is a noun? Write your answer.

REVIEW THE RULES

- A **noun** can name a person, a place, or a thing.

More Practice

A. **Circle nouns that name a person. Underline nouns that name places.**

6. The park has many trees.

7. A woman eats lunch by the pond.

8. A man catches a fish.

9. The children play on the swings.

10. Birds fly in the sky.

B. **Spiral Review** **Draw a line under the subject in each sentence. Circle each noun.**

11. My family visits the park.

12. My sister goes down the slide.

13. The boys sit on the grass.

14. Some fish swim in the pond.

15. Mom feeds the ducks.

Handbook
page 434

Extra Practice
page 129

Writing Activity **Description**

Write about a favorite place. Use details.
APPLY GRAMMAR: Circle each noun.

Proper Nouns

- Proper nouns name special people, pets, and places.

  Aunt Lil and *Patches* live on *Bay Street*.

- A proper noun begins with a capital letter.

Nouns	Special nouns
boy	Miguel
dog	Pepper
street	Elm Street
school	Hillside Day School
city	Riverside

Guided Practice

Name the nouns that need capital letters.

1. My friend nick has a fish. _____

2. The fish's name is pippy. _____

3. I named my cat snowy. _____

4. We live on spring street. _____

5. Flora lives in newtown. _____

THINK AND WRITE

Nouns
Write in your journal how you can tell if a noun is a special noun.

72

Handbook
page 434

Extra
Practice
page 130

REVIEW THE RULES

- Nouns that name special people, pets, and places are proper nouns.

- A proper noun begins with a capital letter.

More Practice

A. Write each proper noun correctly with a capital letter.

6. My brother bill has a pet club. _____

7. I hope paul brings his dog. _____

8. The name of the dog is frisky. _____

9. My friend lisa has a rabbit. _____

10. The vet is in middletown. _____

B. Spiral Review Add commas where they belong. Circle each noun. Write if it names a person, place or thing.

11.–20. A dog a cat and a bird live at our house near the lake. My mother and sister really love our pets!

_____

_____

Writing Activity   Silly Story

Write a silly story about a pet.
APPLY GRAMMAR: Include proper nouns.

Days, Months, and Holidays

RULES

- Some proper nouns name days of the week, months, and holidays.

- The name of each day, month, and holiday begins with a capital letter.

Is Thanksgiving on a Thursday in November?

Days	Months		Holidays
Monday	January	July	Martin Luther
Tuesday	February	August	King Day
Wednesday	March	September	Memorial Day
Thursday	April	October	Thanksgiving
Friday	May	November	
Saturday	June	December	
Sunday			

THINK AND WRITE

Nouns
What kinds of words always begin with a capital letter? Write your answer.

Guided Practice

Name the nouns that need a capital letter.

1. On tuesday everyone will get a part. _____

2. We will practice next friday. _____

3. We will make costumes in november. _____

4. Our play will be about thanksgiving. _____

_____

5. Will we do a play in december? _____

74

REVIEW THE RULES

• Nouns that name days, months, and holidays begin with capital letters.

More Practice

A. Write each proper noun correctly with a capital letter.

6. We have a parade in january. _____

7. The parade is for new year's day. _____

8. We will practice on monday. _____

9. We will march on tuesday. _____

10. Is there a holiday in february? _____

Handbook
page 435

Extra Practice page 131

B. **Spiral Review** Add the correct end mark to each sentence. Write each proper noun correctly.

11. My uncle lives in woodland_____

12. Is his farm on pine street_____

13. Uncle jim has a new pig_____

14. The pig's name is penny_____

15. Did they go to the woodland fair_____

Writing Activity **A Poster**

Make a poster about a holiday or a special event.
APPLY GRAMMAR: Include three proper nouns.

Social Studies Link

Using Capital Letters

RULES

- Begin names of people, pets, and places with capital letters.

    Jessica   Fluffy   Hilltop   Park

- The names of days, months, and holidays begin with capital letters.

    Monday   September   Labor Day

Practice

A. **Write the special nouns that should have a capital letter.**

1. The next concert is on friday. _____

2. Uncle bob likes the music. _____

3. The band plays on main street. _____

4. Please come on july 4! _____

5. The band plays for independence day. _____

B. **Spiral Review** **Add the end mark to each sentence. Write *statement, question, command,* or *exclamation.***

6. Max likes music___ _____

7. Max likes Monday, too___ _____

8. Does Max like the month of May___ _____

9. See Max on Memorial Day___ _____

10. Max loves the M Street Zoo___ _____

Handbook
pages 449-450

Extra
Practice
page 132

THINK
AND WRITE

Nouns

What are some of your favorite special nouns? Write them correctly.

Nouns

REVIEW THE RULES

- A **noun** names a person, place, or thing.

- Nouns that name special people, pets, and places begin with capital letters.

- Nouns that name days, months, and holidays begin with capital letters.

Handbook
pages 449–450

Nouns

How can you tell a regular noun from a special noun? Write your answer.

Practice

A. Write each proper noun correctly with a capital letter.

1. What holidays are in february?

_____

2. We celebrate presidents' day.

_____

3. I wrote about abraham lincoln.

_____

4. Does ann like valentine's day?

_____

5. My sister likes groundhog day.

_____

B. **Challenge** Write the paragraph on a piece of paper. Fill in the blanks with regular and proper nouns.

6.–10. My favorite holidays are _____ and my favorite place to celebrate is _____. I like to celebrate with _____ and _____.

Plural Nouns

--- **RULES** ---

- A **singular noun** names one person, place, or thing. A **plural noun** names more than one person, place, or thing.

  one singer   two singers

- Add *-s* to form the plural of most singular nouns.

  I know one song.

  He knows two songs.

- Add *-es* to form the plural of nouns that end with *s, sh, ch,* or *x.*

  Put your box next to all the other boxes.

THINK AND WRITE

Nouns
How can you tell whether a noun is singular or plural? Write your answer.

Guided Practice

Make the noun in ( ) name more than one.

1. Our (friend) have fun. _____

2. Two (boy) paint pictures. _____

3. Three (girl) play ball. _____

4. We find (bunch) of books. _____

5. One book is about (fox). _____

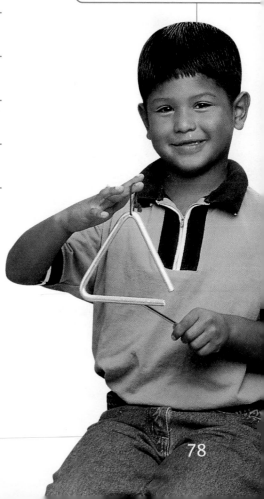

REVIEW THE RULES

- A **singular noun** names one person, place, or thing.

- A **plural noun** names more than one person, place, or thing.

More Practice

A. Make the noun in ( ) name more than one. Write the new noun.

6. We need our (ruler) for math. _____

7. We measure in (inch). _____

8. Our class sings (song). _____

9. We write in our (journal). _____

10. We can tell about our (wish). _____

B. Spiral Review Underline the subject in each sentence. Circle nouns for places.

11. My mom and I visited the city.

12. We went to a museum.

13. The dinosaur room was crowded.

14. Mom saw a bookstore.

15. I chose a new book.

Handbook
page 436

Extra Practice
page 133

Writing Activity A Paragraph

Write a paragraph about something your class enjoys.
APPLY GRAMMAR: Include plural nouns and circle them.

More Plural Nouns

RULES

- To form the plural of nouns ending in a **consonant** and *y*, change *y* to *i* and add *-es*.

  bunny -y + i + es = bunnies

- Some nouns change their spelling to name more than one.

Singular	Plural
man	men
woman	women
child	children
tooth	teeth
mouse	mice
foot	feet

Guided Practice

Change each noun in ( ) to make it name more than one person or thing.

1. Three (woman) play music. _____

2. Some (man) sing songs. _____

3. Meg's two (foot) are flying! _____

4. Do the (pony) like the music? _____

5. All the (bunny) are asleep! _____

THiNK AND WRITE

Nouns
Write how to change a noun ending in *-y* to show more than one.

REVIEW THE RULES

- For the plural form of nouns ending in a **consonant** and **y**, change the **y** to **i** and add **-es**.

- Some nouns change their spelling to name more than one.

More Practice

A. **Make the noun in ( ) name more than one. Write the new noun.**

6. Many (child) come to the party. _____

7. Dad has plenty of party (supply). _____

8. Mom puts (cherry) on the yogurt cups. _____

9. The lemonade makes Pat's (tooth) cold. _____

10. Toss the (penny) in the wishing well! _____

B. **Spiral Review** **Add the correct end mark to each sentence. Circle each plural noun.**

11. What costumes do you like____

12. Costume parties are fun____

13. Look at the funny masks____

14. Can we play guessing games____

15. The party treats taste so good____

Handbook
page 436

Extra Practice page 134

Writing Activity **An Invitation**

Write an invitation to a party.
APPLY GRAMMAR: Include plural nouns.

Singular Possessive Nouns

RULES

- Some nouns show who or what owns or has something.

- This kind of noun is called a **possessive noun**.

- By adding an **apostrophe** (') and an **s**, you can show that a singular noun owns something.

  The bird's song is beautiful.

Singular Noun	Singular Possessive Noun
sky	sky's color
Ben	Ben's pencil
girl	girl's picture

THINK AND WRITE

Nouns

How can you show that a noun owns something? Write your answer.

Guided Practice

Name the possessive form of each singular noun.

1. girl

_____

2. artist

_____

3. Brandon

_____

4. man

_____

5. teacher

_____

6. painter

_____

7. Rita

_____

8. boy

_____

9. dog

_____

10. sister

_____

82

Handbook
page 432

Extra
Practice
page 135

— REVIEW THE RULES —

• Add an apostrophe (') and an **s** to a singular noun to make it a possessive noun.

More Practice

A. **Write the possessive form of the noun in ( ).**

11. (Mona) drawing looks like a spaceship. _____

12. (John) crayons are over there. _____

13. Pam likes (Carmen) picture. _____

14. Did you see (Terry) pictures? _____

15. Look at the (rainbow) colors! _____

B. Spiral Review **Circle each complete sentence. Underline each plural noun.**

16. Our two classes work hard.

17. The children put on an art show.

18. The families will come.

19. Ryan's favorite picture.

20. How many pictures will win?

Writing Activity   A Scrapbook

Make a scrapbook page about a class event. Draw pictures and write about it.
APPLY GRAMMAR: Use possessive nouns.

Plural Possessive Nouns

RULES

- You can show that more than one person or thing owns or has something. If a plural noun ends in *s* or *es*, just add an apostrophe at the end of the word.

  Our two birds' names are Tex and Tiny.

- If a plural noun does not end in s, add an apostrophe and an *s* (*'s*).

  The mice's feet are tiny!

Singular Possessive Noun	Plural Possessive Noun
boy's lunch	boys' team
bat's wings	bats' cave
dog's ball	dogs' dishes

THINK AND WRITE

Nouns

How do you make most plural nouns show they own something? Write the answer.

Guided Practice

Change each plural noun to a plural possessive noun.

1. girls

_____

2. teachers

_____

3. brothers

_____

4. birds

_____

5. tigers

_____

6. mothers

_____

7. goats

_____

8. players

_____

9. doctors

_____

10. friends

_____

REVIEW THE RULES

- Just add an **apostrophe** to make plural nouns that end in *s* possessive.

- Add an **apostrophe** and an *s* to plural nouns that do not end in *s* possessive.

Handbook
page 437

Extra Practice page 136

More Practice

A. Change the nouns in ( ) to plural possessive nouns.

11. Look at the (ants) trail._____

12. The (butterflies) wings are yellow._____

13. The (trees) branches are high._____

14. We see some (birds) nests._____

15. The (children) adventure is fun!_____

B. **Spiral Review** **Underline each plural noun. Use *and* to join each pair of sentences. Write the new sentence on a piece of paper.**

16. Grandma hiked. I hiked.

17. Our legs got tired. Our feet got tired.

18. Trees smelled good. Plants smelled good.

19. Birds chirped. Crickets chirped.

20. Bees flew by. Flies flew by.

Writing Activity   A Postcard

Write a postcard about a trip. Use exact words.
APPLY GRAMMAR: Include one plural possessive.

Letter Punctuation

┌─ **RULES** ──────────────────────────────

Put a **comma** after the greeting of a letter.

Dear Bobby,

Put a **comma** after the closing.

Your friend,

└──

Practice

A. Nate the punctuation that should follow each greeting and closing.

1. Yours truly ____

2. Dear Amanda ____

3. Dear Jacob ____

4. Your friend ____

5. Dear Rory ____

6. Dear Grandpa ____

7. Your grandson ____

8. Dear Taylor ____

9. Sincerely ____

10. With many thanks ____

B. **Spiral Review** Write the proper nouns correctly. Add commas and capital letters where they belong.

11.–15. Dear Mayor cole,

There is litter in greenville. We see

cans bottles and paper on main street.

I think more trash containers would help.

Sincerely,
sasha sims

_____

_____

Handbook
page 462

Extra Practice
page 137

THINK AND WRITE

Nouns
Who would you like to write to? Write a greeting to this person. Write a closing, too.

Grammar

Nouns

REVIEW THE RULES

- Most nouns form the plural by adding -*s*. Add -*es* to form the plurals of nouns that end in *s*, *ss*, *sh*, *ch*, or *x*. If a noun ends in *y*, change *y* to *i* before adding -*es*.

- Add (') and *s* to singular nouns to make them possessive. Put (') after plural nouns.

- Put a comma after the greeting and closing of a letter.

Handbook
page 436

QUICK WRITE

Nouns

Does it help your writing to know more about nouns? Write your ideas.

Practice

A. Make the noun in ( ) name more than one. Write the new noun.

1. Two (class) visit the zoo. _____

2. We ride on two (bus). _____

3. Some (friend) laugh at the monkeys. _____

4. The (child) love the elephants. _____

5. We eat our (lunch) at noon. _____

B. **Challenge** Add commas. Change each word in ( ) to form a possessive noun. Write the new word.

6. Dear Felita

7. My (school) trip was fun. _____

8. An (elephant) feet are so big! _____

9. Two (monkeys) tricks were funny. _____

10. Your friend Kerry

McGraw-Hill School Division

Common Errors with Possessive Nouns

A possessive noun shows who or what owns something. Sometimes writers make mistakes.

Common Error	Examples	Corrected Sentences
A possessive noun does not have an apostrophe (').	The girls nose is red.	The girl's nose is red.
	The girls noses are red.	The girls' noses are red.

REVIEW THE RULES

POSSESSIVE NOUNS

- To form the possessive of a singular noun, add *'s*.
- To form the possessive of a plural noun that ends in *s*, add (').

Practice

Write the possessive form of the noun in ( ).

1. (Ted) class went to the zoo. _____

2. Look at the (elephant) trunk. _____

3. The (giraffes) necks are long. _____

4. Do you see the (lion) mane? _____

5. The (boys) faces are happy. _____

Troubleshooter, pages 422–423

Grammar
COMMON ERRORS

THINK AND WRITE

Nouns
How do you form a possessive noun? Write the answer.

88

Grammar and Usage

Directions

Read the paragraph and choose the word that belongs in each space.

Sample

Frogs have long, strong back legs. In the water, the back __(1)__ kick and help the frog to swim quickly. On land a __(2)__ legs help it to jump and get away from danger. Some frogs can jump up high to catch __(3)__ flying by. Frogs have four legs, but the front legs are short. It's the back legs that do all the work.

1 ○ leg
○ legs
○ leg's

2 ○ frog
○ frogs
○ frog's

3 ○ insect's
○ insectss
○ insects

TIME FOR KIDS Writer's Notebook

RESEARCH

RESEARCH When I do research or need to check information, the **library media center** is the first place I go. The books, magazines, newspapers, and computers there give lots of information. They help me write using correct information.

COMPOSITION SKILLS

WRITING WELL When I write, I make sure the **leads** that start my paragraphs will make readers want to read more. The **endings** that finish each paragraph tell my readers when I finish with an idea.

VOCABULARY SKILLS

USING WORDS Words like grandmother and underground are **compound words**. They are made from two separate words. When I write, I use them to explain a specific idea. What compound words do you know?

Read Now!

As you read the photo essay about emeralds, jot down information that the writer could check in the library media center.

RESEARCH

RESEARCH Write the information in the photo essay on emeralds that the writer could check in the library media center.

_____

_____

_____

_____

_____

_____

_____

_____

_____

_____

_____

_____

EMERALDS

They are green, beautiful, and very hard to find!

EMERALDS!

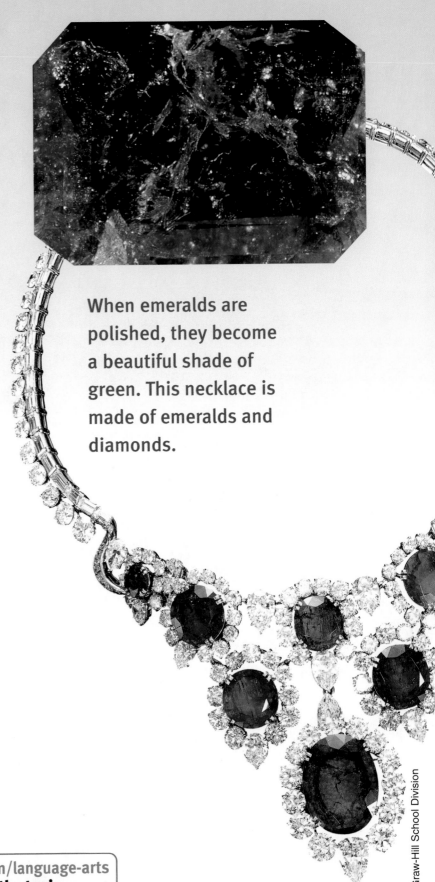

James Hill is very good at finding things hidden deep underground. It all started when he was a child. Back then, James visited his grandmother in Hiddenite, North Carolina. "First I crawled around her front yard," he says. Then he checked out the woods, creeks, and corn fields.

Wherever he went, he looked for buried treasure. One day, Hill discovered a real treasure in Hiddenite. It was a bed of emeralds. Emeralds are beautiful green gemstones.

Hill found the stones with his 8-year-old son. His son asked, "Daddy, did we find a treasure?" Hill told him, "Son, did we ever!"

When emeralds are polished, they become a beautiful shade of green. This necklace is made of emeralds and diamonds.

interNET CONNECTION Go to www.mhschool.com/language-arts for more information on the topic.

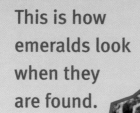
This is how emeralds look when they are found.

Necklace photo:Christies Images
All other photos:Warren F. Dobson/Full Moon Communications, N.C

Hill shows off his emerald. It will be cut and polished.

Write Now!

James Hill and his son were surprised when they found emeralds in the ground. Describe a place where you once found a surprise.

93

Note-taking and Summarizing

When you read a paragraph for information, you can take **notes**. The notes will help you remember what is most important about the paragraph. Read this paragraph about trees. Then read the notes that one student wrote.

Trees

There are many different kinds of trees. Each tree has its own kind of leaf. Sugar maple leaves have five large points. Elm leaves have zigzag edges. The leaves of the ginkgo tree are shaped like a fan.

Notes

Many kinds of trees

Different leaves

maple—5 points

elm—zigzag edges

ginkgo—like a fan

You can use your notes to write a **summary** that tells in a few sentences what the paragraph is about.

Practice

A. Use the notes on page 94 to answer these questions.

1. What is the paragraph about? _____

2. What three different kinds of trees does the

paragraph tell about? _____

3. What is a sugar maple leaf like? _____

4. What is an elm leaf like? _____

5. What is a ginkgo leaf like? _____

B. Write the answer to each question.

6. How does note-taking help you? _____

_____

7. What should you look for when taking notes? _____

_____

8. What can you use your notes to write? _____

_____

9. Is a summary long or short? _____

_____

10. Are the notes or the summary written in complete

sentences? _____

Writing Activity   A Summary

Use the notes on page 94 to write a summary of the paragraph about trees.

95

Vocabulary: Compound Words

DEFINITION

A compound word is a word that is made from two smaller words. Knowing the meaning of the two smaller words can help you figure out the meaning of the compound word.

birth + day = birthday

sea + shell = seashell

sun + light = sunlight

THINK AND WRITE

Compound Words

How can compound words make your writing more interesting? Write your answer in your journal.

Look at the blue compound words below.

Nature is all around me. Pretty bluebirds sing in my backyard. I see red ladybugs in Dad's vegetable garden. The air is filled with the sweet smell of wildflowers. The cool breeze fluffs up my dog's fur. Nature is everywhere.

Practice

A. **Circle the compound word in each sentence.**

1. We visited the pond in the afternoon.

2. The warm sunshine felt good on our faces.

3. Mom laughed at the sound of a bold blackbird.

4. We saw tall cattails leaning toward the water.

5. I watched buttercups move in the breeze.

B. **Make compound words with the words in the box. Use them to complete the sentences.**

moon	man	weather	storms	thunder
sun	beams	light	flash	set

6. The _____ was beautiful last night.

7. The _____ said rain was coming.

8. But no _____ were in sight.

9. After dark, bright _____ lit up the sky.

10. I didn't need a _____ to see.

C. **Grammar Link** **11.–15. The compound words in Practice B are all nouns. Use the compound words in Practice B to write a sentence of your own.**

Writing Activity   Sentences

Write sentences about nature. Use at least two compound words.

APPLY GRAMMAR: Use at least three plural nouns.

Composition: Leads and Endings

You can get your reader's attention with a strong lead and a good ending.

THINK AND WRITE

Leads and Endings

Why is it important to get the interest of your readers at the beginning of your writing?

GUIDELINES

- A **lead** begins a piece of writing.

- The most important idea is often stated in the lead.

- An **ending** finishes a piece of writing.

- The ending sums up the writing or states the main idea again.

Notice how this writer uses a strong lead and a good ending.

A strong lead gets the attention of readers.

The summer I spent at the beach was the best summer of all! During the day I looked for tiny starfish and bright seashells on the sandy shore. At night, Dad built a roaring campfire. I will never forget the smell of fire mixed with salty sea air. After dinner, we would eat sweet blueberries for dessert. How could a summer be better?

A good ending sums up the writing or states the main idea again.

Practice

A. **Write *lead* or *ending* to tell how to use each sentence.**

1. One day Dad and I found a shipwreck. _____

2. Now I will never use the rowboat again. _____

3. My adventure began on a rainy weekend. _____

4. My life changed forever last summer. _____

5. At last, I felt the seashore was my home. _____

B. **Write a lead for each of these topics.**

6. A Trip to the Farm _____

_____

7. The Rainy Day _____

_____

8. My Favorite Animal _____

_____

9. A Special Visitor _____

_____

10. My Funny Friend _____

_____

C. **Grammar Link** **11.–15. Write an ending for each topic in Practice B. Circle the nouns.**

Writing Activity   **A Paragraph**

Write a paragraph about a vacation or a trip. Begin with a strong lead and finish with a good ending. **APPLY GRAMMAR:** Use at least three proper nouns and circle each.

Better Sentences

Directions

Read the paragraph. Some parts are underlined. The underlined parts may be one of the following:

- Incomplete sentences
- Correctly written sentences that should be combined

Choose the best way to write each underlined part.

> **Sample**
>
> If you don't want to drive, why not take a train? Traveling by train is easy. <u>Traveling by train is fun</u>.(1) You can sit in your seat and see the sights. You can walk from the front of the train to the back. There is a car where you can buy food and sit at a table. <u>Even sleep in some</u>(2) <u>trains</u>. A train trip can be a lot of fun!

Remember, some sentences can be combined.

Does the underlined part tell a complete thought?

1 ○ Traveling by train is easy and by train is fun.

○ Traveling by train is easy and fun.

○ By train is easy and fun.

2 ○ You can even sleep. In some trains.

○ Sleep in some trains.

○ You can even sleep in some trains.

Vocabulary and Comprehension

Directions

Read the paragraph. Then read each question that follows the paragraph. Choose the best answer to each question.

Sample

Tony dreamed of going into space. He would put on his <u>spacesuit</u> and wave to people as he walked toward the space shuttle. On board, he would feel the rumble as the engines fired and the shuttle began to lift. Tony wanted to look out the window and see the earth from space, so far away. "I could do it," he thought. "I could be the first kid in space."

Look for two smaller words that make up one word.

1 The word <u>spacesuit</u> in this story means—

○ suit worn for space travel

○ loose-fitting suit

○ a person's favorite suit

2 What detail helps you understand what Tony feels or hears?

○ walked toward the space shuttle

○ the rumble as the engines fired

○ the earth from space, so far away

Seeing Like a Writer

Details in pictures can give you ideas for writing. Look at the details in these pictures. What do you see? What could you hear, smell, taste, or feel if you were there?

Children Playing in Sand in Holland Park by Dora Holzhandler.

Writing from Pictures

1. Write a caption for each picture. Use a word that names a person, place, or thing in each caption.

2. Write a strong beginning sentence for a paragraph that describes one of the pictures.

3. Choose two pictures. What details do they share? Create a title to describe both pictures. Then write a short paragraph about them.

Apply Grammar: Include plural nouns. Circle each plural noun.

Descriptive Writing

Descriptive writing helps you tell your readers what a person, place, or thing is like. You can use descriptive writing to do this. The details you include create "word pictures".

Learning from Writers

Read these examples of descriptive writing. Notice the details in these two pieces of writing. How do the authors use details to create a picture in your mind?

THINK AND WRITE

Purpose

Write why you think authors use descriptive writing.

Beautiful Music

Ben and Sam are talking to a blind man. The blind man plays beautiful music on his harmonica. But he has no friends.

Ben's eyes were closed, and he was smiling. After a while, Sam turned to the man and said, "Would you like to take a walk with us tomorrow?" The music became so soft and quiet they could barely hear it. Then the dark room filled with wild, happy music. It bounced from wall to wall. Sam and Ben looked at each other. They couldn't wait for tomorrow.

— Ezra Jack Keats from *Apt. 3*

McGraw-Hill School Division

Writing from Pictures

1. Write a caption for each picture. Use a word that names a person, place, or thing in each caption.

2. Write a strong beginning sentence for a paragraph that describes one of the pictures.

3. Choose two pictures. What details do they share? Create a title to describe both pictures. Then write a short paragraph about them.

Apply Grammar: Include plural nouns. Circle each plural noun.

Descriptive Writing

Descriptive writing helps you tell your readers what a person, place, or thing is like. You can use descriptive writing to do this. The details you include create "word pictures".

Learning from Writers

Read these examples of descriptive writing. Notice the details in these two pieces of writing. How do the authors use details to create a picture in your mind?

THINK AND WRITE

Purpose
Write why you think authors use descriptive writing.

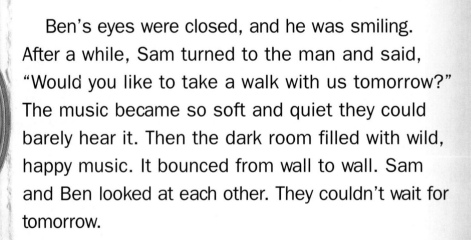

Beautiful Music

Ben and Sam are talking to a blind man. The blind man plays beautiful music on his harmonica. But he has no friends.

Ben's eyes were closed, and he was smiling. After a while, Sam turned to the man and said, "Would you like to take a walk with us tomorrow?" The music became so soft and quiet they could barely hear it. Then the dark room filled with wild, happy music. It bounced from wall to wall. Sam and Ben looked at each other. They couldn't wait for tomorrow.

— Ezra Jack Keats from *Apt. 3*

My Birthday Sleepover

For my birthday this year, I had a sleepover party. My friends came over at 5:00. We ate a yummy meal of chicken and rice. The spicy smell filled the house!

After dinner, I opened presents. My friend Molly gave me a bright pink seashell for my collection. Two other friends gave me a tape of quiet and loud seashore sounds. We listened to the roar of the waves together.

Later, we got into our sleeping bags. We giggled and told funny stories. Everyone enjoyed my sleepover party.

— Josie Hernandez

PRACTICE and APPLY

Thinking Like a Reader

1. How does the music change in "Beautiful Music"?

2. What presents did the author of "My Birthday Sleepover" receive?

Thinking Like a Writer

3. What describing words do you see in "Beautiful Music"?

4. What describing words do you see in "My Birthday Sleepover"?

5. **Reading Across Texts** What picture does each author create for the reader?

Features of Descriptive Writing

DEFINITIONS AND FEATURES

Descriptive writing tells what a person, place, or thing is like. Good descriptive writing does these things:

▶ It uses **details** to create a picture.

▶ It groups details together in **an order that makes sense.**

▶ It uses **describing words** to tell how something looks, sounds, feels, smells, or tastes.

▶ Details

Reread "Beautiful Music" on page 104. What details create a picture of Ben as he listens to the music?

Ben's eyes were closed, and he was smiling.

The words "eyes were closed" and "smiling" help you picture Ben.

▶ Order That Makes Sense

Think about how the music is described in "Beautiful Music." How does the music match the man's changing feelings?

> The music became so soft and quiet they could barely hear it. Then the dark room filled with wild, happy music.

When the music is soft and quiet, the man is thinking. When it turns wild and happy, he seems to be saying he is happy.

▶ Describing Words

Describing words in "Beautiful Music" tell how things look and sound.

> Then the dark room filled with wild, happy music. It bounced from wall to wall.

Which word tells how the room looked? Which words tell how the music sounded?

PRACTICE and APPLY

Create a Descriptive Writing Chart

1. List the features of descriptive writing.
2. Reread "My Birthday Sleepover."
3. Write how the author used each feature.

Features	Examples

Prewrite

You can use descriptive writing to help others imagine what you have seen or done.

Purpose and Audience

Your purpose for writing a description may be to give information. You might describe a special place so that others will want to visit it. The audience would be people who might want to travel.

Choose a Topic

Begin by **brainstorming**. Think of special places you think others might like to visit. Choose one place. Then **explore and list ideas**.

THINK AND WRITE

Audience
Write what feelings you want your audience to have when they read your description.

I found these ideas in my journal.

Pine Mountain Park

trails	sound of stream
signs	fresh air
squirrels	pine needles
chipmunks	parking lot
chirping birds	visitor center

Organize • Sorting

Details in a description are grouped together in an order that makes sense. You can use a star chart to help you organize details by sight, sound, touch, smell, and taste.

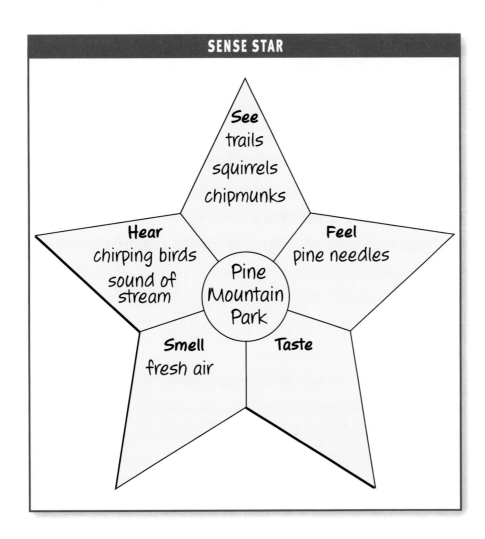

SENSE STAR

See
trails
squirrels
chipmunks

Hear
chirping birds
sound of
stream

Pine
Mountain
Park

Feel
pine needles

Smell
fresh air

Taste

Checklist ✓
Prewriting

☐ Did you think about your purpose and audience?

☐ Did you choose a place to describe?

☐ Did you explore and organize ideas?

☐ Do you need to find out more?

PRACTICE and APPLY

Plan Your Own Description

1. Think about your purpose and audience.

2. Brainstorm ideas for a topic.

3. Choose a topic and explore ideas.

4. Organize your ideas.

Writing PROCESS

Prewrite • Research and Inquiry

▶ Writer's Resources

You may need to do some research for your writing. What do you need to know? List your questions. Then list resources where you can find answers.

What Else Do I Need to Know?	Where Can I Find the Information?
What kind of squirrels did I see in the park?	Go to library to find books about squirrels.
How can I describe the smell of fresh air?	Read magazines about the outdoors.

▶ Use the Library

You can use the library to do research.

STRATEGIES FOR USING THE LIBRARY

• Take your questions with you.

• Use the computer or card catalog to find books about your topic.

• Ask the librarian to help you look for magazines, videos, or CDs about your topic.

• Take notes.

► Study Periodicals

Find magazine pictures of places that look like the one you are describing. The pictures can help you remember details. Read some of the articles. Look for describing words.

Use Your Research

Add information from your research to your chart. This writer learned two new things.

Handbook
pages 456–457

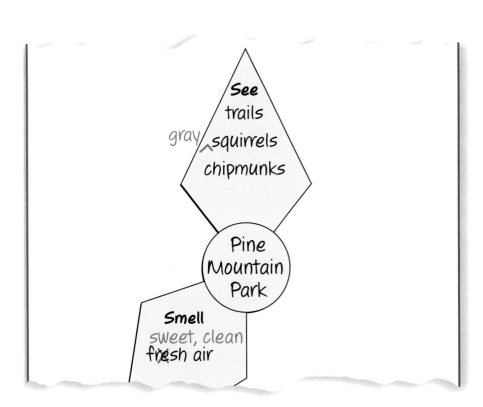

Checklist ✓

Research and Inquiry

☐ Did you list your questions?

☐ Did you find helpful resources?

☐ Did you take notes or check out library materials?

PRACTICE and APPLY

Review Your Plan

1. Look at your prewriting chart.

2. List any questions you have.

3. Decide on resources that will help you.

4. Add new information to the chart.

Draft

You can write your description as a travel guide. Before you start, look at your star chart. Think about a main idea for the description. The details on your chart should tell about it.

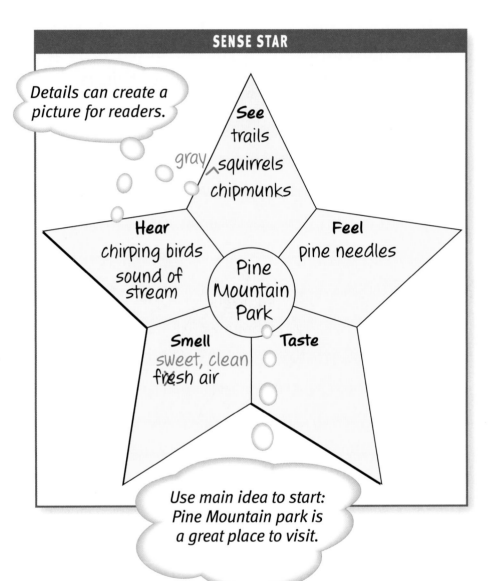

SENSE STAR

Details can create a picture for readers.

See
trails
gray squirrels
chipmunks

Hear
chirping birds
sound of stream

Feel
pine needles

Pine Mountain Park

Smell
sweet, clean fresh air

Taste

Use main idea to start: Pine Mountain park is a great place to visit.

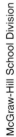

This writer used his ideas to write a draft. He began with a main idea that makes a strong lead. He used details to create a picture. He added a good ending.

DRAFT

Pine Mountain park is a great place to visit!

Pine Mountain park has miles of trails. You can see gray squirrels and chipmunks. Pine Mountain park has birdes chirping. A tiny stream makes noises. The air is sweet and clean. As you walk, you feel pine needles crunch under your feet. I always wear my hiking boots. Come visit soon!

Main idea makes a strong lead.

Details create a picture for readers.

Good ending.

PRACTICE and APPLY

Draft Your Own Description

1. Review your prewriting chart.
2. Write a strong lead.
3. State a main idea.
4. Write details that create a picture.
5. Add a good ending.

TiP!

TECHNOLOGY

Double-space your draft on the computer so you can write in changes later.

Revise

Elaborate

Close your eyes and think about the place you are describing. Make a picture in your mind to help you think of more details.

through green woods

There are miles of walking trails.
^

DESCRIBING WORDS

bubbling

shiny

bumpy

slippery

delicious

Word Choice

Choose the right words for your topic and audience. What words did this writer use to describe how things look, sound, feel, smell, or taste?

Conferencing for the Reader

■ Check your partner's writing to see if it includes:
- details that create a picture
- details grouped in an order that makes sense
- describing words

■ Tell your partner what is good about the writing. Suggest ways to make it better.

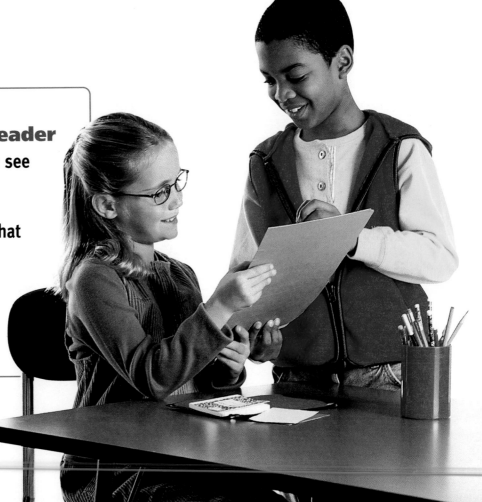

McGraw-Hill School Division

Better Sentences

As you revise your draft, read it aloud. Do some sentences sound the same?

See how this writer made some sentences more interesting.

> **REVISE**
>
> ^ Come to Pine Mountain park
>
> Pine Mountain park is a great place to visit!
> ~~Pine Mountain park has~~ There are miles of trails. through green woods You
>
> can see gray squirrels and chipmunks. ~~Pine~~
> You can hear
> ^~~Mountain park has~~ birdes chirping. A tiny
> bubbling
> stream makes noises. The air is sweet and
>
> clean. As you walk, you feel pine needles
>
> crunch under your feet. ~~I always wear my~~
>
> ~~hiking boots.~~ Come visit soon!

PRACTICE and APPLY

Revise Your Own Description

1. Reread your description.

2. Take out incomplete sentences.

3. Add details to make your "word pictures" clearer.

4. **Grammar** Can you change the way you wrote your sentences?

Checklist ✓
Revising

☐ **Did you keep your purpose and audience in mind?**

☐ **Did you give examples of things to do?**

☐ **Did you use words that tell about the senses?**

☐ **Did you include a strong lead and a good ending?**

☐ **Did you add an interesting title?**

115

Proofread

Proofread your description after you revise it. Look for a different kind of mistake in mechanics, grammar and usage, and spelling.

STRATEGIES FOR PROOFREADING

- Reread your writing several times.

- Check for correct punctuation.

- Check to make sure you have formed proper nouns and plural nouns.

- Check each word for correct spelling.

TiP!

Spelling

When the /s/ is spelled *c*, *c* is always followed by *e*, *i*, or *y*. (*city, center*)

REVIEW THE RULES

GRAMMAR

- A singular noun names one person, place, or thing.

- A plural noun names more than one. You can often make a singular noun plural by adding -*s* or -*es*.

MECHANICS

- The names of special people and places are proper nouns.

- A proper noun begins with a capital letter.

Look at the proofreading corrections made on the draft below. What does ≡ mean? Why is this change needed?

PROOFREAD

Come to Pine Mountain park

#Pine Mountain park is a great place to visit!
There are   through green woods
Pine Mountain park has miles of trails. You

can see gray squirrels and chipmunks. Pine
You can hear   birds
Mountain park has birdes chirping. A tiny
        bubbling
stream makes noises. The air is sweet and

clean. As you walk, you feel pine needles

crunch under your feet. I always wear my

hiking boots. Come visit soon!

PRACTICE and APPLY

Proofread Your Own Descriptive Writing

1. Correct spelling mistakes.

2. Check capital letters and end marks.

3. Indent paragraphs.

Checklist ✓
Proofreading

☐ **Did you begin each proper noun with a capital letter?**

☐ **Did you write plural nouns correctly?**

☐ **Did you indent the paragraph?**

PROOFREADING MARKS

new paragraph

∧ add

↶ take out

≡ Make a capital letter.

/ Make a small letter.

(sp) Check the spelling.

⊙ Add a period.

117

Publish

Good writers review their writing one last time before they publish it. Use this checklist.

✓ Self-Check Descriptive Writing

- ☐ Did I keep my audience and purpose in mind?
- ☐ Did I add a good title?
- ☐ Did I use details to create a picture?
- ☐ Did I put details in an order that makes sense?
- ☐ Did I use describing words?
- ☐ Did I write a strong lead and a good ending?
- ☐ Did I use plural and proper nouns correctly?
- ☐ Did I proofread and correct all mistakes?

This writer used the checklist to review his description. Read and discuss "Come to Pine Mountain Park." Do you think the writing is ready to publish? Why?

Come to Pine Mountain Park

by Eric Parker

Pine Mountain Park is a great place to visit! There are miles of walking trails through green woods. You can see busy gray squirrels and chipmunks. You can hear birds chirping. A tiny stream makes bubbling noises. The air is sweet and clean. As you walk, you can feel pine needles crunch under your feet. Come visit soon!

TiP!

Handwriting

As you write, leave a lot of space around your words. This makes it easier to read.

PRACTICE and APPLY

Publish Your Own Description

1. Check your revised draft once more.

2. Print or write a neat final copy.

3. Add drawings or photographs.

4. Make a cover for your travel guide.

119

Present Your Descriptive Writing

You need to plan before you present your description.

STEP 1

How to Share Your Description

Strategies for Speaking

Your purpose is to make your audience want to visit the place you describe.

- Write your main idea and a few details on a note card to help you remember what to say.
- Look at your audience. Smile.
- Make important points stand out by using body movements.
- Speak so that everyone can hear you.

TiP!

Listening Strategies

- Decide what you want to find out.

- Imagine what the speaker is describing.

- Keep your eyes on the speaker.

- Ask questions at the end of the talk.

Multimedia Ideas

Do you have home videos of the place you are describing? If so, you might want to show them before or after you speak.

STEP 2

How to Show Your Description

Suggestions for Illustration You can make what you have to say more interesting with pictures.

- Show photos or drawings of the place you describe.
- Point out the place on a map.
- If you have small pictures or souvenirs, pass them around.

STEP 3

How to Share Your Travel Guide

Strategies for Rehearsing Practice your presentation before you give it.

- Ask a partner to make suggestions.
- Watch yourself practice in a mirror.
- Tape-record your description. Listen to the tape. How can you make it better?

Viewing Strategies

- Study the pictures carefully.
- Look for details that the speaker does not tell you.
- Watch the speaker for clues about how he or she feels.

PRACTICE and APPLY

Present Your Own Descriptive Writing

1. Make notes to help you remember.

2. Look at your audience as you speak.

3. Use interesting pictures and objects.

4. Practice what you have to say.

Writing Tests

On a writing test, you are given a prompt that asks you to write something. Remember to read the prompt carefully. Look for key words and phrases that tell you what to write about and how to do your writing.

> **Prompt**
>
> **Think about what a room at home looks like.**
>
> **Write a paragraph for your teacher telling what the room looks like or what you might see in that room.**

How to Read a Prompt

Purpose Read the prompt again. Look for the words that tell you the purpose of the writing. In this prompt, the words "what the room looks like" tell you that the purpose is to inform.

Audience The prompt tells who the audience is. The words "for your teacher" let you know that your teacher is the audience.

Descriptive Writing When you are asked to write about what a place looks like, you are writing a description. The words "looks like" and "what you might see" tell you that you should use describing words and details to show what the place is like.

How to Write to a Prompt

Read the following tips to help when you are given a writing prompt.

Before Writing **Content/Ideas**	• Think about your writing purpose. • Remember who your audience is. • Make a list of describing words.
During Writing **Organization/ Paragraph Structure**	• Start with a good topic sentence. • In descriptive writing, use details to make a picture for the reader. • Group details together in an order that makes sense. • Use describing words.
After Writing **Grammar/Usage**	• Proofread your work. • Use correct end marks. • Spell all words correctly. • Be sure you used singular and plural nouns correctly.

Apply What You Learned

Find the words in a prompt that tell you what to write about. Look for purpose and audience. Figure out the order to write your ideas in.

> **Prompt**
>
> Parties have exciting colors, sounds, and smells.
>
> Write a paragraph for your teacher that describes what you might see, hear, or smell at a party.

Grammar and Writing Review

pages 68–71, 78–81 ## Nouns

A. Circle the correct noun in ( ). Name each noun by writing people, places, or things.

1. Two (family, families) are having a picnic. _____

2. Maria carries a big (basket, baskets). _____

3. All the (child, children) are playing games. _____

pages 72–75 ## Proper Nouns

B. Circle proper nouns.

4. Last Sunday we went to visit Grandma.

5. We celebrated Mother's Day and missed you.

6. How do you like Salt Lake City?

pages 82–85 ## Singular and Plural Possessive Nouns

C. Circle the possessive noun in each sentence. Write *S* if it is singular. Write *P* if it is plural.

7. My grandfather's favorite season is winter. _____

8. The trees' branches were heavy with snow. _____

9. How great my brothers' snow fort was! _____

pages 76, 86 ## Mechanics and Usage: Using Capital Letters and Commas

D. Write each sentence or greeting correctly on a piece of paper.

10. On monday, eric got a new pet.

11. dear aunt Ruth

12. Many dogs play in hillside park.

Unit 2 Review

pages 96–97

Vocabulary: Compound Words

E. **Circle each compound word.**

13. Dad and I took a walk this afternoon.

14. We waited until after the thunderstorm.

15. Dad took pictures of the rainbow.

16. I jumped over puddles on the sidewalk.

17. The sunshine soon dried up the puddles.

pages 98–99

Composition: Leads and Endings

F. **Write *lead* or *ending* to tell where each sentence would come in a story.**

18. It was raining hard this morning. _____

19. That was how it all happened. _____

20. Once there was a girl named Daisy. _____

pages 116–117

Proofreading a Description

G. **21.–25. Correct the 5 mistakes. Then write the description correctly on a piece of paper.**

> The Science Museum
>
> on monday, we went to The Science
>
> museum. You can do all kinds of super
>
> things in the children's senter. One room
>
> has a giant tub filled with soapy water

Save this page until you finish Unit 2.

Project File

A Friendly Letter

A **friendly letter** is a letter to someone you know. Think about why each part is needed.

Knowing the form for a friendly letter will help you write your letter in the next unit.

312 Essex Lane
Ames, Iowa 50010
August 3, 20_ _

Dear Marla,

I had a good time with your family last week. Your mom, dad, and sister are really nice. Thank you so much for inviting me to the beach.

Every time I look at the pretty shells, I think of the fun we had. Guess what! When I put the big shell to my ear, I thought I heard the ocean! I really miss the big waves, the noisy gulls, and making sand castles. Most of all, I miss you.

I hope you can visit my family and me this fall. It will be so much fun. Write back soon.

Your friend,
Jody

Heading Gives the address of the person writing the letter.

Date Tells when the letter was written.

Greeting Usually starts with Dear, and the name of the person the letter is to.

Body Is the main part of the letter.

Closing Tells that the letter is ending.

Signature Is the writer's name.

Share your experiences with a pen-pal Wouldn't it be fun to have a pen-pal from another country? Ask your teacher to help you join a pen-pal club, and choose someone to write a letter to.

Write your letter.

PROJECT 2

A Poster

If you were born in May, your birthstone is the emerald. Look in the encyclopedia for a list of the birthstones for each month.

Birthstones Create a poster about birthstones. Write a sentence or two about each stone. Use colorful words.

TIME
FOR KIDS

Nouns

A. **Write the underlined words that are nouns.**

1. <u>Where</u> is the <u>birdhouse</u>? _____

2. <u>Look</u> in the <u>yard</u>. _____

3. The <u>grass</u> <u>is</u> dry. _____

4. <u>Find</u> the <u>hose</u>. _____

5. We <u>need</u> <u>seeds</u>. _____

6. Let's <u>go</u> to the <u>store</u>. _____

7. Where <u>are</u> the <u>keys</u>? _____

8. <u>Get</u> into the <u>truck</u>. _____

9. <u>Put</u> on your <u>seat belt</u>. _____

10. We <u>need</u> <u>birdseed</u>, too. _____

B. **Circle the noun in each sentence.**

11. Do you see the nest?

12. Look up in the tree.

13. The birds are eating.

14. The branch sways.

15. Let's take a picture.

Save this page until you finish Unit 2.

Grammar

More About Nouns

A. Write **person**, **place**, or **thing** to tell what each underlined noun names.

1. Where is my <u>flute</u>? _____

2. The <u>case</u> is empty! _____

3. Is it in the <u>kitchen</u>? _____

4. Did my <u>sister</u> take it? _____

5. My <u>teacher</u> just called. _____

6. I must learn a new <u>song</u>. _____

7. My <u>brother</u> helps me look. _____

8. We look all over the <u>house</u>. _____

9. We check my <u>bedroom</u> last. _____

10. I see it on my <u>desk</u>! _____

B. Circle the noun that names a person or people. Underline nouns that name things.

11. My family likes music.

12. We go to concerts in the park.

13. My mom brings a blanket.

14. We watch the stars in the sky.

15. We listen to the music and crickets.

129

Grammar

Proper Nouns

A. Write the proper nouns in the sentences.
Begin each proper noun with a capital letter.

1. miss ames tells us about the new boy. _____

2. He will start school on tuesday. _____

3. His name is michael bono. _____

4. The bonos are from texas. _____

5. His family has just moved to seaside. _____

6. Our town is in florida. _____

7. The bonos live on shore drive. _____

8. Our house is on dune road. _____

9. I belong to a pet club called feathers. _____

10. Michael has a pet parrot called henry. _____

B. Write each proper noun correctly with capital letters.

11. Ask michael to join our pet club. _____

12. The club meets on friday. _____

13. My friend andy from bayside is coming. _____

14. The pet store is on main street. _____

15. The pet store owner is alan lee. _____

130

Days, Months, and Holidays

A. Write the proper nouns that name days of the week, months, and holidays.

1. January is a busy month. _____

2. February is busy, too. _____

3. Groundhog Day comes first. _____

4. It is on Tuesday this year. _____

5. Mom likes Valentine's Day best. _____

6. March is my favorite month. _____

7. We like to go swimming in July. _____

8. When is President's Day? _____

9. School starts after Labor Day. _____

10. My party is on October 1. _____

B. Write each proper noun correctly with capital letters.

11. I really like independence day. _____

12. The holiday is on the fourth of july. _____

13. The town parade is on saturday. _____

14. We have a picnic on sunday. _____

15. Is there a holiday in august? _____

Using Capital Letters

A. Write each underlined proper noun correctly.

1. My name is <u>greg allen</u>.

2. My family lives in <u>derry</u>.

3. Our house is on <u>oak road</u>.

4. My friend <u>jake</u> has a horse.

5. His horse, <u>patches</u>, is beautiful.

6. I go horseback riding every <u>saturday</u>.

7. The stable is in <u>greenville</u>.

8. I go to riding camp in <u>june</u>.

9. Camp starts around <u>father's day</u>.

10. Camp ends before <u>independence day</u>.

B. Write each proper noun correctly with capital letters.

11. Dad and I drove to ohio.

12. Our friend bill has a farm.

13. He sold his horse flash.

14. We drove home on labor day.

15. School starts in september.

Plural Nouns

A. **Write the underlined word that names more than one.**

1. My <u>sister</u> likes <u>peaches</u>. _____

2. My <u>brothers</u> share an <u>orange</u>. _____

3. Who wants a <u>bag</u> of <u>peanuts</u>? _____

4. I want some <u>pears</u> for <u>lunch</u>. _____

5. My <u>friend</u> only eats <u>bananas</u>. _____

6. I have a <u>box</u> of <u>raisins</u>. _____

7. Are these <u>apples</u> for a <u>pie</u>? _____

8. Here is a <u>bowl</u> of <u>plums</u>. _____

9. Put the <u>pits</u> on your <u>plate</u>. _____

10. Who has the <u>basket</u> of <u>cherries</u>? _____

B. **Make the noun in ( ) name more than one. Write the new noun.**

11. Look at the (row) of grapes. _____

12. We need many (bunch). _____

13. Dad picks ten (box). _____

14. How many (jar) do we need? _____

15. Mom makes two jellies and three (jam). _____

Grammar

More Plural Nouns

A. Circle the noun that names more than one.

1. All the children have a chore.

2. I feed the ponies.

3. What big teeth they have!

4. My brother likes the bunnies best.

5. Ann feeds the hen and the geese.

6. A baby chick hops around her feet.

7. Our barn cat chases mice.

8. Mom and her friend pick berries.

9. The women will make jam.

10. Two men help Dad with the fence.

B. Change the underlined noun from singular to plural. Write the new word.

11. The <u>mouse</u> hid in the barn. _____

12. The <u>child</u> weeded the garden. _____

13. The <u>cherry</u> tasted sweet. _____

14. Our <u>puppy</u> grew quickly. _____

15. His <u>tooth</u> grew strong. _____

Singular Possessive Nouns

A. Write the possessive form of each singular noun.

1. Miss Hart _____

2. Toby _____

3. owl _____

4. Max _____

5. Mom _____

6. Ed _____

7. Lee _____

8. Mr. Romano _____

9. woman _____

10. Dina _____

B. Write the possessive form of the word in ( ).

11. (Everyone) work is so good. _____

12. This (artist) painting is pretty. _____

13. Will (Ryan) drawing win? _____

14. The (winner) name is Carl. _____

15. (Carl) painting wins first prize. _____

Plural Possessive Nouns

A. **Circle the plural possessive noun in each sentence.**

1. My sisters' toys are in the hall.

2. The cats' bowls are in the kitchen.

3. The teachers' meeting starts after lunch.

4. The parents' cars are parked outside.

5. My grandmothers' cookies are the best.

6. The children's pictures hang in the hall.

7. My aunts' store is in the next town.

8. Your friends' fishing trip sounds like fun.

9. We will spend Thanksgiving at our cousins' house

10. Many people are invited to the two families' party.

B. **Change each noun in ( ) to a plural possessive noun. Write each new word.**

11. Welcome to our (family's) picnic. _____

12. My (sisters) friends are here. _____

13. Try my (aunts) tasty dishes. _____

14. Meet my (uncles) children. _____

15. Are these your (dogs) toys? _____

Letter Punctuation

A. Write each greeting and closing. Add commas where they belong.

1. Your cousin _____

2. Dear Grandma _____

3. With thanks _____

4. Very truly yours _____

5. Dear Uncle Ed _____

6. Sincerely _____

7. Your grandson _____

8. Dear Jeff _____

9. Love to all _____

10. Dear Mom and Dad _____

B. Add the correct punctuation to each greeting and closing.

11. Dear Aunt Bea

12. Very sincerely

13. Dear Alex

14. Love

15. Dear Cousin Ken

Verbs and Explanatory Writing

*In this unit you will learn about verbs.
You will also learn how to write to tell how to do
something.*

Art Link   *Learning how to do new things is
exciting. What did the writer learn how to do?*

I liked making things with clay in art class.
You took a fat hunk of it and rolled it into a long
piece and curled it around and put it on top of
another long, curled piece, and another. Then
you smoothed it all out and painted it and
baked it—and took it home to your mother.

from **Higher on the Door**
by James Stevenson

Thinking Like a Writer

Explanatory Writing
Explanatory writing tells
how to do or make
something.

• How did this writer make
things with clay in art
class?

• What did James do last?

Verbs Each sentence above
has a verb that shows
action.

 **QUICK WRITE**
Write the words that tell
the action in each sentence.

Thinking Like a Writer

Explanatory Writing After you read the passage on page 139, write about the way James Stevenson made things with clay in art class. Write what James did last.

_____

_____

_____

_____

_____

_____

_____

_____

⏰ **QUICK WRITE** Write the words that tell the action in each sentence in the passage.

_____

_____

_____

_____

_____

McGraw-Hill School Division

Action Verbs

RULES

- An **action verb** is a word that shows what someone or something is doing.

  I draw a picture.

- Some action verbs tell about actions that are hard to see.

  Mom likes my picture.

- A sentence names the person or thing you are talking about. It also tells what is happening.

  Ted <u>writes</u> a poem. The bell <u>rings</u>.

      ↑   ↑

   action verb   *action verb*

THINK AND WRITE

Verbs

How can you tell if a word is an action verb? Write your answer in your journal.

Guided Practice

Name the action verb in each sentence.

1. Kayla taps the drum. _____

2. Marcus plays the flute. _____

3. Josh and I clap our hands. _____

4. Our teacher enjoys the song. _____

5. We listen to the music. _____

140

REVIEW THE **RULES**

• **Action verbs** tell what someone or something is doing.

More Practice

A. **Circle the action verb in each sentence.**

6. Chad brings a jump rope outside.

7. Kim holds one end of the jump rope.

8. Kim and I swing the jump rope.

9. The rope moves around and around.

10. Maria jumps first.

Handbook
page 438

Extra Practice page 196

B. Spiral Review **Circle the action verb in each sentence. Underline each noun.**

11. Students go to the playground.

12. The class knows a good game.

13. The boy throws the ball.

14. The teacher runs fast.

15. The children cheer loudly.

Writing Activity   A Song

Write a song to sing when you jump rope.
APPLY GRAMMAR: Use action verbs.

 Music Link

Present-Tense Verbs

--- **RULES** ---

- The tense of a verb tells when the action takes place.

- Present-tense verbs tell about actions that happen now.

     The rabbit hops away.

- Add *-s* to present-tense verbs that tell about one person or thing. Add *-es* if the verb ends with *s, ch, sh, x,* or *z*.

Add *-s*	Add *-es*
My cat sleep**s** on a mat.	Dana watch**es** the bee.
Muff like**s** her nap.	The bee buzz**es** by.

THINK AND WRITE

Verbs
How do you know which verbs need the ending *-s* and which need *-es*? Write the answers.

Guided Practice

Name the ending to add to the verb in ( ), *-s* or *-es*. Tell what the new word is.

EXAMPLE: Tina (toss) the ball to her dog.
     Ending: -es, tosses

1. Lucky (catch) the ball. _____

2. The dog (bring) the ball to Tina. _____

3. The girl (hug) her pet. _____

4. Mom (mix) food for Lucky. _____

5. Tina (feed) her good pet. _____

• **Present-tense verbs** tell what is happening now. Add *-s* or *-es* to tell what one person or thing is doing.

More Practice

A. Add *-s* or *-es* to the verb in ( ). Write the new verb.

6. Bill (walk) his puppy to the pet show. _____

7. Nell (put) her kitten in a box. _____

8. Bob (brush) his dog's coat. _____

9. Jed (fix) the cage for his mouse. _____

10. The neighborhood pet show (start). _____

Handbook
page 438

Extra
Practice
page 197

B. **Spiral Review** **Circle the verb in each sentence. Write each proper noun correctly with a capital letter.**

11. Come to our january concert. _____

12. We perform next tuesday. _____

13. Mr. may's class plans the concert. _____

14. Luke and I invite aunt nancy. _____

15. She lives in grovetown. _____

 Writing Activity **A Sign**

Write a sign to tell people about a pet show.
APPLY GRAMMAR: Use present-tense verbs.

🔍 **Science Link**

McGraw-Hill School Division

Subject-Verb Agreement

RULES

- The **subject** and the **verb** in a sentence need to agree, or go together correctly.

- Do not add *-s* or *-es* to a present-tense verb that tells about more than one person or thing.

  One bell rings. Three bells ring.

- If the subject is one person, the verb must tell about one person. If the subject is more than one person, the verb must tell about more than one person.

One	More Than One
Toby walks home.	Toby and I walk home
subject verb	subject verb

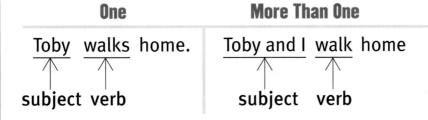

THINK AND WRITE

Verbs

How can you remember when to add *-s* or *-es* to a verb and when not to? Write your answer.

Guided Practice

Name which verb in ( ) is correct.

1. Mr. Crane (test, tests) the water.

_____

2. Ms. Yin (pay, pays) the bills. _____

3. My mom and my aunt (drive, drives) buses.

_____

4. Officer Pat (watch, watches) us cross.

_____

5. Truck drivers (pick, picks) up the trash.

_____

Handbook
page 439

Extra
Practice
page 198

REVIEW THE RULES

- A **subject** and **verb** must agree. Add *-s* or *-es* only if the verb tells about one person or thing.

More Practice

A. Circle the correct verb in ( ).

6. Mr. Hall (teach, teaches) cooking.

7. Dan and I (stand, stands) in the kitchen.

8. We (ask, asks) some questions.

9. Mr. Hall (show, shows) us the pots and pans.

10. The cooks (wash, washes) their hands.

B. **Spiral Review** **Add apostrophes in three possessive nouns. Circle each subject.**

11. Amber and I meet a painter. _____

12. The womans paintings are pretty. _____

13. We learn many things. _____

14. The painters brushes stand in a jar. _____

15. Some brushes tips come to a point. _____

Writing Activity   A Paragraph

Write about a job in which workers help others.
APPLY GRAMMAR: Circle each verb.

Social Studies Link

McGraw-Hill School Division

Abbreviations

RULES

- An abbreviation is a short way of writing a word. Abbreviations start with a capital letter and end with a period.

  Will Mr. and Mrs. Sanchez visit the school?

Practice

A. Correct the abbreviation in each sentence.

1. First, ms Dara made paper birds. _____

2. Next, mr Ling painted pictures. _____

3. Then dr Fish showed a video. _____

4. Mark Ross, jr, sang a song. _____

5. After that, mrs Jones told a story. _____

B. **Spiral Review** **Make the ending of the verb in ( ) go with the subject. Capitalize each proper noun.**

6. Mom, dad, and I (get) ready. _____

7. Mom (drive) us to jefferson school. _____

8. Ms. dowd (greet) everyone. _____

9. Mr. cruz (help) the actors. _____

10. My friend ali (act) in the play. _____

Handbook
page 447

Extra Practice
page 199

Verbs

Why do you think there are abbreviations for people's titles? Write your answer.

Verbs

REVIEW THE RULES

- An action verb is a word that shows action.

- Present-tense verbs tell about actions that happen now.

- Add -s or -es to a present-tense verb only if it tells about one person or thing.

- The subject and the verb in a sentence need to agree, or go with each other correctly.

- An abbreviation is a short way of writing a word.

**Handbook
page 438**

QUICK WRITE

Sentences
Does it help your writing to know about verbs? How?

Practice

A. Circle the action verb in each sentence.

1. James reaches for the telephone.

2. He presses the numbers.

3. Kara's telephone rings.

4. Kara answers the telephone.

5. The two friends make some plans.

B. Challenge Write the sentences on a piece of paper. Fix any verbs that do not go with the subject. Fix any abbreviations that are not correct.

6.–10. Dr Lee is my uncle. His name is Dave Lee, jr He come to see us. I runs to him. He call me Mr. Mighty.

Past-Tense Verbs

Grammar

— **RULES** —

- **Past-tense verbs** tell about actions that happened before now. To tell about actions in the past, add the ending *-ed* to most verbs.

  Last week we visited the zoo.

- If the verb ends in a single consonant, double the consonant and add *-ed*.

  If the verb ends in silent *e*, drop the *e* and add *-ed*.

  Mac dropped his pencil.

  drop + p + ed = dropped

  You traced a picture.

  trace - e + ed = traced

THINK AND WRITE

Verbs
What helps you remember how to write past-tense verbs correctly?

Guided Practice

Tell which verb in ( ) shows action in the past.

1. We (plan, planned) a letter. _____

2. Jill (opened, opens) her letter. _____

3. Dot (finished, finishes) her letter. _____

4. I (pick, picked) up my letter. I folded it. _____

5. Dan (mailed, mails) the letter. _____

REVIEW THE RULES

- **Past-tense verbs** tell about actions in the past. Most past-tense verbs end with *-ed: jumped.*

- For verbs like *hop*, double the final consonant before adding *-ed: hopped.* For verbs like *race*, drop the *e* before adding *-ed: raced.*

Handbook
page 438

Extra Practice page 200

More Practice

A. **Circle the verb in ( ) that shows action in the past.**

6. Lisa (stop, stopped) at my desk.

7. She (hand, handed) me a letter.

8. I (placed, place) the letter in my backpack.

9. Some milk (spill, spilled) on the letter.

10. I (wipe, wiped) off the milk.

B. **Spiral Review** **Underline the action verb in each sentence. Circle each plural noun.**

11. The boys checked their mailbox.

12. Luis hoped for a birthday card.

13. Letters filled the mailbox.

14. The neighbors stopped by.

15. Mr. and Mrs. Cliff helped the children.

Writing Activity A Self-Portrait

Write a self-portrait to tell what you did yesterday.
APPLY GRAMMAR: Use past-tense verbs and circle them.

The Verb *Have*

— RULES —

- The verb *have* has three forms: **have, has,** and **had.** *Has* and *have* tell about present actions.

  Today I have a bike. Lin has one too.

- *Had* tells about the past.

  Yesterday I had a scooter.

- See which form of the verb have goes with certain subjects. Look at the chart.

Who or What	Present	Past
I or you	have	had
one person or thing	has	had
more than one person or thing	have	had

THINK AND WRITE

Verbs

How do you know when to use the verb *have* or *has* in a sentence? Write your answer.

Guided Practice

Circle the correct verb in ( ).

1. The museum (has, have) dinosaur bones.

2. You (has, have) a ticket to go in.

3. I (has, have) a ticket, too.

4. Some dinosaurs (has, had) big teeth.

5. Some dinosaurs (have, had) long necks.

Handbook
page 440

Extra Practice
page 201

— **REVIEW** THE **RULES** —

• Use *have* and *has* for the present tense. Use *had* for the past.

More Practice

A. Circle the correct verb in ( ).

6. Adam and Nina (have, has) toy dinosaurs.

7. Nina's dinosaur (have, has) a collar.

8. I (have, has) a book about dinosaurs.

9. Some dinosaurs (have, had) big heads.

10. The Apatosaurus (has, had) a small head.

B. Spiral Review Write the verb in ( ) to show action in the past. Cirle each singular noun.

11. Yesterday Mom (hand) us a box. _____

12. My brother (lift) the lid. _____

13. He and I (pick) up two dinosaurs. _____

14. We (hug) our mother. _____

15. She (smile) and kissed us. _____

Writing Activity   Journal Entry

Write about a favorite toy. Use exact words.
APPLY GRAMMAR: Use the verbs *have, has,* and *had* in your journal entry.

McGraw-Hill School Division

Combining Sentences: Verbs

RULES

Sometimes the subjects of two sentences are the same. You can use *and* to combine the sentences so you do not repeat words.

> *Ty swings the bat. Ty hits the ball.*

> *Ty swings the bat and hits the ball.*

- Find subjects that are the same. Combine the predicates with *and*.

Our class *plays kickball.*

same   combine with *and*

Our class *wins games.*

Our class *plays kickball and wins games.*

THINK AND WRITE

Verbs
Why would you combine two short sentences with *and* in your writing? Write your answer.

Guided Practice

Use *and* to combine the underlined predicates. Then write the sentences on a piece of paper.

1. Sue <u>sees the ball</u>. Sue <u>hits it</u>.

2. The ball <u>flies</u>. The ball <u>falls</u>.

3. Drew <u>gets the ball</u>. Drew <u>throws it</u>.

4. Sue <u>runs to the base</u>. Sue <u>slides</u>.

5. Al <u>grabs the ball</u>. Al <u>tags Sue</u> .

More Practice

A. Use *and* to combine the underlined predicates. Write the new sentence on a piece of paper.

6. The class <u>gets ready</u>. The class <u>goes outside</u>.

7. Friends <u>stand together</u>. Friends <u>form teams</u>.

8. One team <u>calls a name</u>. One team <u>asks for Deb</u>.

9. Deb <u>hears her name</u>. Deb <u>comes over</u>.

10. The players <u>hold hands</u>. The players <u>make a line</u>.

B. **Spiral Review** Fill in the blank with *have, has,* or *had*. Write each proper noun correctly.

11. Last october we ————— a concert. —————————————

12. Now we ————— the oakwood science fair.

—————————————————————————

13. I ————— a robot in the show. —————————

14. My friend pete ————— some magnets. —————————

15. Jason and jess ————— a model shark. —————————

Handbook
page 433

Extra Practice
page 202

Writing Activity   Directions

Tell how to play a game or make something. Say what to do first, next, and last.

APPLY GRAMMAR: Use *and* to combine sentences.

Commas in Dates

RULES

• Write a comma between the day and the year in a date.

People voted on April 7, 1998.

Practice

A. **Add a comma where it belongs in each date.**

1. The work began on March 30 1999.

2. They dug the hole on April 12 1999.

3. The builders started on May 5 1999.

4. The work ended on July 20 2000.

5. School opened on September 1 2000.

B. **Spiral Review** **Write the letter on piece of paper. Add commas where they belong. Use *and* to combine short sentences.**

6.–10.   May 15 2001

Dear Calvin

    Last week my family went to the playground. Last week my family had fun. I played baseball. I swam in the pool.

Your friend

Carrie

Handbook
page 452

Extra Practice
page 203

THiNK AND WRITE

Verbs
Tell a first grader how to write a date. Write this in your journal.

154

Grammar

Verbs

REVIEW THE **RULES**

- **Past-tense verbs** tell about actions in the past. Add *-ed* to the end of most verbs to make the past tense.

- Use *has* and *have* to tell about the present. Use *had* to tell about the past.

- Use *and* to combine sentences.

- Write a comma between the day and the year in a date.

Handbook
pages 438–441,
452

QUICK WRITE

Verbs
Write to tell how you can tell when a verb is in the past tense.

Practice

A. **Write the past-tense form of each verb in ( ).**

1. Our town (has) a Save Our Earth day. _____

2. We (plan) the event last year. _____

3. Some people (plant) trees. _____

4. Many people (recycle) trash. _____

5. Everyone (use) less water. _____

B. **Challenge** Use *and* to combine each pair of sentences. Write the new sentence on a piece of paper.

6. Mom cuts the grass. Mom pulls weeds.

7. I rake leaves. I make big piles.

8. Joey rakes leaves. Joey bags them.

9. Dad trims trees. Dad clips shrubs.

10. We work together. We have fun.

Common Errors with Subject-Verb Agreement

Sometimes a writer forgets that a subject and verb must go together.

Common Error	Examples	Corrected Sentences
The verb does not agree with the subject.	The boy rush away.	The boy rushes away.
	Our dogs runs fast.	Our dogs run fast.

REVIEW THE RULES

SUBJECT–VERB AGREEMENT

- If the subject is one person or thing (singular), add *-s* or *-es* to most verbs in the present tense.

- If the subject is more than one person or thing (plural), do not add *-s* or *-es* to the verb.

THINK AND WRITE

Verbs
How do you know when to add *-s* or *-es* to a verb? Write the answer.

Practice

Circle the verb in ( ) that agrees with the subject.

1. The train (stop, stops).

2. The doors (open, opens) wide.

3. People (step, steps) off the train.

4. His mother (hold, holds) his hand.

5. A man (look, looks) for his family.

Troubleshooter, page 424-425

Mechanics and Spelling

Directions

Read the passage and decide which type of mistake appears in each underlined section. Choose the correct answer.

Check to see if commas are needed in the date.

Do you have to double the consonant before adding the ending?

Sample

On <u>June 21 2000</u>, Olga rode her bike to the
(1)
pet store. Inside <u>she saw hamsters runing</u> in
(2)
circles on a wheel. She saw lizards crawling
up a stick. She saw snakes curled up in knots.
Then she saw a green and blue parrot that
said, "I see you." <u>That made olga laugh</u>.
(3)

Every proper noun begins with a capital letter.

1 ○ Spelling
　　○ Capitalization
　　○ Punctuation

2 ○ Spelling
　　○ Capitalization
　　○ Punctuation

3 ○ Spelling
　　○ Capitalization
　　○ Punctuation

Test Tip
If you don't understand something, read it again carefully.

TIME FOR KIDS Writer's Notebook

RESEARCH

RESEARCH If I want to find out where a place is, I look at a **map**. Maps help me find cities, towns, mountains, lakes, rivers, and oceans. Sometimes I put a map in my story. Maps show my readers where a place is.

COMPOSITION SKILLS

WRITING WELL When I write a story, I always start at the beginning. Then I tell what happened **in order**. Writing events in order helps readers follow my story.

VOCABULARY SKILLS

USING WORDS Adding a few letters before a word can change its meaning. Those letters are called a **prefix**. Prefixes can help me change the usual into the unusual. Using these words can help me say exactly what I want to say. Can you think of any words with prefixes?

Read Now!

As you read the photo essay about the friendly firehouse, write down words or phrases that tell about the order of events in the essay.

TIME
FOR KIDS

Writer's Notebook

COMPOSITION SKILLS

WRITING WELL Write the words and phrases that tell about the order of events in the photo essay about the friendly firehouse.

_____

_____

_____

_____

_____

_____

_____

_____

_____

_____

_____

_____

TIME FOR KIDS
PHOTO ESSAY

FIRE DEPARTMENT

A Very Friendly Firehouse

Firefighters jump at the idea of having fun with kids.

Firefighters Keep Kids in School

"Good Morning!" A firefighter says hello to a group of kids from the neighborhood.

The firefighters of Engine Company 16 battle fires in Chicago, Illinois. But when they aren't fighting fires, they do something very unusual. They open their firehouse doors to kids.

The story begins about 15 years ago. Back then, children from Hartigan Elementary School were not going to class. Instead, they were visiting the firehouse during school hours.

So firefighter Arthur Lewis had an idea. Kids who started going to school would win a radio. Later, the men gave away old bikes which they rebuilt. The idea worked. Kids stayed in school!

Today, all kinds of stuff goes on at the firehouse. Kids play sports and chess. Kids practice math.

Jeremy Woods drops by the firehouse to play football. "It's my favorite place to come," he says.

interNET CONNECTION Go to www.mhschool.com/language-arts for more information on the topic.

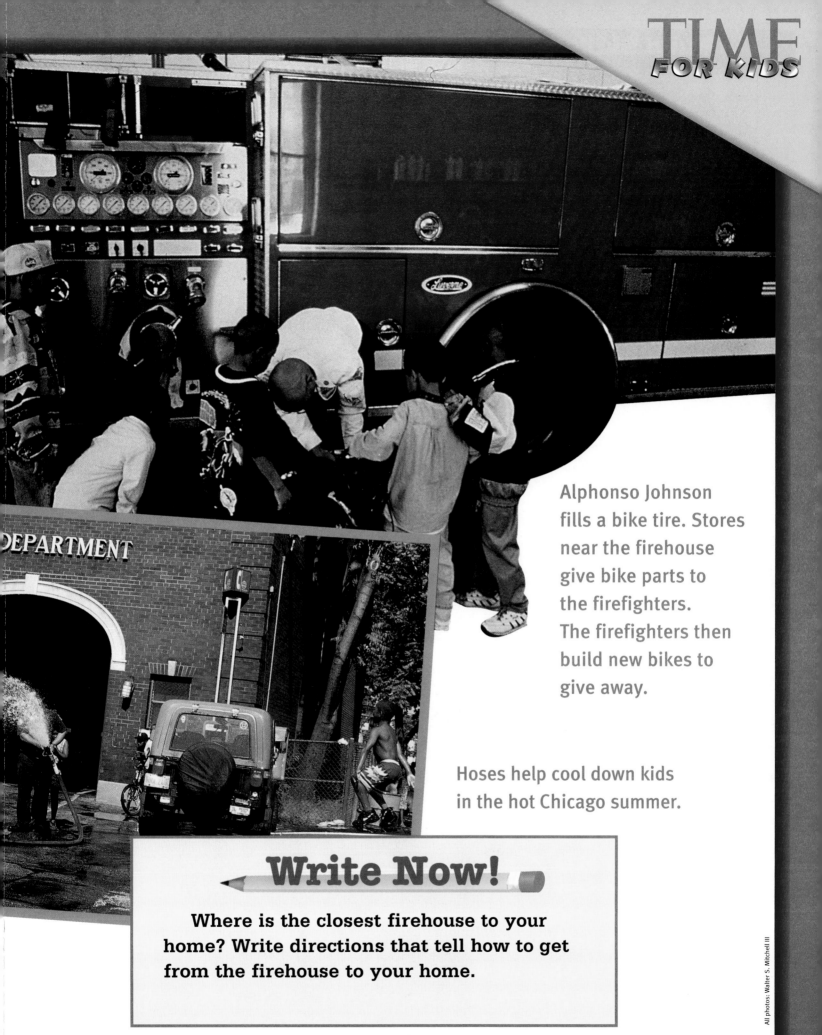

Alphonso Johnson fills a bike tire. Stores near the firehouse give bike parts to the firefighters. The firefighters then build new bikes to give away.

Hoses help cool down kids in the hot Chicago summer.

Write Now!

Where is the closest firehouse to your home? Write directions that tell how to get from the firehouse to your home.

Maps

Maps help you find places. Look at the map of a school building. Find the rooms and hallways.

Some maps have pictures on them called **symbols**. The **key** tells you what each symbol means.

Elm Street School

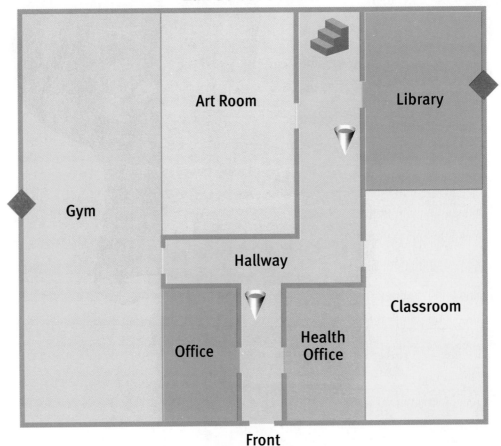

Key

162

Practice

A. Use the map and the key on page 162 to answer these questions.

1. What does this symbol [symbol] show? _____

2. How many exits are there? _____

3. How does a symbol help you?

_____

_____

4. What shows you what each map symbol means?

_____

5. How many different symbols are shown? _____

B. Imagine that you are at the front door of the school on the map. Then answer 6-10.

6. As you walk in the front door, what room is on

the right? _____

7. What room is next to the Art Room? _____

8. What room is to the right of the stairs? _____

9. What room is next to the Health Office? _____

10. What is between the office and the Art Room?

_____

Writing Activity   Directions

Write five sentences telling where to find two or more rooms shown on the school map. Try to use the direction words *left* and *right*.

Vocabulary: Prefixes

DEFINITION

A prefix is a word part added to the beginning of a word. A prefix changes the meaning of a word. You can use prefixes to say things in a shorter way.

Prefix	Meaning	Example
un-	not, do the opposite of	un- + lock = unlock
re-	again, back	re- + fill = refill

THINK AND WRITE

Prefixes

How can using prefixes like *un-* or *re-* make your writing better? Write your answer.

Look at the blue words in the letter below.

Dear Aunt Nancy,

   Our family is unhappy that we were unable to find your new house.

   We were unwise to try to get there without a map. We retraced our path many times. We even had to refill the gas tank!

   You will have to retell the directions to Dad.

                     Love,

                     Laura

McGraw-Hill School Division

Practice

A. Write the word from the box that matches each meaning.

unload	unwind	relock	reload	retie

1. load again _____

2. do the opposite of wind _____

3. lock again _____

4. tie again _____

5. do the opposite of load _____

B. Change the underlined words in each sentence to a word with the prefix *un-* or *re-*.

6. Ron and I were <u>not sure</u> of the way. _____

7. We <u>again opened</u> the map. _____

8. Ron <u>checked</u> the directions <u>again</u>. _____

9. We were <u>not happy</u> about our problem. _____

10. Ron <u>placed</u> the map <u>back</u> in his pocket.

_____

C. Grammar Link **11.–15.** Add a prefix to these verbs: *pack, start, open, close,* and *turn.* Use each new word in a sentence.

Writing Activity   A Checklist

Write a checklist of things to do before a trip.
APPLY GRAMMAR: Use two or three verbs with prefixes.

Composition: Logical Order

When you write to explain, the steps you write should be in an order that makes sense.

GUIDELINES

- **Time-order words**, such as *first, next,* or *last,* help you tell directions in order.

- **Space-order words**, such as *to the right, to the left, above,* or *below* help you tell exactly where people, places, and things are.

- To make sense, each step should lead to the next step.

THINK AND WRITE

Logical Order

Why is it important to keep the steps in order when you give directions?

Notice how the writer of these directions used an order that makes sense.

Space-order words help the reader "see" where places are.

Time-order words show the reader what happens next.

To get to Ray's Pet Shop from Main Street, follow these directions. Go north on Main Street. You will pass Eastman's Hardware Store on the right. Then walk two blocks beyond Eastman's. You will come to Cree Road.

Turn left onto Cree Road. Next, walk one more block. Finally, look across the street. You will see Ray's Pet Shop at 314 Dune Lane.

McGraw-Hill School Division

Practice

A. Write *time order* or *space order* to tell how the underlined words show order.

1. First, check for traffic. _____

2. Look left down Dune Lane. _____

3. Next, turn and check the other way. _____

4. Stay between the lines of the crosswalk. _____

5. Then cross the street to Ray's. _____

B. Write *1, 2, 3, 4,* and *5* to show the order of the sentences.

6. Second, turn right and go to the puppies. _____

7. Now, pick out a colorful leash. _____

8. First, enter Ray's Pet Shop. _____

9. Next to the puppies, you will see leashes. _____

10. Last, go to the counter to pay for it. _____

C. **Grammar Link** On a piece of paper, write the sentences in order. Make the underlined verb match the tense in ( ).

11. Pat wave good-bye. (present)

12. First, Pat open her purse. (past)

13. Now, Ray put Pat's leash in a bag. (present)

14. Then Ray count the money. (past)

15. Next, she place money on the counter. (past)

Writing Activity Directions

Tell how to get to your desk from the classroom door.
APPLY GRAMMAR: Circle each verb.

Better Sentences

Directions

Read the paragraph. Some parts are underlined. The underlined parts may be one of the following:

- Incomplete sentences
- Correctly written sentences that should be combined

Choose the best way to write each underlined part.

Two sentences with many of the same words can be combined.

Is the sentence complete? Is there a subject and a predicate?

Sample

Lin had a brand new bike. <u>The bike had a</u> <u>horn</u>. <u>The bike had a mirror</u>. The bike was painted red and white. <u>Wanted to ride her bike</u> <u>in the parade</u>. Mom and Dad said she could. So she taped a flag to the bike, and off she rode.

(1) ... The bike had a horn.
(2) ... Wanted to ride her bike in the parade.

---

1 ○ The bike had a horn and a mirror.

○ The bike had a horn. A mirror.

○ The horn and the mirror on the bike.

2 ○ Her bike in the parade.

○ Lin wanted to ride her bike in the parade.

○ Lin wanted her bike.

Vocabulary and Comprehension

Directions

Read the paragraph. Then read each question that follows the paragraph. Choose the best answer to each question.

> **Sample**
>
> Are you getting a new puppy? Here's how to get ready for it. First, get a box and some old sweaters to make a soft, warm bed. Next, fill a bowl with water and another bowl with food. Be sure to <u>unfold</u> some newspapers and spread them all around. Then, get a collar and leash ready. Finally, you will be able to run and play with your new dog.

Look for small word parts to help figure out the word's meaning.

1 What is the first thing you need to do to get ready for a puppy?

○ Get a collar and leash.

○ Think of a name.

○ Make a soft, warm bed.

2 In this paragraph, the word <u>unfold</u> means—

○ read

○ make not folded

○ make not full

Seeing Like a Writer

Look at these pictures. How would you explain what the people are doing? What words would you use to describe each step?

Hayley and Her Violin by Patricia Espir.

Writing from Pictures

1. Think about what actions the pictures show. Write three action words for the pictures.

2. Write a caption for one of the pictures. Tell what the children are doing and how to do it.

3. Choose two of the pictures. Write a paragraph telling what the pictures show.

Apply Grammar: Include present-tense verbs that add -*s* or -*es*. Circle each one.

Explanatory Writing

Think about a time when you tried to teach someone how to do something. Explanatory writing is like that. It goes step by step.

Learning from Writers

Read these pieces of explanatory writing.

THINK AND WRITE

Purpose

How can you write directions that are easy to understand? Write your answer.

The Marching Band

Bobby watched the boys and girls on his street march back and forth. Each one played a different instrument. If Bobby had an instrument, he could be in the band, too. Bobby was lucky. His grandma showed him how to make a humming horn.

First, Bobby cut a four-by-four-inch square of waxed paper. Next, he placed the paper over one end of an empty paper tube. He used a rubber band to hold the paper in place. Last, Bobby's Grandma used a sharp pencil to poke holes through the tube.

To play his horn, Bobby held the tube next to his mouth and hummed. He moved his fingers to cover and uncover the holes. Soon, Bobby was humming along with the rest of the band!

— *Dale Ryder*

McGraw-Hill School Division

My Peanut Butter and Jelly Sandwich

Do you want to know what my favorite lunch in the world is? It's a peanut butter and jelly sandwich and a glass of milk! Here's how to make your own.

First, you get two pieces of bread. Next, you get the peanut butter and jelly. Open them up and put them near the bread. Get a butter knife and smush the peanut butter onto one piece of bread. Then, smush the jelly onto the other piece. Smush both pieces together and you have a peanut butter and jelly sandwich. It's delicious!

— Ken Lee

PRACTICE and APPLY

Thinking Like a Reader

1. How did Bobby make the horn?

2. What step comes after putting the peanut butter on the bread?

Thinking Like a Writer

3. Why did Dale Ryder name all the materials for making a horn?

4. What space-order words did Ken Lee use?

5. **Reading Across Texts** Tell how the two explanations are alike. How are they different?

Features of Explanatory Writing

— DEFINITIONS AND FEATURES —

Explanatory writing explains how to do something. Good explanatory writing does these things:

▸ It tells **how to** complete a task.

▸ It gives **step-by-step instructions.**

▸ It uses **time-order** or **space-order words.**

▶ How-To

Reread "The Marching Band" on page 172. What does this story explain how to make?

> Bobby was lucky. His grandma showed him how to make a humming horn.

The author tells how Bobby makes the horn. The instructions teach the reader how, too.

▶ Step-by-Step Instructions

The directions in the story go step by step. The first step has to be completed before going on to the next step.

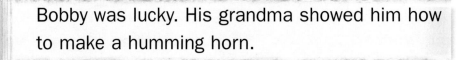

> First, Bobby cut a four-by-four inch square of waxed paper. Next, he placed the paper over one end of an empty paper tube.

McGraw-Hill School Division

▶ **Space-Order Words**

Space-order words add important details to directions. Use words like *on, over, under,* and *near* when you write about how to do something.

> To play his humming horn, Bobby held the tube next to his mouth and hummed.

What space-order words did the author use to help the reader understand how to make a humming horn?

PRACTICE and APPLY

Create a Features Chart

1. List the features of explanatory writing.

2. Reread "My Peanut Butter and Jelly Sandwich" on page 173.

3. Write how the author used each feature.

Features	Examples

Writing PROCESS

Prewrite

Explanatory writing explains how to do something. When you give directions, you are writing to explain.

Purpose and Audience

The purpose of explanatory writing is to inform. Think about who will read your letter. Decide what that person needs to know.

Choose a Topic

Start by **brainstorming** a list of topics. Think of an event coming up at school. Work out the directions for getting there.

Explore and list ideas to put in your letter.

THINK AND WRITE

Audience

How would your invitation be different if you wrote it to someone in your family. Write your answer.

I have lots of ideas for my letter.

Invite Dr. Jones to pet show

Pet show at school on December 17

My dog Rex has brown fur.

Go to the office.

Sign in.

Go through the doors.

Go down the hall.

Go up the stairs.

Turn.

Organize • Sequence

Your invitation will give directions to the event. To plan the order of your directions, use a list-of-steps chart.

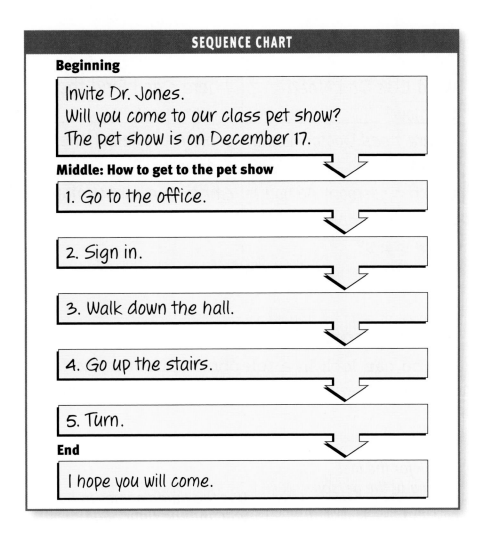

SEQUENCE CHART

Beginning

Invite Dr. Jones.
Will you come to our class pet show?
The pet show is on December 17.

Middle: How to get to the pet show

1. Go to the office.

2. Sign in.

3. Walk down the hall.

4. Go up the stairs.

5. Turn.

End

I hope you will come.

PRACTICE and APPLY

Plan Your Own Explanatory Writing

1. Choose an event and a person to invite.

2. Brainstorm ideas about the event.

3. Put the steps for the directions in order.

Checklist ✓

Prewriting

☐ **Did you tell when the event takes place?**

☐ **Did you think about your purpose and your audience?**

☐ **Did you choose a person to invite?**

☐ **Have you put the steps of your directions in order?**

☐ **Do you need to find out more?**

Prewrite • Research and Inquiry

▶ Writer's Resources

You may need to do some research for your invitation. Start with a list of questions. Then find resources that answer them.

What Else Do I Need to Know?	Where Can I Find the Information?
Where does Doctor Jones live?	Look in the telephone directory.
Which classroom do you pass before you go up the stairs?	Check the school map.

▶ Telephone Directory

You can look in a telephone directory to find someone's address or telephone number. The names are listed in ABC order.

Look for the last name of the person.

Use the guide names to help you find the right page.

| 418 | JONES—JORDAN |

Jones Cathy 22 Washington St	555-0234	Jordan David 155 River Dr	555-2281
Jones Donna 40 Morris Rd	555-1299	Jordan Dennis 602 Lincoln Rd	555-8743
Jones Ellen 33 West Ave	555-6624	Jordan Ed 29 Garden Rd	555-9876
Jones Larry 495 River Dr	555-7543	Jordan Maria 700 Cove Pl	555-2901
Jones Dr. Lisa 37 Garden Rd	555-4675	Jordan Paul 221 River Dr	555-3417

Look for the first name of the person.

McGraw-Hill School Division

▶ A Map

A map can help you make your directions clearer. Include places to look for, so readers can be sure they are going in the right direction.

▶ Use Your Research

Now that you have done your research, you can use it in your invitation. Add details from your research to your chart.

Handbook
pages 458–459

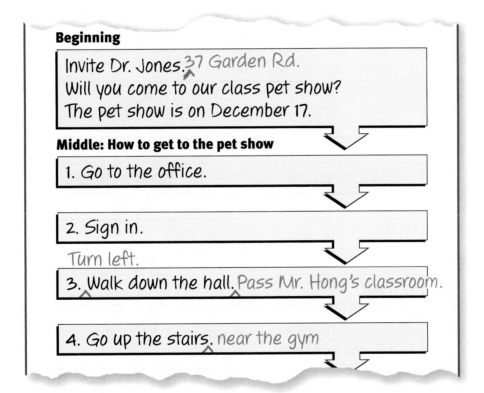

Beginning

Invite Dr. Jones. 37 Garden Rd.
Will you come to our class pet show?
The pet show is on December 17.

Middle: How to get to the pet show

1. Go to the office.

2. Sign in.

Turn left.
3. Walk down the hall. Pass Mr. Hong's classroom.

4. Go up the stairs. near the gym

Checklist ✓

Research and Inquiry

☐ Did you make a list of questions?

☐ Did you use resources to answer your questions?

☐ Did you add your answers to your chart?

PRACTICE and APPLY

Review Your Plan

1. List questions you have about your letter.

2. Use resources to answer your questions.

3. Add new information to your chart.

Draft

Before you write your draft, look over your list of steps. Be sure they are in the right order. You want your audience to be able to follow your directions easily.

Main idea for first paragraph: Inviting Dr. Jones

Main idea for second paragraph: Directions to the pet show

SEQUENCE CHART

Beginning

Invite Dr. Jones. 37 Garden Rd.
Will you come to our class pet show?
The pet show is on December 17.

Middle: How to get to the pet show

1. Go to the office.

2. Sign in.

Turn left.
3. Walk down the hall. Pass Mr. Hong's classroom.

4. Go up the stairs. near the gym

5. Turn.

End

I hope you will come.

This will be a good way to end the letter.

✓ Checklist

Drafting

☐ Did you think about your purpose and your audience?

☐ Does your letter tell how to get to the event?

☐ Does the order of the steps make sense?

☐ Did you use words that make your directions easy to follow?

Look at this draft of a letter. This writer used ideas from her chart and added some details.

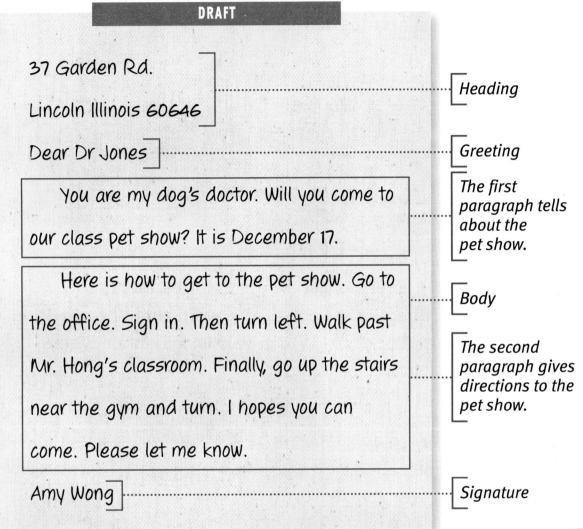

DRAFT

37 Garden Rd.

Lincoln Illinois 60646 — Heading

Dear Dr Jones — Greeting

You are my dog's doctor. Will you come to our class pet show? It is December 17. — *The first paragraph tells about the pet show.*

Here is how to get to the pet show. Go to the office. Sign in. Then turn left. Walk past Mr. Hong's classroom. Finally, go up the stairs near the gym and turn. I hopes you can come. Please let me know. — Body

The second paragraph gives directions to the pet show.

Amy Wong — *Signature*

PRACTICE and APPLY
Draft Your Own Explanatory Writing

1. Look back at your chart.
2. Use words that will make the steps clearer.
3. Use a map to help you give directions.

TECHNOLOGY
Highlight parts of your letter that you might want to move. Then use the cut or paste features.

Revise

Elaborate

In your letter, you can elaborate by adding details to your directions. The writer added important details.

It is December 17. It starts at 1:30.

Sign in. at the desk

SPACE-ORDER WORDS

behind	near
below	next to
beside	north
by	opposite
east	right
in front	south
left	west

Word Choice

Space-order words help readers follow directions. Look at the word this writer added to her draft. Which words tell about where places are?

Finally, go up the stairs near the gym and turn. right

Conferencing for the Reader

- Check to see if your partner's writing
  - gives step-by-step instructions
  - uses time-order words
  - uses space-order words

McGraw-Hill School Division

Better Paragraphs

Think about the main ideas you want to tell. Each main idea should be its own paragraph.

PREWRITE

DRAFT

REVISE

PROOFREAD

PUBLISH

REVISE

37 Garden Rd.

Lincoln Illinois 60646

Dear Dr Jones

You are my dog's doctor. Will you come to our class pet show? It is December 17. It starts at 1:30.

First, Here is how to get to the pet show. Go to the office. Sign in. at the desk Then turn left. Walk past Mr. Hong's classroom. Finally, go up the stairs near the gym and turn right. I hopes you can come. Please let me know.

Amy Wong

Checklist ✓
Revising

- [ ] **Did you keep your purpose and your audience in mind?**
- [ ] **Do you need more details?**
- [ ] **Are the steps in the directions clear?**
- [ ] **Do you have different kinds of sentences?**

PRACTICE and APPLY

Revise Your Own Explanatory Writing

1. Read your draft to yourself.
2. Share your draft with a partner.
3. Add details to make your directions easier.
4. **Grammar** Do your subjects and verbs agree?

Writing PROCESS

Proofread

After you revise your letter, go back and read it again. Look for a different kind of mistake.

TECHNOLOGY

When you work on a computer, a spell checker program can help you find words that are spelled wrong. Check that the new spelling matches the word you want to write.

STRATEGIES FOR PROOFREADING

- **Look for names of people, places, months, and holidays.** Start each with a capital letter.

- **Check for punctuation.** Make sure you added commas after the greeting, closing, between the city and state, and between the day and year.

- **Check your spelling.** Use a dictionary.

REVIEW THE RULES

GRAMMAR

- A **present-tense verb** must match the subject of the sentence. Add *-s* to some present-tense verbs that tell about one person or thing.

- Add *-ed* to most **past-tense action verbs** that tell about the past.

MECHANICS

- Start **abbreviations** in people's titles with a capital letter and end with a period.

- In a **date,** write a comma between the day and the year.

McGraw-Hill School Division

Look at the corrections made on the draft below. What does ∧ mean? Why are those corrections needed?

PROOFREAD

37 Garden Rd.

Lincoln, Illinois 60646

December 8, 2002

∧ Dear Dr. Jones,

You are my dog's doctor. Will you come to

It starts at 1:30.

our class pet show? It is December 17.∧

First,

Here is how to get to the pet show. Go to

at the desk

the office. Sign in. Then turn left. Walk past
∧

Mr. Hong's classroom. Finally, go up the stairs

right #

near the gym and turn. I hopes you can
∧

come. Please let me know.

Sincerely,

∧Amy Wong

PRACTICE and APPLY

Proofread Your Own Explanatory Writing

1. Fix any spelling mistakes.
2. Check punctuation, such as commas.
3. Make sure verbs agree with nouns.
4. Check that proper nouns begin with a capital.

Checklist ✓
Proofreading

☐ **Did you check your spelling?**

☐ **Are commas used correctly?**

☐ **Do your subjects and verbs agree?**

☐ **Did you write abbreviations correctly?**

PROOFREADING MARKS

new paragraph

∧ add

℘ take out

≡ Make a capital letter.

/ Make a small letter.

(SP) Check the spelling.

⊙ Add a period.

185

Publish

Before you publish your letter, go back and check it one more time. A checklist can help you.

✓ Self-Check Explanatory Writing

- ☐ Did I write an invitation my audience will be interested in getting?
- ☐ Did I make my purpose clear?
- ☐ Did I write the steps in order?
- ☐ Did I use different kinds of sentences?
- ☐ Did I use time-order and space-order words?
- ☐ Did I proofread and fix any mistakes?

The checklist helped this writer check her letter. Do you think it is ready to publish?

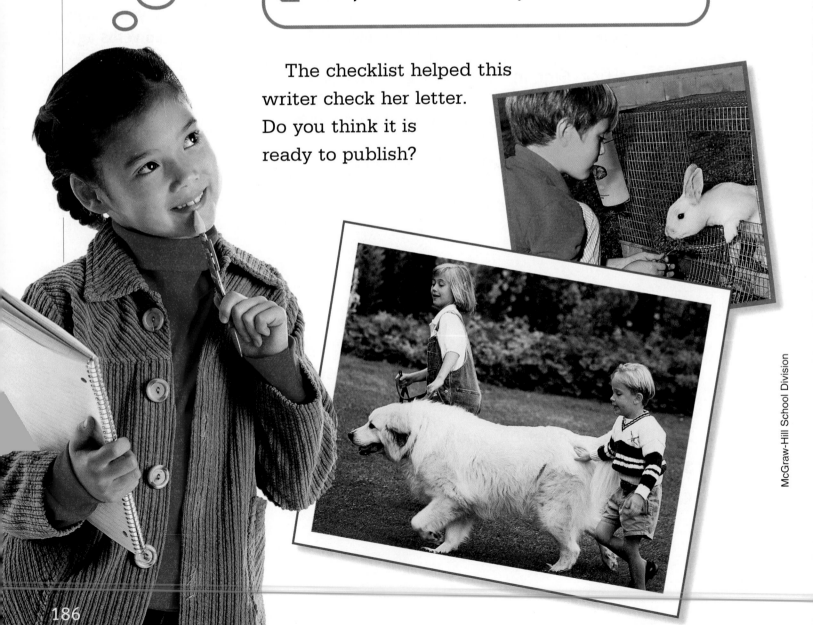

37 Garden Rd.
Lincoln, Illinois 60646
December 8, 2002

Dear Dr. Jones,

    You are my dog's doctor. Will you come to our class pet show? It is December 17. It starts at 1:30.

    Here is how to get to the pet show. First, go to the office. Sign in at the desk. Then turn left. Walk past Mr. Hong's classroom. Finally, go up the stairs near the gym and turn right.

    I hope you can come. Please let me know soon.

                    Sincerely,
                    Amy Wong

PRACTICE and APPLY

Publish Your Own Explanatory Writing

1. Read your invitation and look for any mistakes you missed.

2. Copy your letter neatly.

3. Draw a map or add pictures.

4. Put your letter in an envelope. Address it.

TIP!

TECHNOLOGY

Use the computer to print out another copy of your letter. Send that letter to the person you wrote to.

Present Your Explanatory Writing

Plan how to present your letter.
Use these ideas.

TiP!

Listening Strategies

■ Think about why you are listening. What information do you need to remember?

■ Listen for space-order direction words like *near*, *right*, *left*, and *at*.

■ Draw a map or take notes to help you remember.

STEP 1

How to Give an Invitation Aloud

Strategies for Speaking

Your purpose is to make your listeners feel that they are invited to something really special.

■ Smile at your audience.

■ Use note cards to remember the order of the directions.

■ Speak loudly and clearly.

Multimedia Ideas

You might want to show a videotape. For example, present a tape of last year's event to show what a good time everyone had.

STEP 2

How to Show Your Invitation

Suggestions for Illustrations Show pictures or maps to help your audience.

- Make a poster. List important facts, such as dates and times.
- Show a map of the directions.
- Make your pictures, maps, or posters big enough so that people can see them easily.

STEP 3

How to Share Your Invitation

Strategies for Rehearsing If you practice ahead of time, you'll be ready.

- Find a quiet place to practice.
- Ask a partner or family member to listen to you and give you ideas.

PRACTICE and APPLY

Rehearse Your Invitation

1. Get your note cards together.
2. Find or make pictures you will use.
3. Practice saying your invitation out loud.
4. Smile and sound interested when you speak.

TiP!

Viewing Strategies

- Read the information shown on posters or pictures.
- Make sure you understand maps and diagrams.
- Take notes about important facts and directions.

189

Writing Tests

Remember to read the prompt carefully. Look for key words and phrases that tell you what to write about and how to do your writing.

Look for words that tell if the purpose is to entertain or inform.

What words tell who the audience is?

Look for words that tell what kind of writing this is.

> **Prompt**
>
> **Think of a special activity that you know <u>how to do.</u>**
> **Write a paragraph <u>for your teacher</u> that tells <u>what you can do and how you do it.</u> Be sure to use details to tell about it.**

How to Read a Prompt

Purpose Look for words in the prompt that tell you the purpose of the writing. The words "how to do" tell you that the purpose will be to inform. When you explain how to do something, you give the audience information.

Audience The prompt tells who the audience is. The words "for your teacher" let you know that your teacher is the audience.

Explanatory Writing In explanatory writing, you tell how to do something. The words "what you can do and how you do it" let you know that you should explain what to do step-by-step.

McGraw-Hill School Division

How to Write to a Prompt

Remember these tips when you write to a prompt.

Before Writing **Content/Ideas**	• Think about your writing purpose. • Remember who your audience is. • Make a list of the steps you take to do your activity.
During Writing **Organization/** **Paragraph** **Structure**	• Start with a good topic sentence. • Give step-by-step instructions. • Use time-order or space-order words.
After Writing **Grammar/Usage**	• Proofread your work. • Start each sentence with a capital letter. • Spell words correctly. • Be sure you used verbs correctly.

Apply What You Learned

Find words in a writing prompt that tell you what to write about. Look for the purpose and audience. Plan the best way to organize your ideas.

Prompt

Think about how you get to school in the morning. Do you walk, get a ride, take a bus, or ride a bike?

Write a paragraph for your teacher explaining how you get to school. Be sure to use details to tell about it.

Name _____

Grammar and Writing Review

pages
140–145,
150–151

Present-Tense Verbs

A. Circle the correct verb in ( ).

1. Alex (watch, watches) a bird.

2. The babies (chirp, chirps) loudly.

3. I (take, takes) pictures of the birds.

pages
148–151

Past-Tense Verbs

B. Write the past tense of each underlined verb.

4. We <u>have</u> a book about dogs. _____

5. I <u>like</u> the poodles most of all. _____

6. Tina and I <u>flip</u> through the pages. _____

pages
152–153

Combining Sentences: Verbs

B. Use the word *and* to join each pair of sentences. Write the new sentence on a piece of paper.

7. Sam made a bird feeder. Sam filled it with seeds.

8. We watched. We waited.

9. Birds came. Bird ate the seeds.

pages
146, 154

Mechanics and Usage: Abbreviations and Commas

D. Write each group of words correctly.

10. February 9 2002 _____

11. dr Ortiz _____

12. December 18 2001 _____

pages
164–165

Vocabulary: Prefixes

E. Circle the prefix in each underlined word. Write what the word means.

13. I was <u>unhappy</u> with my photos. _____

14. Some pictures were <u>unclear</u>. _____

15. Dad and I <u>rechecked</u> the camera. _____

16. I <u>reloaded</u> the camera. _____

17. I <u>retook</u> the pictures. _____

pages
166–167

Composition: Logical Order

F. Write 1, 2, and 3 to put the sentences in order.

18. I put all my stuffed animals on a shelf. _____

19. I put the bears beside the lions. _____

20. First, I lined up the wild animals. _____

Proofreading a Letter

pages
184–185

G. 21.–25. Write the letter correctly on a piece of paper. There are 5 mistakes.

> January 30 2002
>
> Dear Ms. Ames,
>
>   Our Author's Day program is march 12.
>
> We are glad you can come. Our shcool is on
>
> Hill Street. Please meet Mr Sosa in the office.
>
>   Yours truly
>
>   Jeff Johnson

Save this page until you finish Unit 3.

Project File

An Article

An **article** presents information on a topic.

You will need to know the form for an article when you write your magazine article in the next unit.

City Birds

Many people live in cities. Did you know that many birds do, too? The city is home to different kinds of birds.

Pigeons and sparrows are common city birds. Pigeons often perch on ledges of high buildings. They look for seeds in grasses at parks. They also peck at crumbs people feed them. Sparrows build nests in park trees and bushes. They eat seeds, insects, or scraps of food left by people.

Gulls are common city birds, too. However, their "hometowns" are near the shore. Gulls build nests by the water. They clean up food scraps from beaches, streets, and sidewalks.

Birds may be different. But they all need food and homes, even in the city.

Topic is stated at the beginning.

Facts are presented clearly.

Main ideas and supporting details Each paragraph gives details about one main idea.

Compare and contrast The writer may compare and contrast things to make them clear.

Ending Sums up the writer's main ideas.

Same or Different When you see something that is flying high up in the sky, how can you tell if it's a bird or a plane? How are birds and planes alike and how are they different?

Write an article that compares birds and planes. Include exact details and put them in an order that makes sense.

PROJECT 2

Directions

Has a firefighter ever talked to you and your classmates about what to do if there is a fire in your home or school?

What to Do in Case of a FIRE Write a set of directions that tells how to get out of your home or school in case of a fire.

Name _____

Grammar

Action Verbs

A. **Circle each underlined word that is an action verb.**

1. My friends <u>walk</u> <u>to</u> my house.

2. <u>First</u>, we <u>eat</u> lunch.

3. Mel and Tom <u>ride</u> their <u>bikes</u>.

4. Greg <u>skates</u> in the <u>driveway</u>.

5. Jack and Dad <u>shoot</u> <u>baskets</u>.

6. Lori <u>and</u> I <u>play</u> jump rope.

7. Mom <u>holds</u> the <u>rope</u>.

8. <u>All</u> my friends <u>clap</u>.

9. Dad <u>cheers</u> <u>for</u> Mom.

10. <u>Dad</u> <u>jumps</u> high, too.

B. **Circle each action verb.**

11. Jack and I wave to our friends.

12. We race to the playground.

13. Mel and Tom run together.

14. Terry skips rope by herself.

15. Luis runs the fastest.

 Save this page until you finish Unit 3.

Present-Tense Verbs

A. Circle the correct word in ( ).

1. My friend (watch, watches) the softball team.

2. Jan (pitch, pitches) for the team.

3. Jan's twin sister (catch, catches) for the team.

4. Ann (buy, buys) a new mitt.

5. The new mitt (fit, fits) Ann's hand.

6. Jan's sister (save, saves) her money.

7. Mrs. Jones (coach, coaches) the girls.

8. The girl's brother (help, helps), too.

9. The team (play, plays) on Saturday mornings.

10. Each player (practice, practices) for the game.

B. Add *-s* or *-es* to the verb in ( ). Write the new verb.

11. The big game (begin) soon. _____

12. Each girl (get) ready. _____

13. Ann (drink) a cup of water before the game. _____

14. Jan (stretch) her arms and legs. _____

15. The coach (wish) everyone luck. _____

Grammar

Subject-Verb Agreement

A. Circle the correct form of the verb in ( ) to complete each sentence.

1. Many people (work, works) in my neighborhood.

2. Miss Simms (deliver, delivers) our mail.

3. We (buy, buys) bread from Mrs. Barton.

4. Ben and Diane (mow, mows) lawns.

5. Mom and Dad (teach, teaches) school.

6. Officer Jones (keep, keeps) us safe.

7. Mr. Sung and Mr. Yin (fix, fixes) cars.

8. Uncle Bob (fight, fights) fires.

9. My sister and I (help, helps) our neighbors.

10. Dr. Ruiz (check, checks) our teeth.

B. Change the verb in ( ) to show action going on now.

11. Dad (need) wood and paint. _____

12. We (drive) to the store. _____

13. Mr. Lee (own) the store. _____

14. Mr. Lee, Dad, and I (load) the truck. _____

15. Now Dad (finish) painting the bookcase. _____

Abbreviations

A. **Circle each word that is an abbreviation.**

1. My dad is Mr. James Lewis.

2. I am James Lewis, Jr.

3. Dr. Ann Lewis is my mom.

4. Our neighbor is Mr. Bell.

5. It is nice to meet you, Ms. Bell.

6. Have you met Mr. Anderson?

7. Mr. and Mrs. Anderson are painters.

8. Dr. and Mrs. Jack Soo live next door.

9. Mrs. Soo has a cute dog.

10. Jack Soo, Jr., is my friend.

B. **Write an abbreviation for each underlined word.**

11. Is <u>Doctor</u> Steven Lewis in his office? _____

12. Lee Soo, <u>Junior</u>, has a sick dog. _____

13. <u>Mister</u> Anderson will drive them. _____

14. Alan Bell, <u>Junior</u>, waits with Fluffy. _____

15. Fluffy belongs to Alan's neighbor,

<u>Mister</u> Anderson. _____

Grammar

Past-Tense Verbs

A. **Read each pair of sentences. Circle the underlined word that shows action in the past.**

1. Our mailman <u>knocks</u>. The dog <u>barked</u>.

2. Mom <u>answered</u> the door. Grandpa <u>says</u> hello.

3. Mr. Lee <u>handed</u> her a box. Mom <u>gives</u> the box to Jenna.

4. I <u>checked</u> the label. We <u>carry</u> it inside.

5. Jenna <u>opened</u> the box. I <u>help</u> her.

6. Inside the box we <u>see</u> a present. I <u>untied</u> the ribbon.

7. Grandpa <u>watches</u> us. I <u>ripped</u> off the paper.

8. We <u>looked</u> in the box. I <u>take</u> out the present.

9. I <u>showed</u> them the train set. We all <u>smile</u>.

10. Mom <u>moved</u> the box. Grandpa <u>helps</u> set up the train.

B. **Write each verb in ( ) to show action in the past.**

11. Mom (smiles) at me. _____

12. I (grin) back at Mom. _____

13. I (hug) my new teddy bear. _____

14. We (mail) a note to Grandma. _____

15. I (thank) her for the present. _____

The Verb *Have*

A. Write *present* if the underlined verb shows action in the present. Write *past* if the underlined verb shows action in the past.

1. Who <u>had</u> the camera last? _____

2. Do you <u>have</u> it? _____

3. Lisa <u>had</u> the camera last. _____

4. Ben <u>has</u> it now. _____

5. May I <u>have</u> it back, please? _____

6. We <u>had</u> some extra film. _____

7. Now we <u>have</u> only one roll. _____

8. Lisa <u>has</u> an old photo of Mom. _____

9. What a funny hat Mom <u>had</u> long ago! _____

10. Lisa still <u>has</u> that hat! _____

B. Circle the correct form of the verb *have*.

11. Do you (have, had) a Labor Day picnic?

12. We (have, has) a picnic every Labor Day.

13. Dad (has, have) photos from the last picnic.

14. What fun he (has, had) that day!

15. I also (have, had) a great time.

201

Combining Sentences: Verbs

A. Use *and* to combine the underlined predicates.
Write the new sentence.

1. Dad <u>unpacked</u>. Dad <u>put up the tent</u>.

_____

2. Jeb <u>saw a snake</u>. Jeb <u>yelled</u>.

_____

3. We <u>swam</u>. We <u>fished</u>.

_____

4. Mom <u>caught six fish</u>. Mom <u>cleaned them</u>.

_____

5. Dad <u>made a fire</u>. Dad <u>fried the fish</u>.

_____

B. Use *and* to combine the predicates. Write the
new sentence.

6. The moon rose. The moon lit up the sky.

_____

7. An owl hooted. An owl flew away.

_____

8. Jeb was tired. Jeb fell asleep.

_____

9. I heard a noise. I got the flashlight.

_____

10. I looked. I saw a skunk!

_____

Commas in Dates

A. Add commas where they belong in the dates.

1. November 19 2002

2. May 6 1994

3. September 30 2001

4. October 7 1994

5. January 3 2000

6. March 4 1996

7. February 2 2000

8. August 27 1998

9. November 22 1999

10. July 14 1998

B. Add a comma in each date.

11. Today is November 16 2002.

12. Last Monday's date was November 6 2000.

13. We will have a party on January 23 2001.

14. We will visit Grandma on November 26 2001.

15. I was born on April 2 1994.

 Save this page until you finish Unit 3.

Name _____

Unit 1 **Sentences**

A. **Circle each group of words that is a sentence.**

1. I see a squirrel.

2. Finds an acorn.

3. A dog barks at the squirrel.

4. The squirrel runs off.

5. Safe on a tree branch.

B. **Add the correct end mark to each sentence. Write whether the sentence is a *statement*, *question*, *exclamation*, or *command*.**

6. Did you see that bird_____

7. What a tiny bird it is_____

8. I wonder what it is_____

9. Ask your mother_____

10. It is a hummingbird_____

C. **Combine each pair of sentences. Write the new sentence on a piece of paper. Draw a line between the subject and predicate.**

11. Ali set the table. Mia set the table.

12. Mom fixed soup. I fixed soup.

13. Dad made salad. Grandpa made salad.

14. Mia poured water. Grandma poured water.

15. My sisters cleaned up. I cleaned up.

D. Circle the words in a series in each sentence.

16. Sara, Max, and I go riding.

17. Blaze, Red, and Star are our horses.

18. Star's tail, mane, and ears are black.

19. The horses eat oats, bran, and hay.

20. Where are my boots, saddle, and helmet?

Unit 2 **Nouns**

A. Circle the noun in each sentence. Write if it names a person, place, or thing. Write if it is singular or plural.

21. The children are hungry. _____

22. Who wants sandwiches? _____

23. Come out to the kitchen. _____

24. Will you call your father? _____

25. Get the glasses, please. _____

B. Write the proper nouns in each sentence correctly.

26. Last monday was independence day. _____

_____

27. I spent the fourth of july in philadelphia. _____

_____

28. We watched the parade on market street. _____

_____

29. Aunt paula took greg and me. _____

30. Her dog sparky barked at the fireworks. _____

Grammar

C. Write the possessive form of each noun.

31. girls _____

32. teacher _____

33. nurses _____

34. family _____

35. friends _____

D. Punctuate each greeting or closing.

36. Dear Uncle Bob

37. With my thanks

38. Dear Grandpa

39. Your best friend

40. Dear Dad

Unit 3   **Verbs**

A. Circle the correct verb in ( ) to complete each sentence.

41. I (brush, brushes) my teeth after meals.

42. Ted and Ben (floss, flosses) at night.

43. Our mom (fix, fixes) healthful meals.

44. Ted, Ben, and I (visit, visits) the dentist.

45. The dentist (check, checks) our teeth.

B. Change the underlined verb in each sentence to the past tense. Write the new verb.

46. Mom <u>has</u> a birthday. _____

47. Dan and I <u>wrap</u> her gifts. _____

48. Dad <u>helps</u> us. _____

49. Mom <u>likes</u> our gifts. _____

50. She <u>hugs</u> both of us. _____

C. Combine each pair of sentences. Write the new sentence on a piece of paper. Underline each verb.

51. Dad grabbed his banjo. Dad played.

52. Mom stood up. Mom sang.

53. We sat in a circle. We listened.

54. Sara clapped. Sara danced.

55. Everyone laughed. Everyone cheered.

D. Write each date correctly.

56. July 4 1776 _____

57. January 1 2000 _____

58. April 9 1865 _____

59. May 5 1961 _____

60. October 12 1492 _____

Verbs and Writing That Compares

In this unit you will learn about verbs. You will also learn how to compare things in your writing.

Science Link   *Birds and bats both fly, but they are not the same. See what makes them different.*

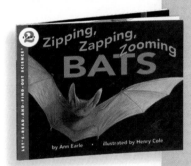

Bats are also good hunters because they are expert fliers. Their wings are different from bird wings. Bat wings have long arm bones with extra-long finger bones. A thin skin called a membrane stretches between the bones. The membrane connects the wing bones to the bat's legs and body.

from ***Zipping, Zapping, Zooming Bats***
by Ann Earle

Thinking Like a Writer

Writing That Compares
Writing that compares tells about two things, places, people, or ideas.

- How are bats different from birds?

Verbs The author uses forms of the verb *be*, such as *am, is,* or *are.*

QUICK WRITE Find a sentence with <u>am</u>, <u>is</u>, or <u>are</u>. Write another sentence using that word.

Thinking Like a Writer

Writing That Compares After you read the passage on page 209, write what you learned about how bats are different from birds.

_____

_____

_____

_____

_____

_____

_____

QUICK WRITE Find a sentence in the passage with a form of the verb *be*. Then write another sentence with that word.

_____

_____

_____

_____

_____

The Verb *Be*

RULES

- The verb *be* has special forms in the present tense and in the past tense.

Subject	Present	Past
I	*am*	*was*
she, he, it	*is*	*was*
you, we, they	*are*	*were*

- *Am*, *is*, and *are* tell about the present time. *Was* and *were* tell about the past.

Present Time	Past Time
I am here.	I was here yesterday.
She is here.	She was here yesterday.
We are here today.	We were here yesterday.

Guided Practice

Write the correct form of the verb *be* in ( ).

1. Last night the sky (is, was) cloudy. _____

2. We (was, were) inside. _____

3. Tonight the stars (are, were) bright. _____

4. The moon (is, are) full. _____

5. Now I (am, was) not sleepy. _____

THiNK AND WRITE

Verbs

How do you know if a sentence is about the present time or the past? Write your answer.

210

Handbook
page 440

Extra
Practice
page 268

REVIEW THE RULES

- The verb *be* has special forms in the present tense (*am, is, are*) and in the past tense (*was, were*).

More Practice

A. Circle the correct form of the verb *be* in ( ).

6. Last night (is, was) very cold.

7. This morning the snow (is, are) deep.

8. Now I (am, was) ready to go outside.

9. Yesterday the streets (are, were) bare.

10. Today the streets (are, am) snowy.

B. Spiral Review Circle each word that is a form of the verb *be*. Draw a line under each action verb.

11. Yesterday the snow was soft.

12. The snowdrifts were very high.

13. Today the snow is sticky.

14. We roll three big snowballs.

15. We make a wonderful snowman!

Writing Activity **A Paragraph**

Write a paragraph about something that is happening now or that happened yesterday.
APPLY GRAMMAR: Circle forms of the verb *be*.

McGraw-Hill School Division

Helping Verbs

RULES

A helping verb helps another verb to show an action. The verbs *be* and *have* can be helping verbs.

Use forms of *be* to tell about things that are happening now.

> We <u>are</u> <u>planning</u> a picnic.

helping verb verb

Use forms of *have* to tell about things that have already happened.

> We <u>have</u> <u>planned</u> a picnic.

helping verb verb

THINK AND WRITE

Verbs
How does a helping verb help another verb? Write your answer.

Guided Practice

Name the helping verb in each sentence.

1. We are playing on the beach. _____

2. We have played here many times before. _____

3. I am swimming in the ocean. _____

4. Aunt Kathy is wading nearby. _____

5. Ben has built a sand castle. _____

REVIEW THE RULES

- A helping verb helps tell about an action.

- *Am, is,* and *are* can help tell about action that is happening now.

- *Has* and *have* can help tell about things that already happened.

Handbook
page 441

Extra Practice
page 269

More Practice

A. Circle the helping verb in each sentence.

6. We have brought a picnic lunch.

7. Dad is giving out the sandwiches.

8. Mom has fixed the beach umbrella.

9. We are sitting in the shade.

10. Let's play after we have rested.

B. Spiral Review Correct the greeting and the closing of the letter. Fill in each blank with the correct form of *be*.

11.–15. Dear Aunt Kathy

How _____ you? Yesterday _____ an

exciting day! Today I _____ tired but happy.

Love
Lucy

Writing Activity   A Journal Entry

Write a journal entry about a special day you had.
APPLY GRAMMAR: Circle each helping verb.

McGraw-Hill School Division

Linking Verbs

RULES

A linking verb is a verb that does not show action.
The verb *be* is a linking verb.

We are happy.
Our dog is a winner.

The verb *be* links the subject to words that
describe something about the subject.

Pixie is proud.   *Pixie stands still.*

linking verb   action verb

THINK AND WRITE

Verbs
What makes a
linking verb
different from
other verbs?
Write your answer
in your journal.

Guided Practice

**Name the verb in each sentence. Tell if the verb is
a linking verb or an action verb.**

1. Yesterday's dog show was exciting. _____

2. My dog Pixie is a toy poodle. _____

3. Toy poodles are small dogs. _____

4. I hold Pixie in my arms. _____

5. Everybody pets Pixie. _____

REVIEW THE RULES

- A **linking verb** is a verb that does not show action.

- The verb *be* is a linking verb.

More Practice

A. Draw a line under each verb. Then write *linking verb* or *action verb*.

6. Mr. King's dog is a boxer. _____

7. Boxers are friendly dogs. _____

8. Mr. King trained his dog Rusty. _____

9. Rusty was a smart puppy. _____

10. Now Rusty works for Mr. King. _____

B. [Spiral Review] Underline the subject. Circle the helping verb.

11. Mom and I have enjoyed dog shows.

12. Mom has ordered our tickets.

13. We are going to the show today.

14. I am brushing Major's shiny coat.

15. Major is waiting for a treat.

Handbook
page 438

Extra Practice
page 270

Writing Activity   A Paragraph

Write about how two pets are alike or different.
APPLY GRAMMAR: Circle each linking verb.

Science Link

Commas in Names of Places

Grammar

RULES

- Use a **comma** between the name of a city and a state.

  Wendy lives in Columbus, Ohio.

Practice

A. **Add a comma where it belongs in each sentence.**

1. The family started in Ames Iowa.

2. They drove to Lincoln Nebraska.

3. Then they went to Topeka Kansas.

4. They stopped in Tulsa Oklahoma.

5. They visited friends in Dallas Texas.

B. **Spiral Review** **Write the three abbreviations correctly. Draw a line under each action verb. Circle each linking verb.**

6. Mr and Mrs Oak live in Arizona. _____

7. They work at the Grand Canyon. _____

8. Mrs Oak is a tour guide. _____

9. She takes people on mule rides. _____

10. Mules are strong animals. _____

Extra Practice page 271

THINK AND WRITE

Commas
Why do you write a comma between the name of a city and state?

Grammar
REVIEW

Verbs

REVIEW THE RULES

- The verb be has special forms. Am, is, and are tell about now. Was and were tell about the past.

- A helping verb helps another verb show action. Be and have are helping verbs.

- A linking verb does not show action. Be links the subject to words that describe it.

- A comma separates a city's name and a state's name.

Handbook
pages 440-441

QUICK WRITE

Verbs

Use linking and helping verbs to write three sentences. Use commas correctly.

Practice

A. Circle the correct verb in ( ).

1. Last week I (was, were) at home.

2. My cousins (was, were) on vacation then.

3. Some mail (is, are) in our mailbox.

4. Now I (am, was) happy.

5. Now two postcards (are, were) on my wall!

B. Challenge Write *am, is, are, was, were, have,* or *has* in each sentence.

6.–10. Lora's friend Carlos _____ gone to camp. Lora _____ sad on the day Carlos left. Mom and Dad _____ seen her sad face. Now they _____ planning a surprise for Lora.

The Verbs *Go* and *Do*

RULES

- Some verbs do not add *-ed* in the past tense.

- The verbs *go* and *do* have special forms in the past tense. They are called irregular verbs.

- The past tense forms of *go* and *do* do not end in *-ed*.

Verb	Past Tense	Example
go	went	I went to school
do	did	I did my homework

Guided Practice

Change the underlined verb to the tense shown in ( ).

1. I <u>go</u> to the library. (past) _____

2. Eva <u>went</u> with me. (present) _____

3. First we <u>do</u> some reading. (past) _____

4. I <u>do</u> an outline. (past) _____

5. Then Eva <u>did</u> a first draft. (present) _____

THINK AND WRITE

Verbs

How are irregular verbs different from other verbs? Write the answer in your journal.

Handbook
page 441

Extra
Practice
page 272

REVIEW THE **RULES**

- The past tense of *go* is *went*.

- The past tense of *do* is *did*.

More Practice

A. Change the underlined verb to the tense shown in ( ).

6. Sometimes the rain <u>goes</u> on for days. (past) _____

7. The showers <u>did</u> not stop. (present) _____

8. The soil <u>does</u> not soak up all the rain. (past) _____

9. After the rain, the clouds <u>go</u> away. (past) _____

10. The puddles <u>did</u> not dry up. (present) _____

B. Spiral Review **Draw a line under each action verb. Circle each linking verb.**

11. The weather changed quickly.

12. Now the sky is dark.

13. The clouds are low and gray.

14. The wind blows.

15. The children run inside.

Writing Activity   An Interview

Write three questions to ask a weather reporter.

APPLY GRAMMAR: Use forms of the verbs *go* and *do*.

🔍 **Science Link**

McGraw-Hill School Division

The Verbs *Say, See,* and *Run*

RULES

- **Irregular verbs** do not add *-ed* to form the past tense.

- *Say, see,* and *run* are irregular verbs.

- The past tense forms of *say, see,* and *run* do not end in *-ed*.

Verb	Past Tense	Example
say	said	We **said**, "Good luck."
see	saw	We **saw** the runners.
run	ran	They **ran** fast.

Guided Practice

Complete each sentence with the past-tense form of the verb in ( ).

1. My friends _____ the race. (see)

2. They _____, "Wow!" (say)

3. They _____ so many riders! (see)

4. I _____, "I don't like bike races." (say)

5. I _____ in a race. (run)

THINK AND WRITE

Verbs
Write to tell why
say, see, and *run*
are called
irregular verbs.

McGraw-Hill School Division

REVIEW THE RULES

- The past tense of *say* is *said.*
- The past tense of *see* is *saw.*
- The past tense of *run* is *ran.*

Handbook
page 441

Extra Practice
page 273

More Practice

A. Fill in the blank with the past-tense form of the verb in ( ).

6. I _____ around the track. (run)

7. I _____ my family cheering for me. (see)

8. Somebody _____, "Here, Snuffy!" (say)

9. I _____ a little dog on the track. (see)

10. It _____ beside me to the finish line. (run)

B. Spiral Review Write the paragraph on a piece of paper. Change the present forms of *go* and *be* to past forms. Add commas where needed.

11.–15. We go to the school track for the race. My brother goes to the starting line. Mr. Cho Ms. Mann and Dr. Jay are the judges.

Writing Activity Story

Write a story about a race or another sport.
APPLY GRAMMAR: Use the past forms of the verbs *say*, *see*, and *run* in your story. Circle the verbs.

The Verbs *Come, Give,* and *Sing*

RULES

- The past-tense forms of irregular verbs do not end in *-ed.*

- *Come, give,* and *sing* are irregular verbs.

- The past tense forms of *come, give,* and *sing* do not end in *-ed.*

Verb	Past Tense	Example
come	came	She came to the stage.
give	gave	She gave everyone smiles.
sing	sang	She sang a silly song.

Guided Practice

Complete each sentence with the past-tense form of the verb in ( ).

1. We _____ out many invitations. (give)

2. Families _____ to the show. (come)

3. Some children _____ songs. (sing)

4. Our school's principal _____, too. (sing)

5. My friend Beth _____ a speech. (give)

THiNK AND WRITE

Verbs
What is the same about the past-tense forms of *give, come,* and *sing?* Write your answer.

REVIEW THE RULES

- The past tense of *come* is *came*.
- The past tense of *give* is *gave*.
- The past tense of *sing* is *sang*.

Handbook
page 441

Extra Practice page 274

More Practice

A. Complete each sentence with the past form of the verb in ( ).

6. Emily _____ a song by herself. (sing)

7. She _____ to the front of the room. (come)

8. She _____ a little bow. (give)

9. Then she _____ very softly. (sing)

10. Everyone _____ her a big cheer. (give)

B. **Spiral Review** Combine each pair of sentences using *and*. On a piece of paper, write each new sentence in the past tense.

11. Max goes to school. Max sees his friends.

12. We see our teacher. We run to her.

13. Mrs. Kato smiles. Mrs. Kato says hello.

14. Tyler sees a bird. Tyler sings to it.

15. Alexa waves. Alexa runs over.

Writing Activity   A Poster

Make a poster about a school show.
APPLY GRAMMAR: Use and circle the verbs *come*, *give*, and *sing* in your poster.

Art Link

Contractions with *not*

RULES

- A **contraction** is a short form of two words.

- An **apostrophe** (') takes the place of the letters that are left out when two words are joined.

  Matt <u>did not</u> pick up his toys.

  ↓

  Matt didn't pick up his toys.

- Remember to put the verb and *not* together to make a contraction.

is not ⟶ *isn't*		*does not* → *doesn't*
are not ⟶ *aren't*		*do not* ⟶ *don't*
has not → *hasn't*		*did not* ⟶ *didn't*
have not → *haven't*		*cannot* ⟶ *can't*

THiNK AND WRITE

Verbs
Why might you choose to use contractions in your writing? Write your answer in your journal.

Guided Practice

Tell how to make the words in ( ) into a contraction. Then write the new word.

1. Matt (cannot) find his book. _____

2. The book (is not) on his desk. _____

3. He (did not) put it on the shelf. _____

4. He (does not) know where it is. _____

5. He (has not) found the book yet. _____

224

REVIEW THE RULES

- A **contraction** is a short form of two words.
- An **apostrophe** takes the place of the letters that are left out.

More Practice

A. **Write the contraction for the underlined words in each sentence.**

6. Matt <u>did not</u> clean his room. _____

7. The room <u>has not</u> been neat for days. _____

8. Matt's books <u>are not</u> on the self. _____

9. Matt's clothes <u>have not</u> been put away. _____

10. The clothes <u>do not</u> belong on the floor. _____

B. **Spiral Review** **Correct the capitalization. Write the past tense of each verb in ( ).**

11. matt (look) under the bed. _____

12. he (lift) up a pile of clothes. _____

13. he (drop) a sweater on the floor. _____

14. then matt (pick) up the sweater. _____

15. at last he (spot) his book. _____

Handbook
pages 443, 453

Extra Practice
page 275

Writing Activity   Paragraph

Write a paragraph about a clean room and a messy room. How are they alike and different?

APPLY GRAMMAR: Use contractions in your paragraph.

Apostrophes

RULES

- An **apostrophe** (') takes the place of letters that are left out in a contraction.

  Marta didn't have skates.

- Add an apostrophe and *s* to make a singular noun possessive. Add an apostrophe to make most plural nouns possessive.

  Marta's dad bought the girls' skates.

Extra Practice page 276

Practice

A. Add the missing apostrophe in each underlined word. Write the word correctly.

1. Gina <u>doesnt</u> save money. _____

2. <u>Ginas</u> bank is empty. _____

3. My bank <u>isnt</u> empty. _____

4. My <u>banks</u> slot is wide. _____

5. My twin <u>brothers</u> banks are full. _____

B. [Spiral Review] Underline each action verb. Circle each linking verb.

6. Susan saves seventy cents.

7. Nell's nine nickels are new.

8. Dan drops dimes on dishes.

9. Bobby's bank is big.

10. Connie counts coins quickly.

THINK AND WRITE

Apostrophes
Write to tell how you know if a word with an apostrophe is a contraction or a possessive noun.

Grammar

Verbs

REVIEW THE RULES

- Some verbs have special forms in the past tense.

  go → went   say → said   see → saw

  run → ran   come → came   give → gave

- A contraction is a short way to write two words. An apostrophe takes the place of the left-out letters.

Handbook
page 441

QUICK WRITE

Verbs

Write five sentences. Use a contraction and the past-tense form of *go, do, say, see, run, come, give,* or *sing*.

Practice

A. Write each underlined verb to show past action.

1. Yesterday Justin and I <u>go</u> to the shore. _____

2. We <u>come</u> to a tide pool. _____

3. I <u>see</u> a crab and <u>say</u>, "Wow!" _____

4. The crab <u>gives</u> Justin a fright. _____

5. Justin <u>runs</u> home. _____

B. **Challenge** **Write each underlined word correctly with an apostrophe.**

6. <u>Lin</u> class is visiting the pond. _____

7. The children see different <u>animals</u> homes.

_____

8. The ducks <u>are not</u> in the water. _____

9. The teacher spots one <u>bird</u> nest. _____

10. The children <u>do not</u> want to get wet. _____

Common Errors with Past-Tense Verbs

Some verbs have special spellings in the past tense. Sometimes a writer adds *-ed* to a verb instead of using the special spelling.

Common Error	Examples	Corrected Sentences
Always adding -ed to form the past tense	He goed home. A bird singed.	He went home. A bird sang.

REVIEW THE RULES

PAST-TENSE VERBS

- Some verbs have special spellings to show the past tense.

- Remember Most past-tense verbs end with *-ed*.

THINK AND WRITE

Verbs
How is the past tense of the verb *run* different from the past tense of the verb *walk*? Write the answer in your journal.

Practice

Write the past tense of the verb in ( ).

1. My grandmother (comes) to my house. _____

2. I (run) to the door. _____

3. Grandmother (sees) me. _____

4. She (gives) me a present. _____

5. I (say) that I liked the gift. _____

Troubleshooter, pages 426–427

Grammar and Usage

Directions

Read the paragraph and choose the word that belongs in each space.

Check to see if the verb should be in the past or present tense.

Some past-tense verbs do not end in -ed.

Sample

I __(1)__ to the park yesterday. Mom and Dad __(2)__ with me. We saw a squirrel eating nuts. The squirrel __(3)__ funny. As soon as it saw us, it scampered away.

See how many things the subject names. The verb must go with the subject.

1 ○ go
　○ goes
　○ went
　○ going

2 ○ came
　○ come
　○ comes
　○ coming

3 ○ am
　○ were
　○ is
　○ was

Test Tip
Read the whole paragraph before choosing the correct word.

TIME FOR KIDS Writer's Notebook

RESEARCH

RESEARCH When I need information for a story, I first check the **encyclopedia**. An encyclopedia is filled with facts and figures about everything! Encyclopedias come in books or on a CD-ROM. The library media center has encyclopedias for me to look at.

COMPOSITION SKILLS

WRITING WELL When I write, I like to make sure that each sentence sounds just right. I want each to be a little different from the others. That helps keep my stories interesting.

VOCABULARY SKILLS

USING WORDS When I add a word or letters to the end of some words, it's called a **suffix**. A suffix changes the meaning of a word. These words help me to say exactly what I want. Can you think of any words with suffixes?

Read Now!

As you read the photo essay about a baby panda, write down two pieces of information that the writer could check in the encyclopedia.

TIME
FOR KIDS
Writer's Notebook

RESEARCH

RESEARCH Write two pieces of information in the photo essay about pandas that the writer could check in the encyclopedia.

_____

_____

_____

_____

_____

_____

_____

_____

_____

_____

_____

_____

A New Mama

A rare giant panda is born at the San Diego Zoo in California.

It's A Girl!

The people at the San Diego Zoo in California were thrilled. On August 21, 1999, a giant panda had a baby girl! The cub is only the fifth panda born in the U.S. And it is the only one who has lived.

The cub came into this world blind and helpless. It weighed only about four ounces. (A full-grown panda weighs as much as 300 pounds.) The panda baby is doing beautifully.

Panda cubs don't open their eyes until they are about 45 days old. When they are born, they are about the size of a stick of butter.

Newborn pandas have white fuzz. They grow black-and-white fur after about a month.

interNET CONNECTION **Go to** www.mhschool.com/language-arts **for more information on the topic.**

Top 5 Biggest Bears

The baby panda looks tiny next to her mom. And giant pandas look small next to polar bears. Here's how a giant panda weighs in against other kinds of bears.

4 Giant Panda
200 to 300 pounds

3 American Black Bear
240 to 330 pounds

2 Brown Bear
850 to 975 pounds

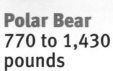

1 Polar Bear
770 to 1,430 pounds

5 Spectacled Bear
180 to 280 pounds

Write Now!

Use the pictures to compare the bears. Which is the biggest? Which is the smallest? How are they alike? How are they different?

The Encyclopedia

An **encyclopedia** is a set of books filled with information about people, places, and things. Each book is called a *volume*. The books are in ABC order.

The letter or letters on each volume show what topics are in the book. The topics are in ABC order.

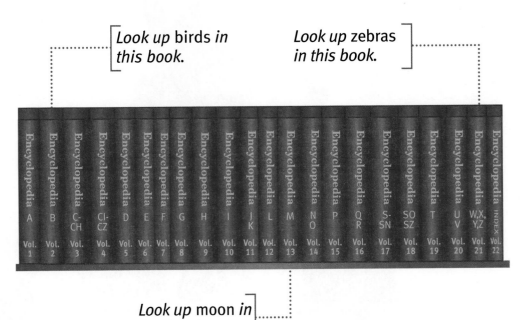

Look up birds *in this book.*

Look up zebras *in this book.*

Look up moon *in this book.*

To look up a topic, use the first letter of its name and find the volume with that letter.

If the topic is the name of a person, look up the person's last name. To find the name of Benjamin Franklin, look up the name Franklin.

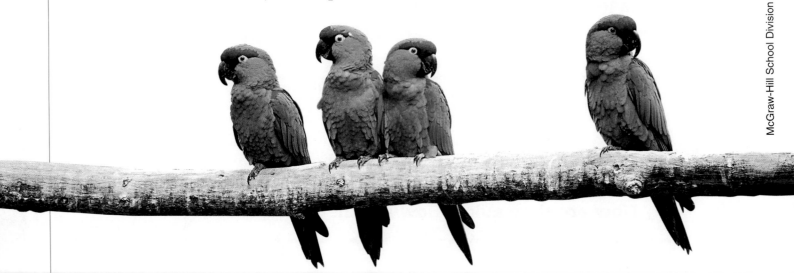

Practice

A. Look at the encyclopedias on page 234.
In what book would you find facts about these topics?

1. dinosaur _____

2. Texas _____

3. elephant _____

4. Africa _____

5. whale _____

B. Write the word you would look up for each
name below.

6. Thomas Jefferson _____

7. Betsy Ross _____

8. Helen Keller _____

9. Mark Twain _____

10. Maria Mitchell _____

Writing Activity   A Report

Use an encyclopedia to look up information about your
favorite animal. Write three sentences about the animal.

Vocabulary: Suffixes

DEFINITION

A **suffix** is a word part that is added to the end of a word. A suffix changes the meaning of the word.

Suffix	Meaning	Examples
-less	without	care + -less = careless
-ful	full of	care + -ful = careful

Think about the meanings of the blue words in this paragraph.

My little cousin Niles likes to be helpful. People think he is kind and thoughtful. But Niles is not very careful. In fact, he is quite careless. Even so, I am always thankful for his help. He always tries hard.

Practice

A. Circle each word that has a suffix. Then write what the word means.

1. At first, people are thankful. _____

2. They are never fearful of Niles. _____

3. They think little boys are harmless. _____

4. They are hopeful he will help. _____

5. They don't know he's not careful. _____

B. Add *-less* and *-ful* to each of these words.

6. color _____   _____

7. care _____   _____

8. hope _____   _____

9. use _____   _____

10. fear _____   _____

C. **Grammar Link** **11.–15. Write five sentences in the past tense. Use five of the new words from Practice B.**

Writing Activity   A Character Description

Describe a person you know who likes to help others. Use two words with the suffix *-ful* and two words with the suffix *-less*. Use long and short sentences.
APPLY GRAMMAR: Write in the present tense.

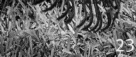

Composition: Sentence Style and Variety

You can vary your sentences by making them different lengths or by using different beginning words.

GUIDELINES

- Write sentences of different lengths.

- Do not begin every sentence in the same way.

- Combine the subjects or predicates of two sentences to make one sentence.

THINK AND WRITE

Sentence Style and Variety

How does using both short and long sentences make your writing more interesting? Write what you think.

See how the writer varied sentences.

Manatees are called "sea cows." How are sea cows like farm cows? Farm cows live on land. Sea cows live in water. Cows on farms have four legs. Sea cows have one pair of flippers. Both animals are plant eaters. They graze. Farm cows graze in pastures. They eat grass and alfalfa. Sea cows graze in shallow water. They eat seaweed and sea grasses.

The sentences begin with different words.

The sentences vary in length.

Nouns were combined to form this sentence.

Practice

A. Underline the part of each pair of sentences that is the same.

1. Sea cows eat plants. Farm cows eat plants.

2. Farm cows live in meadows. Farm cows eat grass.

3. Sea cows live in the sea. Sea cows eat sea grass.

4. Farm cows are mammals. Sea cows are mammals.

5. Sea cows have flippers. Sea cows have a tail fin.

B. Begin these sentences with different words or make them different lengths. Write the new sentences on a piece of paper.

6. My sister and I went to Florida.

7. My sister and I saw many things.

8. A whale leaped.

9. A whale dived.

10. My sister and I had fun.

C. **Grammar Link** Use *and* to join the underlined words. Write the sentence on a piece of paper.

11. <u>Sea cows</u> are mammals. <u>Whales</u> are mammals.

12. <u>Sea cows</u> live in the sea. <u>Whales</u> live in the sea.

13. Both <u>look like fish</u>. Both <u>never leave the water</u>.

14. Both <u>come to the surface</u>. Both <u>need to breathe air</u>.

15. I love to see <u>whales</u>. I love to see <u>sea cows</u>.

Writing Activity A Paragraph

Write about a trip you took with friends or family.
APPLY GRAMMAR: Use linking verbs in your paragraph.

Better Sentences

Directions

Read the paragraph. Some parts are underlined. The underlined parts may be one of the following:

- **Incomplete sentences**
- **Correctly written sentences that should be combined**

Choose the best way to write each underlined part.

Sample

Look up in the sky! It's a horse. No, it's a dragon. <u>Maybe a throne for a king</u>. What you
(1)
see is a cloud picture. You can see anything you want in a cloud if you use your imagination.

<u>A fluffy round shape could be a clown. A fluffy
(2)
round shape could be a sheep</u>. You can see a free show any time there are clouds in the sky.

All you have to do is look up.

A complete sentence has both a subject and a predicate.

Look out for sentences with words that can be combined to make one sentence.

1 ○ Maybe it is a throne for a king.

○ Maybe it is a throne. For a king.

○ Or maybe a throne for a king.

2 ○ A fluffy round shape could be a clown could be a sheep.

○ A fluffy round clown or sheep.

○ A fluffy round shape could be a clown or a sheep.

Test Tip
Remember to read all the answer choices slowly and carefully.

McGraw-Hill School Division

Vocabulary and Comprehension

Directions

Read the paragraph. Then read each question that follows the paragraph. Choose the best answer to each question.

Sample

A zebra is not the same animal as a horse. They both have four legs and can run fast. Their bodies and heads look alike. But a zebra has stripes all over its body. Each has a mane, but the tails are different. A zebra has short hairs at the tip of its tail. A horse's tail is all long hairs. Also, people can ride a horse, but a zebra is not <u>playful</u> and won't like it if you try to go for a ride.

Look for small word parts that help you understand the underlined word.

1 How are a zebra and a horse the same?

- ○ They have stripes.
- ○ They have long tails.
- ○ They have four legs and can run fast.
- ○ You can ride them both.

2 The word <u>playful</u> in this paragraph means—

- ○ becoming angry
- ○ wanting to play
- ○ running quickly
- ○ wearing a saddle

Seeing Like a *Writer*

There are many kinds of animals in the world. We can study them in real life or in pictures. When we do, we can see how they are alike and how they are different.

My Friend by Christian Pierre.

Writing from Pictures

1. These pictures show different animals. Write a sentence about one animal in each picture.

2. Write a sentence about one of the pictures. Tell about two things that are happening.

3. Choose two animals in two different pictures. How are they alike? How are they different? Write a paragraph about them.

Apply Grammar: Include contractions with *not*.

Writing That Compares

Writing that compares tells how things are alike and how they are different. You can compare people, places, or things.

Learning from Writers

Read the following examples of writing that compares. What things are alike in each story? What things are different?

THINK AND WRITE

Purpose

Why is comparing two things a good way to present facts about them? Write your answer.

Night Animals, Day Animals

Day and night, animals live together in many different places...

On a warm summer day, a family of brown bears is playing in the stream. Their mother is catching fish. Bears also eat fruit, nuts, berries, and, of course, honey.

Nearby, high up in a tree, a bobcat sleeps.

When the night comes, the bears are asleep inside a hollow tree on the ground. But it's time for the bobcat to go hunting. It looks for rabbits, mice, and other small animals to eat.

— Judith Lechner

Day School and Oak School

I used to go to Day School, but now I go to Oak School. Some things are the same, but many things are different. Day school is old, and Oak School is brand-new. Both schools have libraries, but Oak School's library is bigger. Day School has a big, outdoor playground. Oak School also has a nice playground, but it is small. I had many friends in Day School. I have a few friends at Oak School, but I hope to meet many more.

— Blake Carson

PRACTICE and APPLY

Thinking Like a Reader

1. How are bears and bobcats different?

2. Which sentence tells the main idea of "Day School and Oak School"?

Thinking Like a Writer

3. How did the author use paragraphs in "Night Animals, Day Animals"?

4. What parts of the schools did the author compare?

5. **Reading Across Texts** What comparing words do both writers use?

Features of Writing That Compares

DEFINITIONS AND FEATURES

Writing that compares tells about two things, places, people, or ideas. Good writing that compares does these things:

▸ It tells how two things are **alike**.

▸ It tells how two things are **different**.

▸ It uses **comparing words**.

▸ How Things Are Alike

Reread "Night Animals, Day Animals" on page 244. How does the author tell you that the animals share something?

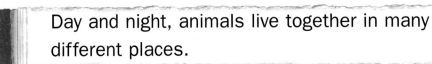

Day and night, animals live together in many different places.

This sentence tells you that the animals share the same habitat.

▶ How Things Are Different

Writing that compares gives different kinds of information about the same topic.

> Their mother is catching fish. Bears also eat fruit, nuts, berries, and, of course, honey.

These sentences tell what bears eat. What does the passage tell you bobcats eat?

▶ Comparing Words

Certain words tell readers that things are being compared. Use comparing words and phrases such as *but, also, like,* and *unlike.*

> When night comes, the bears are asleep inside a hollow tree on the ground. But it's time for the bobcat to go hunting.

What comparing word did the author use?

PRACTICE and APPLY

Create a Category Chart

1. Reread "Day School and Oak School."
2. List the kinds of information you learn.
3. List the facts about Day School.
4. List the facts about Oak School.

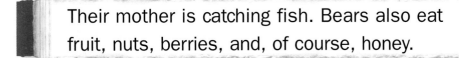

Kind of Information	Day School	Oak School

Prewrite

Writing that compares tells how two things are alike and different. You can compare people, places, or things.

Purpose and Audience

The purpose of writing to compare might be to entertain or inform. Think about your audience. What do you want them to learn?

Choose a Topic

Begin by **brainstorming**. Think of two things that are alike in some ways and different in other ways. **Explore and list** your ideas about the two things.

THINK AND WRITE

Audience

Write what you will have to do to make your audience feel interested in your topic.

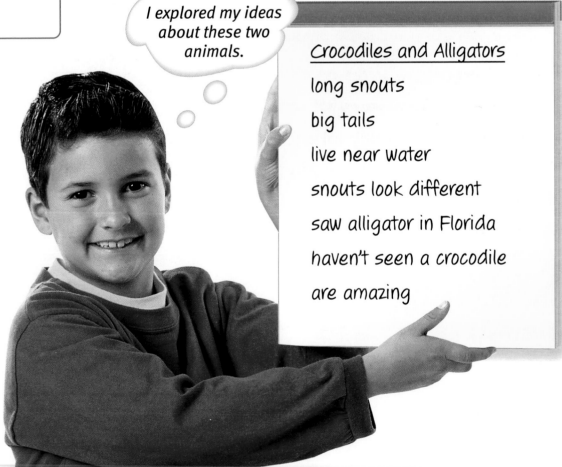

I explored my ideas about these two animals.

Crocodiles and Alligators

long snouts

big tails

live near water

snouts look different

saw alligator in Florida

haven't seen a crocodile

are amazing

Organize • Compare and Contrast

You tell how things are alike and different when you compare. To plan your writing, use a chart like the one below.

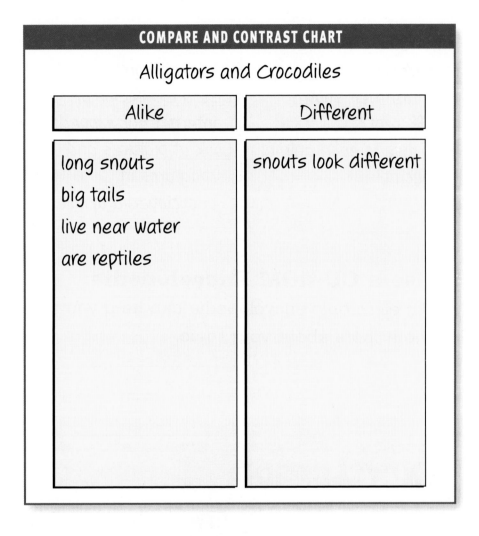

COMPARE AND CONTRAST CHART

Alligators and Crocodiles

Alike	Different
long snouts big tails live near water are reptiles	snouts look different

Checklist ✓
Prewriting

☐ Did you think about your purpose and audience?

☐ Did you choose two things that are alike and different?

☐ Did you explore and organize your ideas?

☐ Do you need to find out more?

PRACTICE and APPLY

Plan Your Writing That Compares

1. Think about your purpose and audience.

2. Brainstorm ideas for a topic.

3. Choose a topic and explore ideas.

4. Organize your ideas in a chart.

Writing
PROCESS

Prewrite • Research and Inquiry

▶ Writer's Resources

Do you have all the information you need for your writing? If you do not, you may have to do research. Make a list of questions.

What Else Do I Need to Know?	Where Can I Find the Information?
How are their snouts different?	Use a CD-ROM or Internet encyclopedia.
How else is each animal special?	Look at pictures and diagrams in encyclopedia articles.

▶ Use a CD-ROM Encyclopedia

An electronic encyclopedia can help you to find out more about your topic.

The writer typed in this key word.

This is the best article for finding out more.

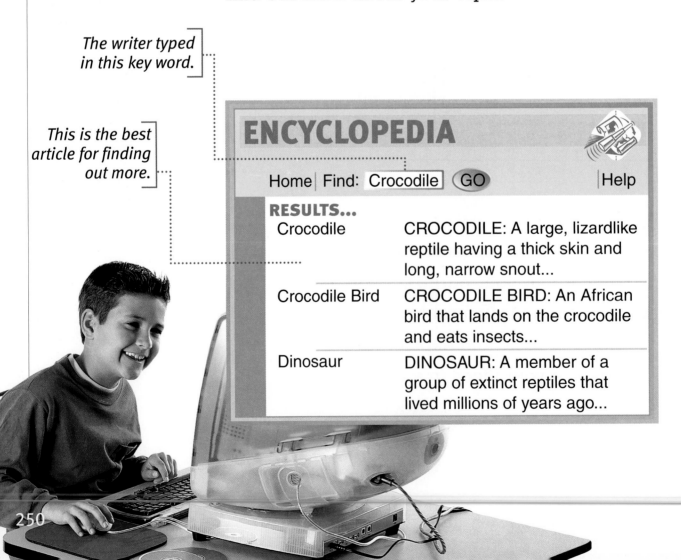

ENCYCLOPEDIA

Home | Find: Crocodile （GO） | Help

RESULTS...

Crocodile	CROCODILE: A large, lizardlike reptile having a thick skin and long, narrow snout...
Crocodile Bird	CROCODILE BIRD: An African bird that lands on the crocodile and eats insects...
Dinosaur	DINOSAUR: A member of a group of extinct reptiles that lived millions of years ago...

McGraw-Hill School Division

▶ Use Diagrams

A diagram is a drawing with labels. The words in the labels tell more about the drawing. Be sure to read all the labels.

Use Your Research

New information from your research can go into your chart.

Alike	Different
long snouts big tails live near water are reptiles	snouts look different Alligators have wide, stubby snouts. Crocodiles have narrow, pointed snouts. Teeth are not the same.

Handbook
page 460–461

Checklist ✓

Research and Inquiry

☐ **Did you list your questions?**

☐ **Did you find the best resources to answer your questions?**

☐ **Did you take notes or print out information?**

PRACTICE and APPLY

Review Your Plan

1. Look at your chart.

2. Make a list of questions and resources.

3. Read to find out new facts.

4. Add new facts to your chart.

Draft

You can use the information you gathered to write a magazine article that compares. Review your chart. Think about making a paragraph for each main idea. Add details.

Main idea for third paragraph:

The two are alike in many ways.

Main idea for first paragraph:

How can you tell the difference between the two animals?

Main idea for second paragraph:

The two are different in some ways.

COMPARE AND CONTRAST CHART

Alligators and Crocodiles

Alike	Different
long snouts	snouts look different
big tails	Alligators have wide, stubby snouts.
live near water	Crocodiles have narrow, pointed snouts.
are reptiles	Teeth are not the same.

✔**Checklist**

Drafting

☐ **Did you think about your purpose and your audience?**

☐ **Does each main idea have details?**

☐ **Did you tell how things are alike and different?**

☐ **Did you write different kinds of sentences?**

Notice how this writer used main ideas and details to tell how things are alike and different.

DRAFT

You see a big reptile with a long snout and tail. Is it an alligator or a crocodile? ⟶ Main idea of first paragraph

Alligators and crocodiles ar different in some ways. ⟶ Main idea of second paragraph

An alligator has a wide, stubby snout, and a crocodile's snout is narrow and pointed. A crocodiles bottom teeth show when its mouth is closed. ⟶ Details tell more about each animal.

⟶ Main idea of third paragraph

Alligators and crocodiles are alike in some ways. They live near water. Both of them are reptiles. They are both very interesting.

PRACTICE and APPLY

Draft Your Writing That Compares

1. Look at your prewriting chart again.
2. Write main ideas and details.
3. Tell how things are alike and different.
4. Use different kinds of sentences.

TECHNOLOGY

If you made your chart on the computer during prewriting, use the same document to start your draft. Turn each thing in your chart into a sentence. You can add more details later.

Revise

Elaborate

One way to make your writing better is to elaborate. Add missing details to make the writing clearer.

> A crocodiles bottom teeth show when its
> *An alligator's teeth dont*
> mouth is closed. ∧

COMPARE/ CONTRAST WORDS

one difference

same

but

also

alike

both

Word Choice

What comparing words did this writer add to his article?

> Alligators and crocodiles are alike in some
> *both*
> ways. They live near the water.
> ∧

Conferencing for the Reader

■ Check to see if your partner's writing
  • explains how two things are alike
  • explains how two things are different
  • uses comparing and contrasting words
■ Tell your partner what's good. And what you think needs to be changed.

Better Sentences

Try to use different kinds of sentences. If a sentence sounds too long, you can make it into two sentences. See how this writer did that.

REVISE

∧Teeth Tails and Snouts

You see a big reptile with a long snout and tail. Is it an alligator or a crocodile?

Alligators and crocodiles ar different in some ways. An alligator has a wide, stubby snout, and a crocodile's snout is narrow and pointed. *Another difference is the teeth.* A crocodiles bottom teeth show when its mouth is closed. *An alligator's teeth dont.*

Alligators and crocodiles are alike in some ways. They live near water. *both* Both of them are reptiles. They are both very interesting.

Checklist ✓
Revising

- ☐ Did you think about your purpose and audience?
- ☐ Do the details tell about things that are alike and different?
- ☐ Did you use words that compare and contrast?
- ☐ Did you make your sentences different?
- ☐ Did you add a title?

PRACTICE and APPLY

Revise Your Writing That Compares

1. Read your draft to yourself.

2. Share your draft with a partner.

3. Elaborate to make your writing better.

4. **Grammar** Did you write contractions correctly?

Proofread

Proofread your article after you revise it. Look for a different kind of mistake each time you read it.

Spelling

Remember, the letter *q* is always followed by the letter *u*. *(quiet)*

STRATEGIES FOR PROOFREADING

• Reread your writing several times.

• Reread for correct capitalization.

• Reread for correct punctuation.

• Make sure the contractions are correct.

• Check for correct spelling. **Look in the dictionary for words you are not sure about.**

REVIEW THE RULES

GRAMMAR

• A contraction is a short form of two words. Write contractions by adding an apostrophe in place of letters that are left out.

MECHANICS

• An apostrophe takes the place of the letters left out of a contraction.

• Apostrophes are also used to form possessives.

Look at the proofreading corrections. What does the ∽ mean? Why is this change needed?

PREWRITE

DRAFT

REVISE

PROOFREAD

PUBLISH

PROOFREAD

∧Teeth, Tails, and Snouts

You see a big reptile with a long snout

and tail. Is it an alligator or a crocodile?

are
Alligators and crocodiles ar different in
∧

some ways. An alligator has a wide, stubby

snout, and a crocodile's snout is narrow and
Another difference is the teeth.
pointed. A crocodiles bottom teeth show when
∧

its mouth is closed.∧
An alligator's teeth dont.

Alligators and crocodiles are alike in some
both
ways. They live near water. Both of them are
∧

reptiles. They are both very interesting.

Checklist ✓
Proofreading

☐ **Did you spell all words correctly?**

☐ **Did you use capital letters correctly?**

☐ **Did you write contractions correctly?**

☐ **Did you indent all paragraphs?**

PROOFREADING MARKS

new paragraph

∧ add

∽ take out

= Make a capital letter.

/ Make a small letter.

(SP) Check the spelling.

⊙ Add a period.

PRACTICE and APPLY

Proofread Your Writing That Compares

1. Fix spelling mistakes.

2. Check capital letters and punctuation.

3. Check how apostrophes are used.

4. Indent paragraphs.

Publish

Review your writing again before you publish it. This checklist can help.

✓ Self-Check Expository Writing

- ☐ Did I keep my audience and purpose in mind?
- ☐ Did I include a main idea and details in each paragraph?
- ☐ Did I write sentences in different ways?
- ☐ Did I tell how things are alike and different?
- ☐ Did I use comparing words to connect ideas?
- ☐ Did I indent all paragraphs?
- ☐ Did I write contractions correctly?
- ☐ Did I proofread and correct all mistakes?

The writer used the checklist to review his article. Do you think it is ready to publish?

Teeth, Tails, and Snouts

by Matt Cooper

You see a huge reptile with a long snout and tail. Is it an alligator or a crocodile?

Alligators and crocodiles are different in some ways. An alligator has a wide, stubby snout. A crocodile's snout is narrow and pointed. Another difference is the teeth. A crocodile's bottom teeth show when its mouth is closed. An alligator's teeth don't.

Alligators and crocodiles are alike in some ways. They both live near water. Both of them are reptiles. They are both very interesting.

TiP!

Handwriting

Put all the letters in a single word close together and leave space before and after the word. This way the reader can tell when a word begins and ends.

PRACTICE and APPLY

Publish Your Writing That Compares

1. Check your revised draft one more time.

2. Make a neat final copy.

3. Add drawings or pictures.

Present Your Writing That Compares

Before you present your article, you need to plan.

Listening Strategies

- **Set a purpose.** Listen to find out information, for enjoyment, or both.

- Try to picture how things are alike and different.

- Don't interrupt.

- Keep your eyes on the speaker.

STEP 1

How to Explain Your Article

Strategies for Speaking Your purpose is to entertain and inform. As you speak, help your audience "see" the things you are comparing.

- Write main ideas on cards. Add notes to help you remember details.
- Speak in a clear, loud voice.
- Remember to smile and relax.
- Plan to leave some time for your listeners to ask questions.

Multimedia Ideas

Does your classroom have an overhead projector? If so, you might show drawings that tell about facts in your article.

How to Show Your Article

Suggestions for Visuals

Show pictures or objects.

- Drawings and photos can show how things are alike and different.
- A diagram can show facts.
- Models made from clay can show how things really look.

How to Share Your Article

Strategies for Rehearsing Be sure to practice before you give your presentation.

- Practice speaking in front of a mirror.
- Make an audiotape of your speech. Do you need to speak more slowly?
- Ask a friend to listen and give you tips.

Viewing Strategies

- Study the materials on display.
- Ask yourself how the pictures and diagrams can help you understand information.
- Look for details that are not in the speech.

PRACTICE and APPLY

Present Your Writing That Compares

1. Make notes about what you want to say.

2. Use pictures, photographs, or diagrams to show important points.

3. Practice alone or with a friend.

4. Relax and give your ideas clearly.

Writing Tests

Remember to read the prompt on a writing test carefully. Look for key words and phrases that tell you what to write about and how to do your writing.

Sometimes a prompt does not name the audience.

Look for words that tell the purpose of the writing.

Look for words that tell what kind of writing this is.

Prompt

Think about what you know about a house cat and a lion.

Write one or two paragraphs describing a house cat and a lion. Give <u>details and facts</u> telling <u>how they are alike and how they are different.</u>

How to Read a Prompt

Purpose Look for key words that tell you the purpose of the writing. The words "details and facts" tell you that the purpose of this writing is to inform. When you use details and facts, you are informing your audience.

Audience When the prompt does not tell who the audience is, you can think of your teacher as the audience.

Writing to Compare The words "how they are alike and how they are different" tell you that this will be the kind of writing that compares two things. When you write to compare two things, you use facts and details to tell how they are alike and different.

How to Write to a Prompt

Here are tips that can help you take a test that has a writing prompt.

Before Writing **Content/Ideas**	• Think about your writing purpose. • Remember who your audience is. • Make lists for "Alike" and "Different."
During Writing **Organization/** **Paragraph** **Structure**	• Start with a good opening sentence. • In writing to compare, explain how the things are alike and different. • Use a good ending sentence.
After Writing **Grammar/Usage**	• Proofread your work. • Start sentences with capital letters. • Use correct end marks. • Use the correct forms of verbs.

Apply What You Learned

Find words in a writing prompt that tell you what to write about. Look for the purpose and audience. Think about how to organize your ideas.

> **Prompt**
>
> Think about how a bicycle and a car are alike and different.
>
> Write a paragraph or two that compares a bike and a car. Tell how they are alike and different.

Name _____

Grammar and Writing Review

pages
210–215
Helping Verbs and Linking Verbs

A. Circle the correct verb in ( ).

1. Omar (has, is) invited Sara to his party.

2. Sara (is, has) excited about the party.

3. Omar's parents (are, have) hired a clown.

pages
218–223
Irregular Verbs

B. Write the past tense of each verb in ( ).

4. We (go) to a concert. _____

5. Everyone (sing) well. _____

6. I (see) some friends there. _____

pages
224–225
Contractions with *not*

C. Write the contraction for the underlined words.

7. This message <u>does not</u> make sense. _____

8. The message <u>is not</u> written with words. _____

9. I <u>cannot</u> figure out the code. _____

page
216, 226
Mechanics and Usage: Commas and Apostrophes

D. Add commas and apostrophes where they belong.

10. Marge cant stay in Austin Texas.

11. Irene didnt visit Chicago Illinois.

12. Little Rock Arkansas isnt far away.

pages 236–237

Vocabulary: Suffixes

E. **Underline the word that has a suffix. Then write what the word means.**

13. What a wonderful day it is! _____

14. The sky is blue and cloudless. _____

15. We're thankful for the good weather. _____

16. We are hopeful the day will stay nice. _____

17. We are helpless to change the weather! _____

pages 238–239

Composition: Sentence Style and Variety

F. **Use *and* to join the subjects or predicates. Write the new sentence on a piece of paper.**

18. Dean rode a bike. Dean could skate well.

19. The town had a picnic. The town held a bike race.

20. Dean entered the race. Marge entered the race.

Proofreading a Magazine Article

pages 256–257

G. **21.–25. Use proofreading marks to correct the 5 mistakes. Then write the article correctly on a piece of paper.**

foxes

Foxes are members of the dog family. The two most common foxes are the red fox and the gray fox. The gray fox isnt qwite as big as the red fox. Both foxes eat mice bugs, and berries.

Save this page until you finish Unit 4.

Project File

A Biography

A **biography** is the story of a real person's life written by someone else.

> You will need to know what to include in a biography when you write one in the next unit.

Young Inventor Louis Braille
by Marylou Taylor

Thanks to young Louis Braille, people without sight can know the joy of reading.

Louis Braille was born in France in 1809. At three, he hurt his eyes. Soon after, young Louis lost the sight in both eyes.

Louis's parents sent him to a special school when he was 10 years old. Louis was a good student. He liked science and music. He even learned to play the organ.

Louis wanted to find a way to read. He invented a code of raised dots that stand for letters and numbers. Later, he worked out a way of reading music. You read by touching the dots with your fingertips. We call this code braille in honor of its young inventor.

Title Gives the subject of the biography.

Topic sentence Tells the main idea of the biography.

Facts Includes facts about the subject's life.

Time order Tells events in the subject's life in the order.

Main ideas and details Each paragraph contains details about one main idea.

Write a short biography Have you ever wondered who invented such things as earmuffs, the basketball, zippers, or ballpoint pens? Choose an invention. Then find out about the inventor.

Write about the inventor. Include some interesting facts about the person's life.

PROJECT 2

A Scrapbook

It's hard to believe that a 300-pound panda only weighed four ounces at birth. How much have you changed since you were born?

Growing and Changing
Create a scrapbook about yourself called "Then and Now." Write about how you are the same and different now. Include photos.

Grammar

The Verb *Be*

A. In each sentence, circle the word that is a form of *be*.

1. I am glad to hear from you.

2. How are you?

3. How is camp?

4. Friday was cold.

5. Saturday and Sunday were rainy.

6. We were inside all weekend.

7. I was ready to go home.

8. Today is much better.

9. The sun is out.

10. We are ready to go on a hike.

B. Draw a line under the correct form of *be*.

11. Tonight the moon (is, were) full.

12. Tonight the stars (are, is) bright.

13. Yesterday it (were, was) foggy.

14. Last night the stars (was, were) dim.

15. Now the sky (is, are) clear.

 Save this page until you finish Unit 4.

Helping Verbs

A. **Write the underlined word that is a helping verb in each sentence.**

1. I <u>am</u> <u>planning</u> a surprise. _____

2. My brother <u>is</u> <u>helping</u>. _____

3. We <u>are</u> <u>fixing</u> breakfast. _____

4. Mom and Dad <u>are</u> <u>sleeping</u>. _____

5. Dan and Ben <u>have</u> <u>set</u> the table. _____

6. Juan <u>is</u> <u>making</u> the juice. _____

7. He <u>has</u> <u>squeezed</u> the oranges. _____

8. I <u>am</u> <u>stirring</u> the oatmeal. _____

9. Juan <u>has</u> <u>buttered</u> the toast. _____

10. Mom and Dad <u>have</u> <u>come</u> downstairs. _____

B. **Draw a line under the helping verb.**

11. Mom and Dad are smiling at us.

12. They have just finished breakfast.

13. Dan has cleared the table.

14. Jim is loading the dishwasher.

15. I am planning the next surprise.

Grammar

Linking Verbs

A. Write **L** if the underlined verb is a *linking* verb.
Write **A** if it is an action verb.

1. I <u>am</u> a bird-watcher. _____

2. My favorite bird <u>is</u> the bluebird. _____

3. Sometimes a robin <u>sits</u> on our windowsill. _____

4. Robins <u>are</u> brown. _____

5. A robin <u>lives</u> in our yard. _____

6. The bird <u>makes</u> a chirping sound. _____

7. Some birds <u>eat</u> tiny insects. _____

8. Bluebirds <u>are</u> pretty. _____

9. Today I <u>saw</u> a bluebird. _____

10. I <u>took</u> a picture of the bluebird. _____

B. Circle each verb. Write *linking verb*
or *action verb*.

11. I am a nature lover. _____

12. I bought a hummingbird feeder. _____

13. The bird feeder was in my garden. _____

14. Robins come every day. _____

15. Birds are fun to watch. _____

Commas in Names of Places

A. Put a comma between the name of each city and each state.

1. Tiffin Ohio

2. San Jose California

3. Dewey Beach Delaware

4. Cape May New Jersey

5. Houston Texas

6. Orlando Florida

7. Las Vegas Nevada

8. Norman Oklahoma

9. Jackson Mississippi

10. Chicago Illinois

B. Put a comma in the correct place in each sentence.

11. Let's visit Denver Colorado.

12. We'll fly from Ann Arbor Michigan.

13. We can drive to Provo Utah.

14. I'd like to see Seattle Washington.

15. I'm thinking about going to Atlanta Georgia.

Grammar

The Verbs *Go* and *Do*

A. Circle the word in ( ) that tells about action in the past.

1. Mom and I (go, went) to the city.

2. We (went, go) by bus.

3. Mom (did, does) some shopping.

4. What (do, did) you buy?

5. I (do, did) not buy a thing.

6. Then we (went, go) to lunch.

7. I (do, did) not know what to eat.

8. After lunch we (go, went) to a movie.

9. My sister (does, did) not come along.

10. My sister (did, does) her homework instead.

B. Change the verb in ( ) to show action in the past. Write each new verb.

11. Mom and I (go) home after the movie. _____

12. We (do) not take the bus. _____

13. We (go) by train instead. _____

14. We (do) not get home until late. _____

15. I (go) right to bed. _____

The Verbs *Say, See,* and *Run*

A. **Change the underlined verb to tell about an action in the past. Write the new verb.**

1. Mom <u>says</u>, "Please walk Rags." _____

2. My sister and I <u>say</u>, "Okay." _____

3. Our dog <u>sees</u> a squirrel. _____

4. Rags <u>runs</u> after the squirrel. _____

5. My sister <u>says</u>, "Let's follow him." _____

6. Rags <u>runs</u> through the yards. _____

7. We <u>run</u> after him. _____

8. Our friend Ben <u>sees</u> us. _____

9. He <u>says</u>, "I'll help you." _____

10. We <u>see</u> Rags down the street. _____

B. **Change the verbs to tell about an action in the past. Write each new verb.**

11. I see the squirrel. _____

12. The animal runs up a tree. _____

13. We run toward the tree. _____

14. We finally see Rags! _____

15. We all say, "Hooray!" _____

Grammar

The Verbs *Come*, *Give*, and *Sing*

A. **Change the underlined verb to tell about an action in the past. Write the new verb.**

1. The Fourth of July <u>comes</u> at last. _____

2. We <u>give</u> a big party in the backyard. _____

3. Everyone in the family <u>comes</u> to the party. _____

4. Grandma from Texas <u>comes</u>, too. _____

5. The family <u>sings</u> songs about America. _____

6. Later, Grandpa <u>gives</u> a speech. _____

7. We <u>give</u> Grandpa a big cheer. _____

8. Our friends <u>come</u> over with a pie. _____

9. Then we <u>sing</u> a special song we wrote. _____

10. Grandpa <u>sings</u> loudest of all! _____

B. **Change the verb in each to tell about an action in the past. Write each new verb.**

11. My aunt and uncle come late. _____

12. Uncle Mike gives me a hug. _____

13. Aunt Nancy comes from far away. _____

14. Everyone sings one last song. _____

15. Then we give thanks for America. _____

McGraw-Hill School Division

Contractions with *not*

A. **Circle each contraction.**

1. Tina can't find Sage.

2. The cat didn't touch her food.

3. Sage doesn't come when Tina calls.

4. It isn't like Sage to get lost.

5. Mom and Dad aren't worried.

6. "Don't worry," say Mom and Dad.

7. Sage hasn't run away.

8. Sage isn't hurt.

9. Tina hasn't seen the kittens.

10. "Don't forget to look in the tree," says Mom.

B. **Write a contraction for the words in ( ).**

11. Tina (cannot) believe how small the kittens are.

_____

12. "(Are not) they cute?" asks Mom. _____

13. "Why (did not) the kittens want to eat?" asked Tina.

_____

14. Sage (has not) eaten all her food. _____

15. "Why (do not) you get her milk?" says Mom.

_____

275

Grammar

Apostrophes

A. Add an apostrophe to the underlined word. Write the word correctly.

1. <u>Sues</u> sandwich is tasty. _____

2. Cora <u>cant</u> cook carrots. _____

3. <u>Idas</u> uncle eats rice. _____

4. Lizzy <u>isnt</u> hungry. _____

5. <u>Daves</u> dad drove to the store. _____

6. They <u>didnt</u> have any more corn. _____

7. Mr. <u>Stones</u> cart was empty. _____

8. Harry <u>hasnt</u> heard from Hanna. _____

9. Fran fed <u>Freds</u> fish. _____

10. Arthur and Arnold <u>arent</u> at home. _____

McGraw-Hill School Division

B. **Add an apostrophe where it belongs in each sentence.**

11. Willy wears Wallys watch.

12. Petes paintings are pretty.

13. Sids sister sips soup.

14. Donnas dog likes to dig.

15. Tims truck is a tanker.

16. Hans hasnt had a hamburger.

17. Petes pet parrot is in a parade.

18. Jim and Jenna dont like to juggle.

19. Carmen cant copy Carrie.

20. Allie and Alice arent always on time.

Pronouns and Expository Writing

In this unit you will learn about pronouns. You will also learn how to give facts and information in your writing.

🔍 **Science Link**   *Sam is putting something important together. What is it?*

Sam spends hours and hours digging for fossils. Once, Sam found a few tiny pieces of bone. Sam knew he had found something important. So he spent the day on his hands and knees looking for more bone. He picked up all the tiny pieces he could find. Then he glued them together. The pieces made up a dinosaur tooth. The dinosaur had lived millions of years ago!

〰 "Are You a Fossil Fan?" from ***Time for Kids***

Thinking Like a Writer

Expository Writing
Expository writing gives facts and information about a topic.

• What facts add up to the main idea of the passage?

Pronouns These words take the place of nouns.

⏰ **QUICK WRITE** Write the pronouns in the passage above.

Thinking Like a Writer

Expository Writing After you read the passage on page 279, write the facts that tell about the main idea of the passage.

_____

_____

_____

_____

_____

_____

_____

QUICK WRITE Write the words that take the place of nouns in sentences in the passage.

_____

_____

_____

_____

_____

Pronouns

RULES

- Pronouns take the place of nouns. Pronouns tell about one person or thing.

    Tina grows corn. She sells corn.

- Pronouns can tell about more than one person or thing.

    The apples are ripe. They taste good.

- Pronouns must match the words they replace. Look at the chart to see which pronouns replace which words.

One Person or Thing			More Than One	
she	he	it	they	we
↓	↓	↓	↓	↓
Eva	Ed	apple	Eva and Ed	Ed and I

THINK AND WRITE

Pronouns
Why might you use pronouns instead of nouns in your writing? Write the answer in your journal.

Guided Practice

Write a pronoun to take the place of the underlined words.

1. Mom and I are farmers. _____

2. Mom sells apples to the market. _____

3. Mr. Ray owns the market. _____

4. Mom and Mr. Ray talk about apples. _____

5. Apples will be on sale today. _____

Handbook
page 442

**Extra
Practice**
page 336

REVIEW THE RULES

- A **pronoun** takes the place of one or more nouns.

- Pronouns must match the noun or nouns they replace.

More Practice

A. Write pronouns to replace the underlined words.

6. Troy's Fruit Store sells fresh fruits. _____

7. Grandma and Grandpa shop there. _____

8. Grandpa and I pick out peaches. _____

9. A peach is a fruit. _____

10. Grandma buys some apples. _____

B. Spiral Review Circle the correct verb in ( ) to show past action. Circle each pronoun.

11.–15. Dear Grandma,

How are you? Yesterday Dad and I

(go, went) to the fair. We (see, saw)

so many people and had so much fun!

Love,

Arthur

Writing Activity   **A Paragraph**

Write a paragraph about a family activity.
APPLY GRAMMAR: Use pronouns in your paragraph.

I and *Me*

RULES

- Use the pronouns *I* and *me* to tell about yourself.

- Use *I* in the subject of a sentence.

  Paul and I learn about the sun.

- Use *me* after an action verb.

  The teacher asks me a question.

- Look at the chart to see where *I* and *me* are used in sentences.

In the Subject	After the Verb
Dad and I read a book.	Dad shows me pictures.
↑	↑
subject	action verb

THINK
AND WRITE

Pronouns
How do you know when to use *I* and when to use *me*? Write your answer.

Guided Practice

Choose *I* or *me* to complete each sentence.

EXAMPLE: (I, me) do my science homework.
Pronoun: I

1. My dad teaches (I, me) about the sun. _____

2. Dad and (I, me) look at pictures of the sun. _____

3. The sun makes (I, me) feel warm. _____

4. Dad tells (I, me) some interesting facts. _____

5. Now (I, me) know more about the sun. _____

Handbook
page 442

Extra
Practice
page 337

— REVIEW **THE** RULES

- Use *I* to tell about yourself in the subject of a sentence. Use *me* after an action verb.

More Practice

A. **Circle the correct pronoun in ( ).**

6. (I, me) will write a science report.

7. Mrs. Sing gives (I, me) a book.

8. Amy and (I, me) read the book.

9. Amy helps (I, me) with my notes.

10. Now (I, me) can write my report.

B. **Spiral Review** **Replace the words in ( ) with the correct pronoun. Circle each helping verb.**

11. (The children) have started a garden. _____

12. (Sarah) has planted some seeds. _____

13. (Mike) has not planted any seeds yet. _____

14. (Suki and I) are growing beans. _____

15. (The sun) is shining on our plants. _____

Writing Activity An Invitation

Write to invite a friend to do something with you.
APPLY GRAMMAR: Use *I* and *me* in your invitation.

We and Us

RULES

- Use *we* and *us* to talk about yourself and another person.

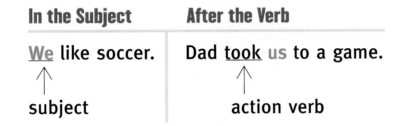

Jill and I play ball.　　*Mom watches Jill and me.*
↓　　　　　　　　　　　　　　　↓
We play ball.　　　　　*Mom watches us.*

- Use *we* in the subject of a sentence. Use *us* after an action verb.

In the Subject	After the Verb
<u>We</u> like soccer.	Dad <u>took</u> us to a game.
↑	↑
subject	action verb

Guided Practice

Choose *we* or *us* to replace the underlined words.

1. <u>Jill and I</u> run fast and kick the ball. _____

2. Rico sees <u>Jill and me</u>. _____

3. <u>Rico, Jill, and I</u> play ball together. _____

4. Jill gives <u>Rico and me</u> the ball. _____

5. <u>Rico and I</u> kick the ball to each other. _____

THiNK AND WRITE

Pronouns
How do you know when to use *we* and when to use *us*? Write your answer.

284

- Use *we* in the subject to talk about yourself and others. Use *us* after an action verb.

More Practice

A. Write *we* or *us* in place of the underlined words.

6. Fran teaches <u>Rita and me</u> to swim. _____

7. <u>Rita and I</u> have fun. _____

8. <u>Fran, Rita, and I</u> swim at the pool. _____

9. Fran's sister likes <u>Rita and me</u>. _____

10. Fay takes <u>Fran, Rita, and me</u> to the

    beach. _____

B. | Spiral Review | Circle the correct pronoun in ( ). Add apostrophes where they belong.

11.–15. Come and see (I, me) play ball. Today (I, me) play at my schools playground. My friends and (I, me) play ball almost every day. We cant wait for our big neighborhood game!

Handbook
page 442

Extra Practice
page 338

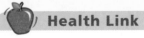

Writing Activity **A Description**

Write about what you do to stay healthy. Include important details.
APPLY GRAMMAR: Use the pronouns *we* and *us*.

Health Link

McGraw-Hill School Division

Using *I* and *Me*

RULES

- The pronoun I is always a capital letter.

  Luis and I will make a bird house.

- Name yourself last when talking about yourself and another person.

  Dad will help Luis and me.

Practice

Extra Practice page 339

A. **Tell if the sentence uses *I* or *me* correctly. If it does not, write the correct sentence on a piece of paper.**

1. Luis and i go outside.

2. Dad follows me and Luis.

3. I and Luis work with Dad.

4. Dad shows Luis and me what to do.

5. Dad, Luis, and i made a bird house.

B. **Spiral Review** **Write S for *statement*, Q for *question*, C for *command*, or E for *exclamation*. Write a pronoun for the underlined words.**

6. Come with Grandpa and me. _____

7. Grandpa and I will show you something. _____

8. Two ducks live near the pond. _____

9. Can Grandpa see the ducks' nest? _____

10. How high the duck flies! _____

THiNK AND WRITE

Pronouns
Why is it important to use a capital letter when you write *I* ?

Pronouns

— REVIEW THE RULES

- A **pronoun** takes the place of one or more nouns. Pronouns match the nouns they replace.

- Use **I** in the subject of a sentence. Use **me** after an action verb. Use **we** in the subject of a sentence. Use **us** after an action verb.

- Name yourself last when talking about yourself and another person.

Handbook
page 442

Pronouns
Write 5 sentences. Use different pronouns in each sentence. Use *I, me, we,* and *us* correctly.

Practice

A. Write pronouns to replace the underlined words.

1. <u>Grandma</u> lives near a rain forest. _____

2. Grandma takes <u>Luke and me</u> there. _____

3. <u>Luke and I</u> hear the birds. _____

4. <u>Luke</u> sees a big parrot. _____

5. <u>The parrot</u> has green feathers. _____

B. **Challenge** **Write the sentences on a piece of paper. Change the words in ( ) to make each sentence correct.**

6. (Me and Kate) pretend to be in the rain forest.

7. A big tiger surprises (Kate and I).

8. (The tiger, I, and Kate) stand very still.

9. (Kate and i) like the tiger.

10. The tiger doesn't bother (me and Kate).

Pronoun-Verb Agreement

RULES

- **Pronouns** and **verbs** must agree, or work together, in sentences.

- When the pronoun *he, she,* or *it* is in the subject of a sentence, add *-s* to most verbs in the present tense. When the pronoun is *I, you, we,* or *they,* do not add *-s*.

  Pam plays tag. Mark and I play, too.
  ↓   ↓
  She plays tag. We play, too.

- See how the verb goes with the pronoun in the subject of the sentence.

One person or Thing	More Than One
I/You hide	We/You hide
He/She/It hides	They hide

THiNK AND WRITE

Pronouns
How do you know when to add *-s* to a verb? Write your answer in your journal.

Guided Practice

Name the correct verb in ( ).

1. He (run, runs) to Masako. _____

2. They (sit, sits) by the door. _____

3. We (see, sees) Jessica behind the tree.

_____

4. You (stay, stays) near the fence.

_____

5. I (race, races) to the goal. _____

288

REVIEW THE RULES

- If a pronoun in the subject is singular, add *-s* to the verb. If it is *I, you,* or plural, do not add *-s*.

Handbook
page 442

Extra Practice
page 340

More Practice

A. Circle the correct verb in ( ) in each sentence.

6. I (learn, learns) how to roller-skate.

7. You (hold, holds) my hand.

8. He (give, gives) me some good advice.

9. She (run, runs) beside me.

10. Then we (skate, skates) together.

B. Spiral Review Circle the subject in each sentence. Circle the correct verb in ( ).

11. Holly and Bill (come, comes) to our party.

12. My brother (do, does) a funny trick.

13. Aunt Pat (give, gives) Joe a present.

14. I (say, says) "hello" to everyone.

15. We (sing, sings) and clap our hands.

Writing Activity A Clapping Chant

Write a song you can sing in a clapping game.
APPLY GRAMMAR: Circle each pronoun in your song.

Music Link

McGraw-Hill School Division

Possessive Pronouns

RULES

- A **possessive pronoun** takes the place of a possessive noun. A possessive pronoun shows who or what owns or has something.

  Sarah's family is going to Washington, D.C.
  ↓
  Her family is going to Washington, D.C.

- A possessive pronoun can take the place of a possessive noun.

One Person or Thing	More Than One
my	our
your	your
his, her, its	their

THINK AND WRITE

Pronouns
How can you tell when to use the word *his* or the word *her*? Write your answer.

Guided Practice

Write the possessive pronoun to replace the underlined words.

1. <u>People's</u> voices seem loud in the hall. _____

2. Mom holds <u>my sister's</u> hand. _____

3. We listen to <u>a man's</u> voice on tape. _____

4. <u>The Capitol's</u> rooms have many paintings. _____

5. <u>Mom's</u> postcard is beautiful. _____

┌───┐
│ ── **REVIEW** THE **RULES** ────────────── │
│   │
│ • Use a possessive pronoun to show who or what │
│   owns something.   │
│   │
└───┘

More Practice

A. **Write a possessive pronoun for the underlined words in each sentence.**

6. The museum's rooms are big. _____

7. Today the visitors' guide is Ms. Hunt. _____

8. My family likes Ms. Hunt's tour. _____

9. The room's furniture is so interesting! _____

10. My brother's feet are getting tired. _____

Handbook
page 443

Extra Practice page 341

B. | Spiral Review | **Replace the underlined words with *we* or *us*. Add a comma in the name of a place.**

11. Dad takes Mom, Josh, and me to Arlington Virginia. _____

12. My friend and I like the space museum. _____

13. My mom shows Josh and me a rocket. _____

14. Mom, Josh, and I see a special movie. _____

15. The movie thrills Josh and me! _____

Writing Activity   A Biography

Write a paragraph about a famous person from the past.
Put your sentences in a clear order.
APPLY GRAMMAR: Use possessive pronouns.

Social Studies Link

Contractions: Pronoun and Verb

RULES

- A **contraction** is the short form of two words.

- An **apostrophe** (') takes the place of the letters that are left out when the words are combined.

  I am thinking of a riddle.
  ↓
  I'm thinking of a riddle.

- See which letter each apostrophe replaces.

Singular		Plural	
I am	= I'm	We are	= We're
You are	= You're	You are	= You're
She is	= She's	They are	= They're
He is	= He's		
It is	= It's		

THINK AND WRITE

Contractions
Why do you use an apostrophe when you write a contraction? Write the answer.

Guided Practice

Change the underlined words to a contraction.

1. <u>We are</u> making up math riddles. _____

2. <u>She is</u> helping, too. _____

3. <u>He is</u> telling a riddle to the class. _____

4. <u>They are</u> figuring out the riddle. _____

5. <u>I am</u> ready for another riddle. _____

REVIEW THE RULES

- A **contraction** is a short form of two words.

- An **apostrophe** (') takes the place of the letters that are left out in the contraction.

Handbook
page 443

Extra Practice
page 342

More Practice

A. Write the contraction that replaces the underlined words in each sentence.

6. <u>I am</u> thinking of a number. _____

7. <u>You are</u> asking me five questions. _____

8. <u>It is</u> a number under twenty. _____

9. <u>They are</u> guessing the number. _____

10. <u>She is</u> right! _____

B. | Spiral Review | Write the words in ( ) correctly. Circle each action verb.

11. (Me and Ellie) write riddles. _____

12. Our dad helps (Ellie and I). _____

13. (Dad, I, and Ellie) like riddles. _____

14. Ellie asks (me and Dad) a new riddle. _____

15. (Dad and i) guess the answer right away. _____

Writing Activity   Riddle

Write a riddle about an animal.
APPLY GRAMMAR: Use contractions in your riddle.

Social Studies Link

McGraw-Hill School Division

Contractions and Possessive Pronouns

RULES

- An **apostrophe** takes the place of letters left out in a contraction.

  You're a pilot.

- A possessive pronoun never has an apostrophe.

  Your job is to fly the plane.

Extra Practice page 343

Practice

A. Circle the correct word in ( ) to complete each sentence.

1. Look at the plane. (It's, Its) wings are huge!

2. (They're, Their) checking the plane.

3. (They're, Their) job is important.

4. (You're, Your) seat is next to mine.

5. Now (you're, your) ready to fly.

B. Spiral Review Write the paragraph on a piece of paper. Make each verb in ( ) agree with each subject. Replace the underlined words with possessive pronouns.

6.–10. Mrs. Fox (work) at my school. She (take) care of the school's computers. Mrs. Fox's tools (is) in a special kit.

THiNK AND WRITE

Pronouns
Why are *it's/its*, *you're/your*, and *they're/their* harder to tell apart in speaking than in writing?

Pronouns

REVIEW THE RULES

- A present-tense verb must go with the pronoun in the subject of the sentence.

- Use possessive pronouns to take the place of possessive nouns.

- A contraction is a short form of two words. A possessive pronoun never has an apostrophe.

Handbook
pages 442–443

QUICK WRITE

Pronouns

Write five sentences
Use pronouns,
possessive pronouns,
and pronoun-verb
contractions.

Practice

A. Circle the correct word in ( ) to complete each sentence.

1. We (like, likes) jigsaw puzzles.

2. Sometimes (we, our) puzzles are hard.

3. She always (find, finds) the pieces.

4. She shows me (she, her) plan.

5. I (fit, fits) the pieces together, too.

B. ▉ Challenge ▉ Circle the word in ( ).

6. (You're, Your) mom fixes cars.

7. She says (it's, its) not a hard job.

8. Mom fixes (they're, their) tire.

9. (It's, Its) hole needs a patch.

10. (They're, Their) happy with the work.

Common Errors with Pronouns

Sometimes writers use the wrong pronoun as the subject of a sentence or after an action verb.

Common Error	Example	Corrected Sentence
Using me *or* us *as the subject of a sentence*	Bob and me play.	Bob and I play.
Using I *or* we *in the predicate*	Dad watches Bob and I.	Dad watches Bob and me.

REVIEW THE **RULES**

PRONOUNS

- Use *I* or *we* in the subject of a sentence.

- Use *me* or *us* after an action verb.

THINK AND WRITE

Pronouns
How do you know when to use *I* or *me* in a sentence? Write the answer in your journal.

Practice

Circle the correct pronoun in ( ).

1. Ms. Han paints with Ken and (I, me).

2. Ken and (I, me) make a big picture.

3. (We, Us) hang it in the main hallway.

4. The principal visits Ms. Han and (we, us).

5. Ken and (I, me) show him the picture.

Troubleshooter, pages 428–429

Mechanics and Spelling

Directions

Read the paragraph and decide which type of mistake, if any, appears in each underlined part. Choose the correct answer. If there is no mistake, choose "No mistake."

Sample

Check to see if any of the underlined words need to be capitalized.

I lost a book that I had borrowed from

the <u>library. Dad and i searched</u> the house for it.
(1)

<u>Dad finally found it</u>. My little brothers had
(2)

<u>put it in they're room</u>.
(3)

Does the underlined part have any mistakes? Sometimes there is no mistake.

A possessive pronoun is never spelled with an apostrophe.

1 ○ Spelling
○ Capitalization
○ Punctuation
○ No mistake

2 ○ Spelling
○ Capitalization
○ Punctuation
○ No mistake

3 ○ Spelling
○ Capitalization
○ Punctuation
○ No mistake

Test Tip
Remember, read all of the answers before you make your choice.

TIME FOR KIDS Writer's Notebook

RESEARCH

RESEARCH If I am looking for information in a book, I turn to the book's **index**. The index lists everything that is in the book. It also gives the page numbers where I can find the information. The index is in ABC order. It is at the end of a book.

COMPOSITION SKILLS

WRITING WELL The **main idea** of a story is what the story is about. But when I write, I need to say more than the main idea. I want to "paint a picture" with words. These "word pictures" are called **details**. Details bring my story to life!

VOCABULARY SKILLS

USING WORDS Smart, bright, clever are words that mean the same. These words are **synonyms**. Synonyms help make my stories more interesting. They also help me say just what I want to say. Can you think of any synonyms for the word pretty?

Read Now!

As you read the photo essay, write down the main idea. Then write down some details that make the story more interesting to you.

TIME
FOR KIDS
Writer's Notebook

COMPOSITION SKILLS

WRITING WELL Write the main idea of the photo essay about wolves. Then write some of the interesting details.

_____

_____

_____

_____

_____

_____

_____

_____

_____

_____

_____

_____

Cry of the Wolf

Gray wolves have returned to Yellowstone National Park. Will they be able to stay there?

Cry of the Wolf

For a long time, gray wolves lived in the forests of the U.S. West. Then, in the 1800s, farmers and ranchers moved in. Wolves sometimes killed farmers' animals. People worried that wolves might kill humans too. So wolves were shot. By the early 1930s, no wolves were left in Yellowstone Park's woods.

In 1995, 31 wolves were caught in Canada. They were sent to Yellowstone. The animals did well.

But many ranchers and farmers think the wolves might kill their animals. People are coming up with a plan to keep the farmers happy and the wolves in Yellowstone.

Cover: Darren Bennett/Animals Animals
All photos William Campbell

Scientists put a radio collar on a wild wolf pup. The radio signals help park workers keep track of the wolves. If a wolf makes trouble for a rancher, it can be moved.

McGraw-Hill School Division

interNET CONNECTION Go to www.mhschool.com/language-arts for more information on the topic.

Wolves live in groups called packs. Each pack has two to 15 members. This male wolf is the leader of a pack.

Gerard Lacz/Animals Animals

Wolves usually have five to nine babies, or pups, at a time. Wolves live about 15 years.

Write Now!

Write a paragraph about wolves using the information you just read. Include details such as the ones on this page to make your paragraph interesting to a reader.

301

Alphabetical Order

A B C D E F G H I J K L M
N O P Q R S T U V W X Y Z

You can put words in ABC order by their first letter. When words begin with the same letter, use the second letter to put them in ABC order.

ball   **best**   **bird**

When words begin with the same two letters, use the third letter to put them in ABC order.

beat   **best**   **better**

Practice

A. Write each group of words in ABC order. Use the first, second, or third letter, as needed.

1. junk, drive, nine _____

2. breeze, balloon, berry _____

3. carrot, cape, catcher _____

4. soap, snake, ship _____

5. trip, tray, trunk _____

B. Write the answer to each question.

6. If you were looking up *toad* in the encyclopedia, would it come before or after *tomato*? _____

7. Would the word *frame* come before or after *fox* in the dictionary? _____

8. Does the word *star* or *six* come before the word *space* in the dictionary? _____

9. If you were looking up *moose* in the encyclopedia, would it come before or after *monkey*?

_____

10. Would the word *panda* come before or after *paper* in the dictionary? _____

Writing Activity Make a Dictionary

Make a dictionary of birds. List all the birds you know in ABC order. Then use an encyclopedia to find out about the birds. Write sentences about them.

303

Vocabulary: Synonyms

DEFINITION

A synonym is a word that has the same or almost the same meaning as another word.

begin/start	shiny/bright
end/finish	sleepy/tired
little/tiny	kind/good
big/huge	dull/boring
glad/happy	high/tall

Notice the synonyms in blue.

THINK AND WRITE

Synonyms

How can synonyms help make your writing more interesting to read? Write your answer.

My brother Jack thinks rainy days are boring. I showed him an indoor game that is not dull. First I hid a shiny coin in the house. Then I told him to search for something bright. I drew a treasure map to help him. The X on the map told him where to start. He began to search for the coin. When he found it, it was his turn to hide the coin for me. He drew another map that helped me discover where he put it.

McGraw-Hill School Division

Practice

A. Write *yes* if the underlined words are synonyms. Write *no* if they are not.

1. I <u>like</u> mysteries and <u>enjoy</u> solving them. _____

2. This <u>hard</u> riddle is <u>difficult</u> to figure out. _____

3. I wondered how the <u>healthy</u> pet got <u>sick</u>. _____

4. The <u>old</u> trick was <u>new</u> to me. _____

5. The movie <u>ended</u> with a surprise <u>finish</u>. _____

B. Write the word from the box that is a synonym for the underlined word.

> small   tall   glad   caring   large

6. My mom is a <u>kind</u> person. _____

7. Mom was <u>happy</u> to help my uncle. _____

8. My uncle has a <u>tiny</u> dog. _____

9. The dog chases <u>huge</u> cars. _____

10. They built a <u>high</u> fence. _____

C. **Grammar Link** **11.–15.** Rewrite each sentence from Practice B on a piece of paper. Replace nouns with pronouns. Use different synonyms.

Writing Activity   Sentence Pairs

Write pairs of sentences about something you had to figure out. Use synonyms in your sentences.
APPLY GRAMMAR: Use one pronoun in each pair.

Composition: Main Idea and Supporting Details

Good writers use a main idea sentence to tell the most important idea in a paragraph. They write details to support the main idea.

McGraw-Hill School Division

THINK AND WRITE

Main Idea and Supporting Details

Write about why details must support the main idea.

GUIDELINES

- A **main idea** is the most important idea in a piece of writing.

- **Supporting details** tell more about the main idea.

- All the sentences in a **paragraph** should tell about one main idea.

Notice the main idea and details in this paragraph.

A main idea sentence states the most important idea.

Colonial Americans had many problems that we don't have today. There was no electricity. Candles gave dim light. Cooking was not easy because it had to be done in a fireplace. Many things had to be made by hand. It was hard work. Often people would raise sheep for wool. Then they would spin the wool into yarn and weave it into material for clothes.

Detail sentences give more information about the main idea.

Practice

A. **Write *yes* or *no* to tell if each sentence supports the main idea.**

> *Main Idea:*
> Settlers in America built different kinds of houses.

1. Early homes looked like cottages. _____

2. Most furniture was made of wood. _____

3. Stone homes were built in New England. _____

4. Pioneers built log cabins. _____

5. The weather in the north was cold. _____

B. **Write a main idea sentence for each title.**

6. A Great American

7. Why History Is Important

8. Problems Americans Have Today

9. What Life Will Be Like in the Future

10. Why I Love My Country

C. **Grammar Link** **11.–15. Write a detail sentence for each main idea sentence from Practice B. Replace some nouns with pronouns.**

Writing Activity A Paragraph

Write a paragraph about how you solved a problem. State the main idea and use details to support it.
APPLY GRAMMAR: Circle each pronoun you use.

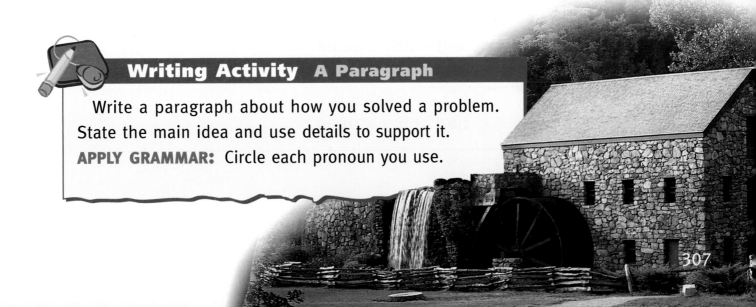

Better Sentences

Directions

Read the paragraph. Some parts are underlined. The underlined parts may be one of the following:

- Incomplete sentences
- Correctly written sentences that should be combined

Choose the best way to write each underlined part.

> **Look for sentences with similar words that can be combined.**

> **Check to see if the group of words is a complete sentence.**

Sample

Peter saw a cowboy hat in the store window. It had feathers around the band. It had shiny (1) stones around the band. Peter wanted that hat. Dad said he had to earn the money. Peter took out the trash. He swept the floor. Soon enough (2) money! He raced to the store and paid for the hat. But when he put it on, it fell down over his eyes and nose.

---

1 ○ Band of feathers and shiny stones.

   ○ It had feathers and shiny stones around the band.

   ○ It had feathers. It had shiny stones.

2 ○ Enough money!

   ○ Soon he had enough money!

   ○ Soon he had. Enough money!

> **Test Tip**
> Read the whole paragraph before choosing your answers.

Vocabulary and Comprehension

Directions

Read the paragraph. Then read each question that follows the paragraph. Choose the best answer to each question.

> **Sample**
>
> Long ago there was a big ocean. Dinosaurs walked on the shore of this <u>huge</u> ocean. They left their footprints in the mud. The footprints hardened. The mud turned to stone. Millions of years later people found the footprints. They showed how dinosaurs walked and where they lived. People can learn about dinosaurs by studying their footprints.

See if other words have almost the same meaning as the underlined word.

1 In this paragraph, the word <u>huge</u> means—

- ○ small
- ○ sandy
- ○ big
- ○ shallow

2 What is the main idea of this paragraph?

- ○ Long ago there was an ocean.
- ○ Dinosaurs are very old.
- ○ People like to see footprints.
- ○ People can learn about dinosaurs from their footprints.

Seeing Like a Writer

Imagine yourself in these pictures. What ideas for writing do they give you? Think about how you would explain what is happening in each one.

Mother and Child by Leslie Braddock.

Writing from Pictures

1. Write a caption for each picture that tells what the people are doing.

2. Write a main idea sentence and a detail sentence for one of the pictures.

3. Choose the two pictures you think are most alike. Write a short paragraph telling how they are the same or similar.

Apply Grammar: Use pronouns. Underline each pronoun you use.

Focus on Expository Writing

Have you ever written a report? This kind of writing is called expository. It gives facts and information about a topic.

Learning from Writers

Here are two examples of expository writing. Notice how the writers use main ideas and supporting details.

THINK AND WRITE

Purpose
Write in your journal when you might use expository writing.

Fossils

Some fossils are actual parts of plants or animals that have turned to stone. Sometimes a fossil is only an imprint of a plant or animal.

Millions of years ago, a leaf fell off a fernlike plant. It dropped onto the swampy forest soil, which is called peat. The leaf rotted away.

But it left the mark of its shape in the peat. The peat, with the imprint of the leaf, hardened. It became a rock called coal. Coal is a fossil, too.

— Aliki, from *Fossils Tell of Long Ago*

Abraham Lincoln

Abraham Lincoln didn't let problems stop him. When he was young, he lived in a log cabin. He wanted to learn about things. But he could only go to school for less than a year. So Lincoln walked long distances to borrow books from other people. He read those books by firelight. Lincoln even made his own arithmetic book! Later, he used what he had learned from the books in some of his speeches.

— Max Carter

PRACTICE and APPLY

Thinking Like a Reader

1. How did the leaf make a fossil?

2. What is the main idea of "Abraham Lincoln"?

Thinking Like a Writer

3. Where might Aliki have found facts about fossils?

4. Why are details about Lincoln important?

5. **Reading Across Texts** What words do the authors use to connect ideas in their paragraphs?

Features of Expository Writing

DEFINITIONS AND FEATURES

Expository writing tells true information. Reports and biographies are expository writing. Good expository writing does these things:

► It gives **facts** and **information** about a topic.

► It has a **main idea and details.**

► It uses **connecting words** to go from one idea to the next.

► **It summarizes information** from more than one source.

► Facts and Information

Reread "Fossils" on page 312. What facts does the author give?

Some fossils are actual parts of plants or animals that have turned to stone.

► Main Idea and Details

A main idea tells the most important idea of a paragraph. What is the main idea below?

The peat, with the imprint of the leaf, hardened. It became a rock called coal. Coal is a fossil, too.

▶ Connecting Words

Writers use connecting words to go from one idea to the next. How can these words make information clearer?

> Millions of years ago, a leaf fell off a fernlike plant.

The words "Millions of years ago" connect ideas. They help the reader understand how long it takes to make a fossil.

▶ Summarizes Information

Where might the author have found out this information?

> Sometimes a fossil is only an imprint of a plant or animal.

The author might have used information from an encyclopedia or from nonfiction books.

PRACTICE and APPLY

Create an Expository Writing Chart

1. List the features of expository writing.
2. Reread "Abraham Lincoln" on page 313.
3. Write how the author used each feature.

Features	Examples

315

Prewrite

Expository writing gives readers facts and information. You can use expository writing to share information with other people.

Purpose and Audience

The purpose of expository writing is to inform. You might write a biography to help others learn about a person's life.

Who will be reading your writing? How can you order the information so that it will be clear?

Choose a Topic

Begin by **brainstorming** a list of interesting people. Choose one to write about. **Explore and list** what you know about that person.

THINK AND WRITE

Audience
Write in your journal what kind of audience might enjoy your biography.

I explored ideas about Benjamin Franklin.

Benjamin Franklin

flew kite in storm

started newspaper

born in Boston

invented things

was smart

did experiments

signed Declaration of Independence

liked science

helped in Revolutionary War

Organize • Main Idea and Details

Expository writing may have more than one paragraph. Each paragraph has a main idea and details. You can use an outline to help you organize your paragraphs.

OUTLINE

Topic: Benjamin Franklin

A. Early Life of Benjamin Franklin
 1. Born in Boston
 2. Started newspaper

B. Helped in Revolutionary War
 1. Signed Declaration of Independence

C. Franklin Liked Science
 1. Did experiments
 2. Invented things

Checklist ✓
Prewriting

☐ Did you think about your purpose and audience?

☐ Did you choose an interesting person?

☐ Did you begin an outline?

☐ Do you need to find out more?

PRACTICE and APPLY

Plan Your Expository Writing

1. Think about your purpose and audience.

2. Choose a topic and explore ideas.

3. Put your ideas in an outline.

Prewrite • Research and Inquiry

▶ Writer's Resources

You may need to do research to get more information. Start a list of questions. Then decide where you can find the answers.

What Else Do I Need to Know?	Where Can I Find the Information?
When was Benjamin Franklin born?	Look in the index of nonfiction books.
What other important things did Franklin do?	Read about Benjamin Franklin in an encyclopedia.

▶ Use an Index

An index lists all the subjects in a book. The subjects are in alphabetical order.

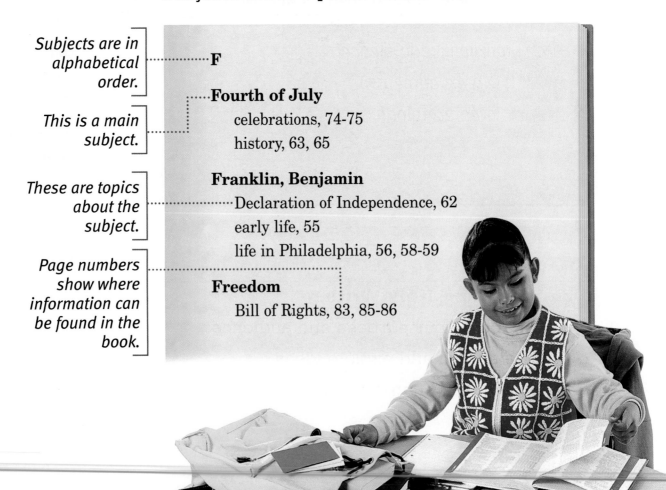

Subjects are in alphabetical order. ┈┈ **F**

This is a main subject. ┈┈ **Fourth of July**
celebrations, 74-75
history, 63, 65

These are topics about the subject. ┈┈ **Franklin, Benjamin**
Declaration of Independence, 62
early life, 55
life in Philadelphia, 56, 58-59

Page numbers show where information can be found in the book. ┈┈ **Freedom**
Bill of Rights, 83, 85-86

▶ Alphabetical Order

Many resources list information in ABC order. To find a subject, look under the letter it begins with. For example, to find Benjamin Franklin in the encyclopedia, look in the "F" book. Since all the words begin with *f*, look at the next letter, too. If there are other words that begin with *fr*, keep looking until you find *fra*.

Use Your Research

Write notes to summarize information from more than one resource. Add these facts to your outline.

Handbook
pages 462–463

> **A.** Early Life of Benjamin Franklin
>
>   **1.** Born in Boston — in 1706
>
>   **2.** Started newspaper
>
> **B.** Helped in Revolutionary War
>
>   **1.** Signed Declaration of Independence
>
>   **2.** Helped write the Constitution

PRACTICE and APPLY

Review Your Plan

1. List any questions you have.

2. Find books and encyclopedias that will help you.

3. Summarize what you learn in each source.

4. Add information into your outline.

Checklist ✓

**Research
and Inquiry**

☐ Did you list
your questions?

☐ Did you find
helpful
resources?

☐ Did you take
notes from the
resources?

☐ Did you add
new information
to your outline?

Draft

Writing PROCESS

Before you begin writing, review your outline. Make a paragraph for each main idea. Add details that support the main idea.

✓ **Checklist**

Drafting

☐ **Did you think about your purpose and audience?**

☐ **Have you written an interesting beginning?**

☐ **Did you summarize information from more than one source?**

☐ **Does each paragraph have a main idea?**

☐ **Did you add details?**

OUTLINE

"A" shows main idea for first paragraph.

Topic: Benjamin Franklin

A. Early Life of Benjamin Franklin
 1. Born in Boston—in 1706
 2. Started newspaper

B. Helped in Revolutionary War
 1. Signed Declaration of Independence
 2. Helped write the Constitution

C. Franklin Liked Science
 1. Did experiments
 2. Invented things

"C" shows main idea for third paragraph.

"B" shows main idea for second paragraph.

McGraw-Hill School Division

Here is how the writer used what she learned from her resources.

DRAFT

Ben Franklin enjoyed science. He did experiments with electricity. He invented things.

Benjamin Franklin liveed long ago. He was born in Boston in 1706. He went to philadelphia. There he helped the city set up it's fire department and library.

Franklin took part in the Revolutionary War. He signed the Declaration of Independence. He helped write the Constitution. Benjamin Franklin died in 1790.

Main idea of first paragraph

Main idea of second paragraph

Important facts and information added

Main idea of third paragraph

PRACTICE and APPLY
Draft Your Own Expository Writing

1. Review your prewriting chart.
2. Add what you learned from all your resources.
3. Write a main idea for each paragraph.
4. Add details.

TECHNOLOGY

If you typed your outline on the computer, you can use that document to begin your draft. Add words to make complete sentences.

Revise

Elaborate

You can elaborate to make your writing better. Put in extra details and examples to make your writing interesting.

> the lightning rod.
> He invented things.

Word Choice

In expository writing, it is important to use words that connect each idea to the next idea. What word did this writer use to connect ideas?

> Later
> He helped write the constitution.

CONNECTING WORDS

later	soon
when	now
but	after
first	before

Conferencing for the Reader

- Are all the parts of expository writing included in your partner's biography?
  - facts and information about the topic
  - main idea and details in each paragraph
  - words that connect ideas
  - information summarized from more than one resource

Better Paragraphs

As you revise your draft, read your paragraphs aloud. Do any of the paragraphs seem out of order? Look how this writer moved paragraphs around to put events in order.

PREWRITE

DRAFT

REVISE

PROOFREAD

PUBLISH

REVISE

Benjamin Franklin

Ben Franklin enjoyed science. He did experiments with electricity. He invented ~~things~~. the lightning rod.

Benjamin Franklin liveed long ago. He was born in Boston in 1706. He went to philadelphia.

There he helped the city set up it's fire department and library.

Franklin took part in the Revolutionary War. He signed the Declaration of Independence. Later He helped write the Constitution. Benjamin Franklin died in 1790. He was a great American.

PRACTICE and APPLY

Revise Your Own Expository Writing

1. Read your draft to yourself.

2. Share your draft with a partner.

3. Elaborate to make it more interesting.

4. **Grammar** Did you use pronouns correctly?

Checklist ✓
Revising

☐ Did you think about your purpose and audience?

☐ Did you add details for each main idea?

☐ Did you use connecting words?

☐ Do your paragraphs fit together well?

☐ Did you add an interesting title?

Writing PROCESS

Proofread

After you revise your biography, you will need to proofread it. Look for a different kind of mistake each time you read it.

STRATEGIES FOR PROOFREADING

- Reread for correct capitalization.

- Reread for correct punctuation.

- Make sure you used pronouns correctly.

- Check for spelling mistakes.

TIP!

Spelling

When words end in silent *e*, drop the *e* when adding an ending that begins with a vowel. *(lived)*

REVIEW THE RULES

GRAMMAR

- A pronoun is a word that takes the place of a noun. Use pronouns correctly by making sure they agree with the nouns they replace.

MECHANICS

- The pronoun *I* is always capitalized.

- *I* and *me* come last if joined by *and* with another pronoun or noun.

McGraw-Hill School Division

Look at the corrections below. What does the / mean? Why is this change needed?

PROOFREAD

Benjamin Franklin

Ben Franklin enjoyed science. He did experiments with electricity. He invented things. the lightning rod.

Benjamin Franklin lived long ago. He was born in Boston in 1706. He went to philadelphia. There he helped the city set up it's fire department and library.

Franklin took part in the Revolutionary War. He signed the Declaration of Independence. Later He helped write the Constitution. Benjamin Franklin died in 1790. He was a great American.

Checklist ✓
Proofreading

☐ Did you spell all words correctly?

☐ Did you correctly capitalize words?

☐ Did you write pronouns correctly?

☐ Did you indent each paragraph?

PROOFREADING MARKS

⌗ new paragraph

∧ add

ℒ take out

≡ Make a capital letter.

/ Make a small letter.

(SP) Check the spelling.

⊙ Add a period.

PRACTICE and APPLY

Proofread Your Own Expository Writing

1. Correct spelling mistakes.
2. Use capital letters correctly.
3. Check the use of pronouns.
4. Indent paragraphs.

Writing PROCESS

Publish

Good writers review their writing one last time before they publish it. This checklist can help.

> ✓ **Self-Check** Expository Writing
>
> ☐ **Did I keep my audience and purpose in mind?**
>
> ☐ **Did I write a main idea for each paragraph? Did I add interesting details?**
>
> ☐ **Did I summarize facts from more than one source?**
>
> ☐ **Did I use connecting words to help the reader make sense of when things happened?**
>
> ☐ **Did I indent all paragraphs?**
>
> ☐ **Did I proofread and fix any mistakes?**

The writer used the checklist to review her biography of Benjamin Franklin. Do you think it is ready to publish?

Benjamin Franklin

by Marisa Montez

Benjamin Franklin lived long ago. He was born in Boston in 1706. He went to Philadelphia. There he helped the city set up its library and fire department.

Ben Franklin enjoyed science. He did experiments with electricity. He invented the lightning rod.

Franklin took part in the Revolutionary War. He signed the Declaration of Independence. Later he helped write the Constitution.

Benjamin Franklin died in 1790. He was a great American.

PRACTICE and APPLY
Publish Your Own Expository Writing

1. Check your revised draft one more time.

2. Make a neat final copy. Add a cover.

3. Include some pictures of your subject.

TiP!

TECHNOLOGY

Does your school have a web site on the Internet? If so, you may want to publish your work on it.

Present Your Expository Writing

Plan before you present your biography.

STEP 1

How to Give Your Biography as a Speech

Strategies for Speaking When you present your biography, your purpose is to inform. Think about what you want listeners to learn. Make your speech as interesting as possible.

- Write main ideas and details on note cards.
- Look at your audience. Speak loudly and clearly.
- Use your voice to stress important points.

Listening Strategies

- **Set a purpose. Why are you listening?**

- **Listen for main ideas and interesting details.**

- **Keep your eyes on the speaker.**

- **Raise your hand to ask questions at the end of the talk.**

Multimedia Ideas

You might want to use sound effects and music you find on the Internet. Tape-record the sounds yourself and play them during the speech.

How to Show Your Biography

Suggestions for Illustrations Pictures can help bring a presentation to life.

- A portrait can help others "see" the person in your biography.
- Maps and drawings can help the audience imagine important events.

STEP 3

How to Share Your Biography

Strategies for Rehearsing It is a good idea to practice before you give a speech.

- Tape-record yourself. Then listen to the tape. How can you improve your presentation?
- Practice in front of a mirror.
- Rehearse in front of family members or a friend. Ask for suggestions.

Viewing Strategies

- Study the materials on display.
- Use drawings to help you understand information.
- Look for facts that the speaker does not tell you directly.

PRACTICE and APPLY

Present Your Own Expository Writing

1. Write notes about main ideas and details.
2. Practice your presentation.
3. Vary your tone of voice as you speak.
4. Use pictures and photographs.
5. Add sound effects or music.

Writing Tests

Read the prompt on a writing test carefully for key words and phrases that tell what to write about and how to do your writing.

Who will the audience be?

Look for words that tell if the purpose of the writing is to inform or entertain.

What does this tell you about the kind of writing?

> **Prompt**
>
> Think about all the things that can be done with ice.
> Write one or two paragraphs <u>for your teacher</u> that <u>tell things to do with ice</u>. Include <u>facts and details</u> about the ways ice is used.

How to Read a Prompt

Purpose Look for key words in the prompt that tell you the purpose of writing. The words "tell things to do with ice" let you know that one purpose is to inform.

Audience The prompt might tell you who the audience is. The words "for your teacher" let you know that your teacher is the audience.

Expository Writing The words "facts and details" are clues that this is expository writing. In expository writing, you give information about something. Your writing should have a main idea, and should give facts and details to support the main idea.

Test Tip
Read all the parts of a writing test slowly and carefully.

How to Write to a Prompt

Here are some tips to remember when you are given a prompt in a writing test.

Before Writing **Content/Ideas**	• Think about your writing purpose. • Remember who your audience is. • Make a list of things you know about the topic.
During Writing **Organization/ Paragraph Structure**	• Start with a good main idea. • Give details about the main idea. • Put your ideas in an order that makes sense. • Give your writing a good ending.
After Writing **Grammar/Usage**	• Proofread your work. • Use end marks correctly. • Use pronouns correctly.

Apply What You Learned

Find words that tell you what to write about. Look for the purpose and the audience. Think about how you will present your ideas.

> **Prompt**
>
> Think about what you know about whales.
>
> Write one or two paragraphs for your teacher telling what you know about whales. Give details about where they live, what they eat, and what they do.

Grammar and Writing Review

pages
280–285,
288–289

Pronouns and Pronoun-Verb Agreement

A. Write a pronoun to replace the underlined words.

1. <u>My sister</u> plays the piano. _____

2. <u>My mother and I</u> sing along. _____

3. My father claps for <u>Jan, Mom, and me</u>. _____

Possessive Pronouns

pages
290–291

B. Write a possessive pronoun for the underlined words.

4. <u>My grandfather's</u> stories are interesting. _____

5. <u>The story's</u> ending was a surprise. _____

6. <u>My sister's</u> laughter was loud. _____

Contractions: Pronoun and Verb

pages
292–293

C. Write the contraction for the underlined words.

7. <u>We are</u> going to the play. _____

8. <u>It is</u> at our school. _____

9. <u>I am</u> bringing my camera. _____

Mechanics and Usage: Contractions and Possessive Pronouns

page
294

D. Circle the correct contraction or possessive pronoun in ( ).

10. (Its, It's) a good day to work in the garden.

11. Did you bring (your, you're) tools?

12. Jill and Dan brought (their, they're) rakes.

pages
304–305

Vocabulary: Synonyms

E. **Circle the synonym in ( ) for the underlined word.**

13. Dance classes <u>begin</u> very early. (start, end)

14. It seems <u>chilly</u> in this room. (warm, cool)

15. My new tap shoes are <u>shiny</u>. (dull, bright)

16. New steps are not <u>easy</u>. (simple, hard)

17. I feel <u>sleepy</u> after class. (tired, lively)

pages
306–307

Composition: Main Idea and Details

F. **Underline only the sentences that support this main idea: Many countries have folk dances.**

18. Step dancing is a favorite in Ireland.

19. My brother likes to dance.

20. The United States has the square dance.

Proofreading a Report

pages
324–325

G. **21.–25. Use proofreading marks to correct the 5 mistakes. Then write the article correctly on a piece of paper.**

Square Dancing

Many people in the United states like

to square dance. Its so much fun! You

need four pairs of danceers for a square

dance. They faces each other in a square.

A caller sings or calls out they're moves.

Save this page until you finish Unit 5.

Project File

A Humorous Story

A **story** tells about made-up characters and events. A funny story entertains its readers.

> You will need to know the form of a story when you write your story in the next unit.

Corky's Mixed-up Morning

Corky Crocodile woke up and smiled. "I have a feeling that today will be a good day!" he said.

First, Corky squeezed the toothpaste tube. All the toothpaste squirted out. There was toothpaste everywhere! "Oh, no!" said Corky. He cleaned up the mess and went to the kitchen.

Next, Corky poured a glass of milk. He dropped the milk carton. There was milk everywhere! "Oh, no!" said Corky. He cleaned up the mess. Then he headed back to his room.

"Where are you going, Corky?" his mother asked.

"I'm going back to bed," said Corky. "My morning started out all wrong. I'd better start over!" With that, he jumped into his bed and then got up again.

Beginning tells who the story will be about.

Middle tells what happens in the story.

Time-order words help explain the order of events.

End tells how everything turns out.

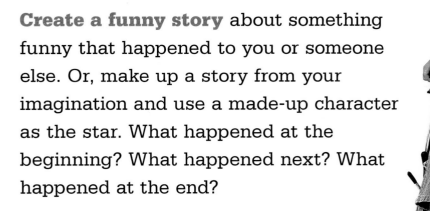

Create a funny story about something funny that happened to you or someone else. Or, make up a story from your imagination and use a made-up character as the star. What happened at the beginning? What happened next? What happened at the end?

PROJECT 2

A Realistic Article

Scientists have been working to save the wolves at Yellowstone. Interview experts at a zoo or search the Internet to find out more about the animals that are in danger of becoming extinct.

Animals in Trouble Choose one group of animals. Write an article about how people are helping to save these animals.

Grammar

Pronouns

A. Circle the correct pronoun in ( ) for the underlined words.

1. A backyard picnic is fun. (It, They)

2. My friends and I had a picnic. (They, We)

3. Felipe and Carmen fixed sandwiches. (You, They)

4. Mario made lemonade. (He, You)

5. Ana peeled some carrots. (They, She)

6. Mom and I baked cookies. (She, We)

7. Dad carried the picnic basket. (We, He)

8. The basket was very heavy. (She, It)

9. Ana spread out the blanket. (They, She)

10. My friends sat on the blanket. (We, They)

B. Write pronouns to replace the underlined words.

11. Peanut butter sandwiches make me thirsty. _____

12. Carmen poured the lemonade. _____

13. The lemonade tasted cold and sweet. _____

14. Felipe and I took some cookies. _____

15. My dog Charlie snatched a cookie. _____

 Save this page until you finish Unit 5.

I and *Me*

A. Circle *I* or *me* to complete each sentence.

1. My brother and (I, me) like music.

2. Kurt and (I, me) take piano lessons.

3. Mr. Herman teaches Kurt and (I, me).

4. (I, me) always practice after school.

5. Our teacher gave (I, me) a new song to learn.

6. Sometimes (I, me) sing and play at the same time.

7. Mom likes to listen to Ben and (I, me) play.

8. Yesterday (I, me) went to a concert.

9. Mr. Herman gave (I, me) tickets.

10. Dad took Kurt and (I, me) to the concert.

B. Choose *I* or *me* to fill in the blank.

11. _____ practice an hour a day.

12. Kurt and _____ are in a show.

13. Kurt will play a song with _____.

14. Mom drives Kurt and _____ to our lessons.

15. Kurt and _____ ride home with Dad.

Grammar

We and Us

A. Circle the correct pronoun in ( ) to replace the underlined words.

1. <u>Lisa and I</u> went to see Mrs. Ruiz. (We, Us)

2. <u>My sister and I</u> brought cookies. (We, Us)

3. Mrs. Ruiz asked <u>Lisa and me</u> to come in. (we, us)

4. She hugged <u>my sister and me</u>. (we, us)

5. Her dog greeted <u>Lisa and me</u>, too. (we, us)

6. <u>Lisa and I</u> patted Pepito. (We, Us)

7. Sometimes <u>she and I</u> walk Pepito. (we, us)

8. <u>My family and I</u> mow the lawn. (We, Us)

9. <u>Mrs. Ruiz and my family</u> are neighbors. (We, Us)

10. Mrs. Ruiz once babysat for <u>Lisa and me</u>. (we, us)

B. Write *we* or *us* in place of the underlined words.

11. Mrs. Ruiz made <u>Lisa and me</u> cocoa. _____

12. <u>Lisa and I</u> served the cookies. _____

13. Pepito barked at <u>Mrs. Ruiz, Lisa, and me</u>. _____

14. <u>Mrs. Ruiz, Lisa, and I</u> laughed. _____

15. <u>Lisa and I</u> gave Pepito a special treat. _____

Using *I* and *Me*

A. **Circle the correct word or words in ( ) to complete each sentence.**

1. My sister and (i, I) like to bake.

2. Mom gave (Sarah and me, me and Sarah) a cookbook.

3. Sarah and (i, I) checked the recipes.

4. (I and she, She and I) picked one.

5. Mom worked with (Sarah and me, me and Sarah).

6. Sarah, Mom, and (I, me) made bread.

7. (Mom and I, Mom and i) found the bowls.

8. She showed (Sarah and me, me and Sarah) the mixer.

9. (Mom and i, Mom and I) poured the batter.

10. (Sarah and I, Sarah and me) learned how to turn on the oven.

B. **Change the sentences that do not use *I* and *me* correctly. Write each sentence correctly on a piece of paper.**

11. Dad asked Sarah and I for a taste of the bread.

12. Mom sliced the bread for me.

13. Sarah and me gave Dad a slice.

14. Dad gave Sarah and I a hug.

15. Sarah and I are good bakers.

Grammar

Pronoun-Verb Agreement

A. Underline the pronoun. Circle the verb.

1. I like baseball most of all.

2. We play all summer long.

3. I see Max and Yoko.

4. They wait for us at the field.

5. He plays ball all the time.

6. He always brings a bat and ball.

7. She takes her glove everywhere.

8. We still need more players.

9. You call Jack, Ed, and Eli.

10. They live down the block.

B. Circle the correct form of the verb in ( ).

11. I (throw, throws) the first pitch to Sara.

12. She (hit, hits) the ball hard.

13. It (land, lands) over the fence.

14. She (send, sends) two runners home.

15. They all (cheer, cheers) for Yoko.

McGraw-Hill School Division

Possessive Pronouns

A. Draw a line under each possessive pronoun.

1. Her class is at the White House.

2. His office and home are here.

3. All of its curtains are new.

4. His mother works for the President.

5. Her office is in the West Wing.

6. Their rooms are private.

7. Their guide leads the way.

8. Her name is Ms. Gomez.

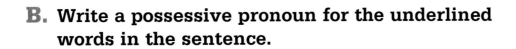

9. Look at its beautiful paintings.

10. Where is her office?

B. Write a possessive pronoun for the underlined words in the sentence.

11. The children's friends saw the President.

_____

12. The President's family arrived in Delaware.

_____

13. The First Lady's parents live there.

_____

14. The house's gardens are beautiful.

_____

15. Juan grandma lives next door.

_____

Grammar

Contractions: Pronoun and Verb

A. Draw a line under each contraction.

1. We're reading a really good book.

2. You're going to like it.

3. It's about a boy and his friends.

4. They're all in the second grade.

5. He's always having adventures.

6. I'm writing a report about the author.

7. She's one of my favorite authors.

8. I'm reading a book by Maurice Sendak.

9. He's another of my favorite authors.

10. You're welcome to read my books.

B. Write the contraction that replaces the underlined words.

11. It is fun to go to the library. _____

12. I am going there with Jan and Ed. _____

13. She is looking for books by Tomie dePaola. _____

14. He is doing a report on the American flag. _____

15. We are leaving in a few minutes. _____

Contractions and Possessive Pronouns

A. Circle the correct word in ( ).

1. (You're, Your) friends are in science class.

2. (Their, They're) learning about the wind.

3. I read (their, they're) report on storms.

4. (Its, It's) really interesting.

5. (Your, You're) doing a good job, too!

6. (Your, You're) report is great!

7. (Its, It's) steps are easy to follow.

8. (Its, It's) hard to catch raindrops.

9. (Their, They're) not really like teardrops.

10. (Their, They're) shapes are different.

B. Correct the underlined word if it is wrong. Write the word correctly.

11. Its time to go. _____

12. Their going to the weather museum. _____

13. It's my favorite place to visit. _____

14. Your class will like it. _____

15. Your going next week. _____

Adjectives, Adverbs, and Writing a Story

In this unit you will learn about adjectives and adverbs. You will also learn how to write a story.

Social Studies Link *Look for describing words as you begin this story about Tomás and his family.*

It was midnight. The light of the full moon followed the tired old car. Tomás was tired too. Hot and tired. He missed his own bed, in his own house in Texas.

Tomás was on his way to Iowa again with his family. His mother and father were farm workers. They picked fruit and vegetables for Texas farmers in the winter and for Iowa farmers in the summer.

~~~ from ***Tomás and the Library Lady*** by Pat Mora

Thinking Like a Writer

A Story A story tells about people and how they solve their problems.

- What have you learned about Tomás?

- What have you learned about his family?

Adjectives The author uses describing words called adjectives to tell about Tomás.

⏰ **QUICK WRITE** Find an adjective in the story and use it in a sentence.

Thinking Like a Writer

Writing a Story After you read the passage on page 345, write what you have learned about Tomás and his family.

_____

_____

_____

_____

_____

_____

_____

_____

QUICK WRITE Write a sentence with an adjective from the passage.

_____

_____

_____

_____

_____

Adjectives

RULES

- An adjective describes a noun.

  Memorial Day is a special day.

- Some adjectives tell what kind.

  We see a big parade.

- Adjectives help paint a picture.

  I see a flag. ⟶ *I see a blue flag.*

  We hear music. ⟶ *We hear loud music.*

THiNK AND WRITE

Adjectives
How can adjectives make your writing better? Write your answer.

Guided Practice

Write the adjective in each sentence.

1. Debbie buys a red balloon. _____

2. We stand on the busy sidewalk. _____

3. Harry beats his new drum. _____

4. The clowns do a funny dance. _____

5. The band plays a happy tune. _____

---— **REVIEW** THE **RULES** ———————

> • An **adjective** describes a noun. It can tell what kind.

More Practice

A. **Circle the adjective in each sentence.**

6. Earth Day is an important day.

7. Our class plants a small tree.

8. The tree has green leaves.

9. We dig a deep hole in the ground.

10. Nicole and I pat the soft soil.

B. **Spiral Review** **Circle the correct pronoun in ( ). Circle each adjective.**

11.–15. (Our, We) class plans a special day. The children bring in (they're, their) favorite books and tapes. (You're, Your) invited to come.

Handbook
page 444

Extra Practice
page 404

Writing Activity A Description

Write a paragraph about a special day you like.
APPLY GRAMMAR: Circle the adjectives you use.

Adjectives That Tell How Many

---- **RULES** ----

- Some adjectives tell how many.

  That mango costs two dollars.

- Here is one way to tell if a word is an adjective. Ask yourself, "How many?"

Sentence	How Many?
Some <u>vegetables</u> are on sale	some
One <u>fruit</u> is on sale	one

THINK AND WRITE

Adjectives
Why is it helpful to use adjectives that tell how many?

Guided Practice

Write the adjective that tells how many.

1. Dad picks out four apples. _____

2. There are many oranges in a bag. _____

3. The bananas weigh one pound. _____

4. I choose two new fruits for us. _____

5. Dad and I buy several pears and figs.

_____

- Some adjectives tell how many.

More Practice

A. Underline the adjective that tells how many.

6. The toy sale lasts for one hour.

7. All toys and games are on sale.

8. The store has many model planes.

9. The children look at some models.

10. Eight children buy model kits.

Handbook
page 444

Extra Practice
page 405

B. Spiral Review **Circle the correct verb in ( ). Circle each adjective that tells what kind.**

11. The shop (sell, sells) beautiful kites.

12. Ling and I (want, wants) a big kite.

13. We (have, has) four dollars.

14. Ling (like, likes) the colorful kites.

15. She and I (buy, buys) a red kite.

Writing Activity   A Shopping List

Write a food shopping list with five things on it.
APPLY GRAMMAR: Circle the adjectives you use.

Math Link

Articles: *a, an*

RULES

- The words *a* and *an* are special adjectives called articles.

- Use *a* before a word that begins with a consonant sound.

  Last night I read a <u>s</u>tory.

- Use *an* before vowel sounds.

  The story was about an <u>e</u>lephant.

- Use *an* only if the next word begins with a vowel sound.

  The elephant saw a <u>m</u>ouse.

  ⊤

  <u>consonant</u>

  The mouse looked up and saw an <u>e</u>lephant.

  ⊤

  <u>vowel sound</u>

THINK AND WRITE

Adjectives
When do you use *an* instead of *a* before a word? Write your answer.

Guided Practice

Name the correct article: *a* or *an*.

1. Mom and I saw (a, an) owl. _____

2. The owl sat in (a, an) tree. _____

3. We found (a, an) old nest. _____

4. In the nest was (a, an) egg. _____

5. Later we saw (a, an) baby owl. _____

Handbook
page 444

Extra Practice
page 406

REVIEW THE RULES

- The words *a* and *an* are articles.

- Use *a* before consonant sounds. Use *an* before words that begin with vowel sounds.

More Practice

A. Circle the correct article in ( ).

6. Jan has (a, an) book about animals.

7. (A, An) picture shows animals in trees.

8. (A, An) ape is in the picture.

9. One page shows (a, an) empty nest.

10. The nest sits on (a, an) branch.

B. Spiral Review Underline each pronoun. Circle each adjective that tells *how many*.

11. I wrote about some whales.

12. The whales swim many miles.

13. They eat fish every day.

14. One whale is a baby.

15. What did you write about?

Writing Activity **A Character Sketch**

Choose a story character and write about him or her.
APPLY GRAMMAR: Circle each *a* and *an* you use.

Adjectives That Compare

RULES

- You can use adjectives to compare nouns. Add *-er* to an adjective to compare two nouns.

  This tree is taller than that one.

- Add *-est* to an adjective to compare more than two nouns.

  This tree is the tallest one of all.

One	This tree is tall.
Compare two. Add *-er*	That tree is taller than this one.
Compare more than two. Add *-est.*	Our tree is the tallest of them all.

THINK AND WRITE

Adjectives
When do you add *-er* or *-est* to an adjective? Write your answer.

Guided Practice

Add the ending *-er* or *-est* to each adjective in ( ). Then write the new word.

1. Mr. Lock's yard is (wide) than our yard. _____

2. Our lawn is the (green) one around. _____

3. Is the oak tree (tall) than the elm? _____

4. This week is the (warm) this spring. _____

5. Your backyard is (cool) than mine. _____

REVIEW THE RULES

- To compare two nouns, add *-er* to an adjective. To compare more than two nouns, add *-est*.

More Practice

A. Add *-er* or *-est* to the adjective in ( ). Write the new adjective.

6. My plant is the (small) one here. _____

7. This plant looks (sick) than that plant. _____

8. These leaves are the (brown) of all. _____

9. Victoria's plant is (tall) than mine. _____

10. This dirt feels (damp) than that dirt. _____

B. **Spiral Review** **Fill in the blank with *a* or *an*. Circle each action verb.**

11. Yesterday was _____ rainy day.

12. _____ inch of rain fell.

13. Al and I looked out _____ open window.

14. _____ cloud moved away from the sun.

15. Then _____ rainbow appeared in the sky.

Writing Activity   A Weather Report

Compare today's weather with yesterday's weather.
APPLY GRAMMAR: Use adjectives that compare.

Science Link

Handbook
page 445

Extra Practice
page 407

Writing Book Titles

┌─ **RULES** ─────────────────────────────┐

• Use capital letters for the first word and all the important
words in a book's title. Draw a line under all words in the title.

I read <u>The Wonders of Space</u>.

└──────────────────────────────────────┘

Practice

A. Write each sentence correctly. Use capital letters
where they belong. Underline the words in each
book title.

1. Sam read an adventure in orbit.

_____

2. I liked blastoff to splashdown.

_____

3. Lena read to pluto and beyond.

_____

4. Did you read women in space?

_____

5. Tyler read the milky way.

_____

B. **Spiral Review** Circle the correct verb in ( ). Fill in each
blank with *a* or *an*.

6. I (am, is) writing _____ book.

7. My book (is, are) about _____ adventure.

8. The characters (is, are) in _____ rocket.

9. One character (was, were) from _____ planet far away.

10. (Is, Are) you _____ author, too?

**Extra
Practice
page 408**

**THINK
AND WRITE**

Adjectives
Write to tell how
capital letters and
lines under the
titles of books are
helpful.

354

Adjectives

REVIEW THE RULES

- An adjective is a word that describes a noun. Adjectives can tell *what kind* or *how many*.

- Use the article *a* before a consonant sound. Use *an* before a vowel sound.

- Add *-er* to adjectives when you compare two nouns. Add *-est* to adjectives when you compare more than two nouns.

Handbook
pages 444–446

Pronouns

Write five sentences. In each sentence, use an adjective that tells *what kind* or *how many* to describe a noun.

Practice

A. Underline each adjective. Circle the adjective if it tells how many.

1. My grandmother bought the blue bike.

2. Now Grandma has two bikes.

3. I like Grandma's old bike.

4. Grandma loves long rides.

5. Grandma and her friends ride for one hour.

B. **Challenge** **Write each underlined adjective correctly.**

On most days, Jake is the <u>faster</u> bike rider in our family. On the bike path he was <u>slow</u> than Sue. Sue is two years <u>youngest</u> than Jake. Today Mom was the <u>quicker</u> rider in the family. Mom thinks this was the <u>great</u> trail ride ever!

6. _____   **9.** _____

7. _____   **10.** _____

8. _____

Adverbs

RULES

- An **adverb** tells more about the verb in a sentence.

- An adverb can tell *how*, *when*, or *where*.

   The sun is shining **brightly**.

- Adverbs tell when, where, or how the action takes place.

When ⟶ We raised the flag **early**.

Where ⟶ The flag flies **high**.

How ⟶ The flag flaps **softly** in the wind.

THINK AND WRITE

Adverbs
What can an adverb tell you about a verb? Write your answer in your journal.

Guided Practice

Tell if each underlined adverb tells how, when, or where.

1. We are drawing pictures <u>today</u>. _____

2. We color the pictures <u>carefully</u>. _____

3. Everyone works <u>quietly</u>. _____

4. <u>Soon</u> I will finish my drawing. _____

5. You can see our drawings <u>everywhere</u>. _____

356

More Practice

A. Write *how, when,* or *where* to say what the adverb tells about.

6. The art show <u>finally</u> begins. _____

7. Miranda holds a painting <u>up</u>. _____

8. We all start working <u>quietly</u>. _____

9. Ed speaks <u>clearly</u> about Mexico's art. _____

10. <u>Later</u> we each tell about our drawings. _____

Handbook
page 442

Extra
Practice
page 409

B. [Spiral Review] Add *-er* or *-est* to the adjective in ( ). Write the new adjective. Then write the two book titles correctly.

11. The (great) book I have read is a new world.

_____

12. Is this book (small) than that one? _____

13. More tiny tales is the (small) book here. _____

_____

14. Your book is (thick) than mine. _____

15. Is Josh a (fast) reader than Jeff? _____

Writing Activity   Instructions

Write a list of steps for how to do something.
APPLY GRAMMAR: Use adverbs in your instructions.

Adverbs That Tell How

RULES

- Some adverbs tell **how** an action is done.

  The snake moves slowly.
  It carefully hides in a hole.

- Many adverbs that tell how end with *-ly*.

  The lion <u>runs</u> <u>quickly</u>.
  ↑ ↑

  <u>What does the lion do?</u> <u>How does it run?</u>

Guided Practice

Name the verb. Then name the adverb that tells how the action is done.

1. A mother tiger gently lifts her cubs.

_____ _____

2. The cubs play happily in the den.

_____ _____

3. The mother listens closely for other animals.

_____ _____

4. Mother tiger roars loudly.

_____ _____

5. Suddenly the cubs stop.

_____ _____

THINK AND WRITE

Adverbs
How can adverbs make your writing more interesting? Write your answer in your journal.

358

REVIEW THE RULES

- Some adverbs tell how an action is done.

More Practice

A. Circle each verb. Underline the adverb that tells about it.

6. In the zoo, the lion walks proudly.

7. The elephants march slowly into the pen.

8. The hippos sink quietly into the water.

9. The monkeys chase each other playfully.

10. The bear cubs play roughly.

B. **Spiral Review** Circle the correct form of the verb in ( ) so that it agrees with the pronoun in the subject of the sentence.

11.–15. We (visit, visits) the new marine park.

Suddenly I (see, sees) a dolphin. It (swim, swims) happily.

Handbook
page 445

Extra Practice
page 410

Writing Activity A Journal Entry

Write a journal entry about a visit to a zoo, a marine park, or an aquarium. Include details.
APPLY GRAMMAR: Use adverbs that tell how.

Science Link

Adverbs That Tell When or Where

RULES

- Some adverbs tell *when* an action happens.

  Now I read my book.

- Some adverbs tell *where* an action happens.

  I read *upstairs*.

- Ask yourself: *When does this action happen? Where does this action happen?*

Sentence	When	Where
It rained today.	today	
We played inside.		inside

THINK AND WRITE

Adverbs
How do adverbs that tell where and when help your writing?

Guided Practice

Write the verb and the adverb in each sentence. Tell if the adverb tells where or when.

1. Grandpa lives nearby. _____

_____

2. We always play in the park. _____

_____

3. We run the bases first. _____

_____

4. We sit down for a rest. _____

_____

5. Then Grandpa watches the sky. _____

_____

REVIEW THE RULES

• Adverbs can tell when or where an action happens.

More Practice

A. Circle each verb and underline each adverb. Write *where* if the adverb tells where. Write *when* if the adverb tells when.

6. Yesterday we went to a new place._____

7. My family drove far._____

8. My sister and I looked around._____

9. Soon we saw three baby lambs._____

10. Later we returned to the city._____

B. **Spiral Review** Write a contraction for the two words in ( ). Circle the three adverbs that tell *how*.

11. Today (we are) learning a new song._____

12. (It is) a beautiful song about the wind. _____

13. (He is) singing the song happily._____

14. (They are) clapping their hands softly. _____

15. (I am) gently tapping the drum. _____

Writing Activity   A Comparison

Write a comparison of two things you like to do.
APPLY GRAMMAR: Use adverbs that tell where or when.

McGraw-Hill School Division

Quotation Marks

┌─ **RULES** ─────────────────────────────────┐
│   │
│ • Use quotation marks (" ") at the beginning and at │
│   the end of the words a person says.   │
│   │
│   *The doctor asked, "How do you feel?"*   │
│   │
└──┘

Practice

A. Add quotation marks where they belong.

1. Breathe in, said the doctor.

2. Dr. Zim said, I will listen to your lungs.

3. Joe asked, Can you hear my heart?

4. Yes, said the doctor.

5. Dr. Zim said, You have a cold.

B. **Spiral Review** Write the contraction for the words in ( ). Write *when* or *where* for each underlined adverb.

6. I (do not) know much about lungs._____

7. Your body has two lungs <u>inside</u>._____

8. <u>First</u> your lungs take air <u>in</u>._____

9. <u>Then</u> your lungs let the air <u>out</u>._____

10. Wow! <u>Now</u> I understand!_____

Grammar

Extra Practice
pages 412-413

THiNK AND WRITE

Quotation Marks
Why is it important to remember to use quotation marks? Write your answer.

362

Adverbs

REVIEW THE RULES

- An adverb tells more about a verb.

- Adverbs tell *how*, *when*, or *where* an action happens.

- Use quotation marks at the beginning and at the end of the words a person says.

Handbook
pages 444–446

QUICK WRITE

Pronouns
Write three sentences. Use each kind of adverb in a sentence to describe *how*, *when*, or *where* an action takes place.

Practice

A. Write what the underlined adverb tells: *how*, *when*, or *where*.

1. Yesterday I made up a scary story._____

2. I quietly told it to my brothers._____

3. Alexander listened closely._____

4. Andrew leaned forward._____

5. The boys always like my stories._____

B. **Challenge** Add quotation marks where they are needed. Circle adverbs.

6. Marta said, It's early.

7. Please tell me a story now, she begged.

8. Okay. Go upstairs, said Grandma.

9. Grandma asked cheerily, What's your favorite story?

10. Marta looked up and said, I like happy stories.

Common Errors with Adjectives

Some writers forget when to add *-er* and when to add *-est* to an adjective.

Common Errors	Examples	Corrected Sentences
Using -est for comparing two nouns	Pat's dog is biggest than my dog.	Pat's dog is bigger than my dog.
Using -er for comparing more than two	Ty's dog is the bigger dog of all.	Ty's dog is the biggest dog of all.

REVIEW THE RULES

ADJECTIVES THAT COMPARE

- Add *-er* to an adjective to compare two nouns.

- Add *-est* to compare more than two nouns.

Practice

Add *-er* or *-est* to the adjective in ( ). Write the new adjective.

1. Sam's dog is (smart) than that dog. _____

2. Jack's dog is the (small) dog in town. _____

3. My dog has the (long) hair of all. _____

4. Lita's dog is (short) than this one. _____

5. Your dog is (old) than my dog. _____

Troubleshooter, page 430

THINK AND WRITE

Adjectives
How do you know when to add *-er* to an adjective? Write the answer.

Grammar and Usage

Directions

Read the paragraph and choose the word or words that belong in each space.

Add -er to adjectives when you compare two nouns.

Use a before a consonant sound. Use an before a vowel sound.

Sample

Jason is learning to skate. His skates are ___(1)___ than mine. He practices in ___(2)___ parking lot every day. He learns ___(3)___. Soon he will be a very good skater.

Adverbs tell about an action. They sometimes end in ly.

1 ○ new
○ newer
○ most new
○ newest

2 ○ a
○ an
○ and
○ those

3 ○ quickly
○ more quick
○ quicker
○ quickest

Test Tip
Read through the paragraph. Think of a word to fit in each space.

TIME FOR KIDS Writer's Notebook

RESEARCH

RESEARCH When I need to know what a book is about, I use the **table of contents**. It is in the book's first few pages. It lists each chapter title. The table of contents also shows on which page each chapter begins. It's my guide to the inside of a book! Look at a table of contents in a book. How does it help you figure out what the book is about?

COMPOSITION SKILLS

WRITING WELL Before I start to write, I read lots of articles about the subject. Then I shape my story so it has a **beginning**, a **middle**, and an **end**. I move the facts around like puzzle pieces, until they fit just right.

VOCABULARY SKILLS

USING WORDS <u>Down</u> and <u>up</u>, <u>in</u> and <u>out</u>, <u>sad</u> and <u>glad</u>. These words are **antonyms**. An antonym is a word that means the opposite of another word. I use antonyms to show clear differences.

Read Now!

As you read the photo essay about a very special hotel, find three pairs of antonyms and write them down.

TIME FOR KIDS Writer's Notebook

VOCABULARY SKILLS

USING WORDS Write three pairs of antonyms used in the photo essay about an underwater hotel.

_____

_____

_____

_____

_____

_____

_____

_____

_____

_____

_____

_____

McGraw-Hill School Division

AN UNDERWATER HOTEL

Visit a place where people look out and fish look in!

GET SOME SLEEP IN THE DEEP

One hotel in Florida is all wet. But guests still stay nice and dry! The hotel is 21 feet underwater.

The hotel has two bedrooms, a bathroom, and a living room. Guests arrive in diving suits. They enter and leave through a small pool. Once inside, guests breathe normally. They can watch TV. And if they feel like fish for dinner, they can order room service.

Giant round windows let guests look out at big and small fish. The fish look in at the humans.

At night, soft bubbling sounds make it easy to sleep. Rick Ford works at the hotel. He says, "Most people say it's one of the best night's sleep they've ever had."

Guests enter and leave through a small pool. They have to put on a diving suit first.

John J. Lopinot/Silver Image

interNET CONNECTION Go to www.mhschool.com/language-arts for more information on the topic.

Dry on the inside, wet on the outside. A guest looks out a window.

A hotel worker brings guests' belongings in a waterproof case.

Write Now!

If you could sleep any place in the world, where would you choose? The desert? The mountains? In space? Imagine that you are in that place. Write to tell about your first night there.

Parts of a Book

Books have many different parts. The first page of a book is the **title page**. It tells the name of the book and the names of the author and illustrator.

All About Frogs ··········· Title of book
written by Mary Lou Keller ········ Author of book
illustrated by Logan Peck ········· Illustrator of book

The **table of contents** follows the title page. It lists the name and page number of each chapter in the book. Here is the table of contents of a book called *All About Frogs* by Mary Lou Keller.

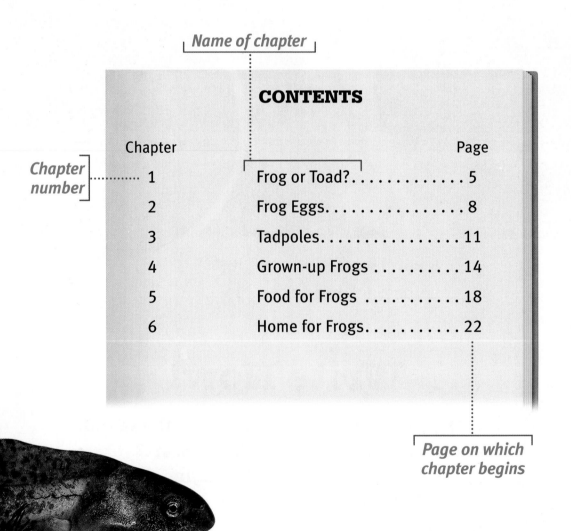

Name of chapter

CONTENTS

Chapter		Page
Chapter number 1	Frog or Toad?.	5
2	Frog Eggs.	8
3	Tadpoles.	11
4	Grown-up Frogs	14
5	Food for Frogs	18
6	Home for Frogs.	22

Page on which chapter begins

An **index** is found at the back of most books that gives facts. It helps you find information quickly. The index lists in ABC order all the topics in the book and their page numbers.

Practice

A. Use the title page and table of contents to answer these questions.

1. What is the title of the book? _____

2. Who is the author? _____

3. How many chapters are in the book? _____

4. What is the name of Chapter 3? _____

5. Which chapter might tell how frogs and toads are alike and different? _____

6. On what page does Chapter 2 begin? _____

7. Which chapter tells about frog eggs? _____

8. Which chapter would you look in to find out what frogs eat? _____

9. On what page would you begin reading about tadpoles? _____

10. What is Chapter 4 about? _____

*inter***NET**
CONNECTION

Go to
www.mhschool.
com/language-arts

for more information about parts of a book.

Writing Activity **A Story**

Write a story about a favorite animal. Use the ideas in your story to make up chapter titles for a book.

Vocabulary: Antonyms

DEFINITION

Antonyms are words with opposite meanings.

young/old	hot/cold	good/bad
tall/short	inside/outside	wild/tame
old/new	wet/dry	few/many
quiet/noisy	hard/soft	dirty/clean

THINK AND WRITE

Antonyms

Write how you can use antonyms to make your writing more interesting.

Look at the blue antonyms in the story below.

> One morning Sam saw some people move into the empty house next door.
>
> Sam could see two people talking quietly. One looked old and the other looked young. The old man walked inside. The young boy stayed outside. Sam looked down from his window.
>
> Suddenly a bird chirped noisily. The boy looked up. He saw Sam in the window and waved.

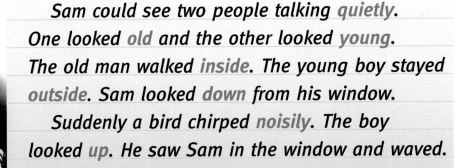

McGraw-Hill School Division

Practice

A. **Circle the two antonyms in each row.**

1. easy   top   small   hard

2. small   day   far   near

3. big   dirty   clean   good

4. tall   short   first   evening

5. right   sad   fine   happy

B. **Write an antonym from the box to replace the underlined word.**

tidy	high	kind
wet	loose	wild
best	first	quickly
hard		

6. Ned says it is <u>easy</u> to move.

   _____

7. The <u>last</u> thing to do is make friends.

   _____

8. Sam thinks Ned is <u>mean</u>. _____

9. The boys become friends <u>slowly</u>. _____

10. Ned is now Sam's <u>worst</u> friend. _____

C. **Grammar Link** **Write the antonym of each underlined word.**

11. The boys do <u>few</u> things together. _____

12. They play on <u>different</u> teams. _____

13. Ned is a <u>slow</u> runner. _____

14. Sam is <u>sad</u> for Ned when Ned wins. _____

15. Each day they find <u>less</u> to like. _____

Writing Activity **A Character Description**

Write about someone that you really like. Use at least one pair of antonyms. Choose describing words.

APPLY GRAMMAR: Draw a line under each adjective.

Composition: Beginning, Middle, End

If a writer writes a clear beginning, middle, and end, it is easy to follow what happens.

GUIDELINES

- The **beginning** is the start of the story. Describe the characters and the problem.

- The **middle** tells what happens as the characters try to solve the problem.

- The **end** is the last part of the story. It tells how the problem gets solved.

THINK AND WRITE

Beginning, Middle, End

Write about why it is important for a story to have a clear beginning, middle, and end.

Read this story. Notice how the writer made the beginning, middle, and end very clear.

A clear beginning tells about the characters and the problem.

Millie is a white mouse. She lives in a big cage in Mr. Berg's classroom. Millie has toys and children to play with her, but she is BORED!

The middle tells what happens.

Millie plans to run away. When Sam opens the cage to play with her, Millie slips out the door. She hops to the floor and races away.

In the end, the problem is solved.

The children chase after Millie. They laugh and try to catch her. Millie is not bored any more.

McGraw-Hill School Division

Practice

A. Write *beginning, middle,* or *end* to tell where it belongs in the story.

1. Annie goes to a pet store to look for a kitten. _____

2. Annie wants a new kitten. _____

3. Annie sees a kitten named Fluff. _____

4. Annie takes Fluff home. _____

5. Annie's mom buys Fluff for her. _____

B. On a piece of paper, write beginning sentences for stories with these titles.

6. Fuzzy's Haircut

7. The Runaway Sled

8. A Terrible Sound

9. Where's My Bed?

10. One Dog Too Many

C. **Grammar Link** Use *and* to combine the underlined words. Write the new sentences on a piece of paper.

11. Sid sits quietly. He sits calmly.

12. He wags his long tail.
    He wags his fluffy tail.

13. Sid barks loudly. He barks happily.

14. Sid jumps up. He jumps down.

15. Sid lets the friendly child pat him.
    Sid lets the quiet child pat him.

Writing Activity A Story Ending

Write an ending for one of the stories you started in Practice B. Check your spelling and punctuation.

APPLY GRAMMAR: Use one adjective and one adverb.

375

Better Sentences

Directions

Read the paragraph. Some parts are underlined. The underlined parts may be one of the following:

- Incomplete sentences
- Correctly written sentences that should be combined

Choose the best way to write each underlined part.

Sample

Many bears go to sleep in the winter. A mother and her cubs might sleep in a cave. A mother and her cubs might sleep in a hole. **(1)**

They don't eat much. They eat a lot the rest of the year. Hungry when they wake up in the **(2)** spring. That's why people sometimes say, "I'm as hungry as a bear."

Two sentences with many of the same words can be put together.

An incomplete sentence needs to have words added.

Test Tip
Remember to read the underlined parts carefully.

1 ○ A mother and her cubs. Sleep in a cave or in a hole.

○ A mother and her cubs might sleep in a cave or in a hole.

○ A mother. Cubs sleep in a cave.

2 ○ When they wake up in the spring and are hungry.

○ Hungry when they wake up. It is spring.

○ They are hungry when they wake up in the spring.

McGraw-Hill School Division

Vocabulary and Comprehension

Directions

Read the paragraph. Then read each question that follows the paragraph. Choose the best answer to each question.

Sample

Beany was a baby whale. All of Beany's friends were seals. Beany wanted to join the seal games, but he couldn't clap his flippers. He couldn't bark like a seal. Beany sadly turned away.

"The only thing I can do is this," thought Beany, and he blew out a tall stream of water. It sprayed all over the seals. They laughed and splashed and swam with Beany. Now Beany <u>gladly</u> played with his friends.

Look for a word that is the opposite of the underlined words.

1 Name the characters in this story.

○ Beany and the mother whale

○ Beany and the seals

○ seals and friends

○ Beany and the whales

2 What is a word that means the opposite of <u>gladly</u>?

○ sadly

○ badly

○ happily

○ loudly

Seeing Like a Writer

Each of these pictures tells a story. What stories do you see? Tell about the characters in your stories and the problems they have to solve.

The Hit by Lance Richbourg.

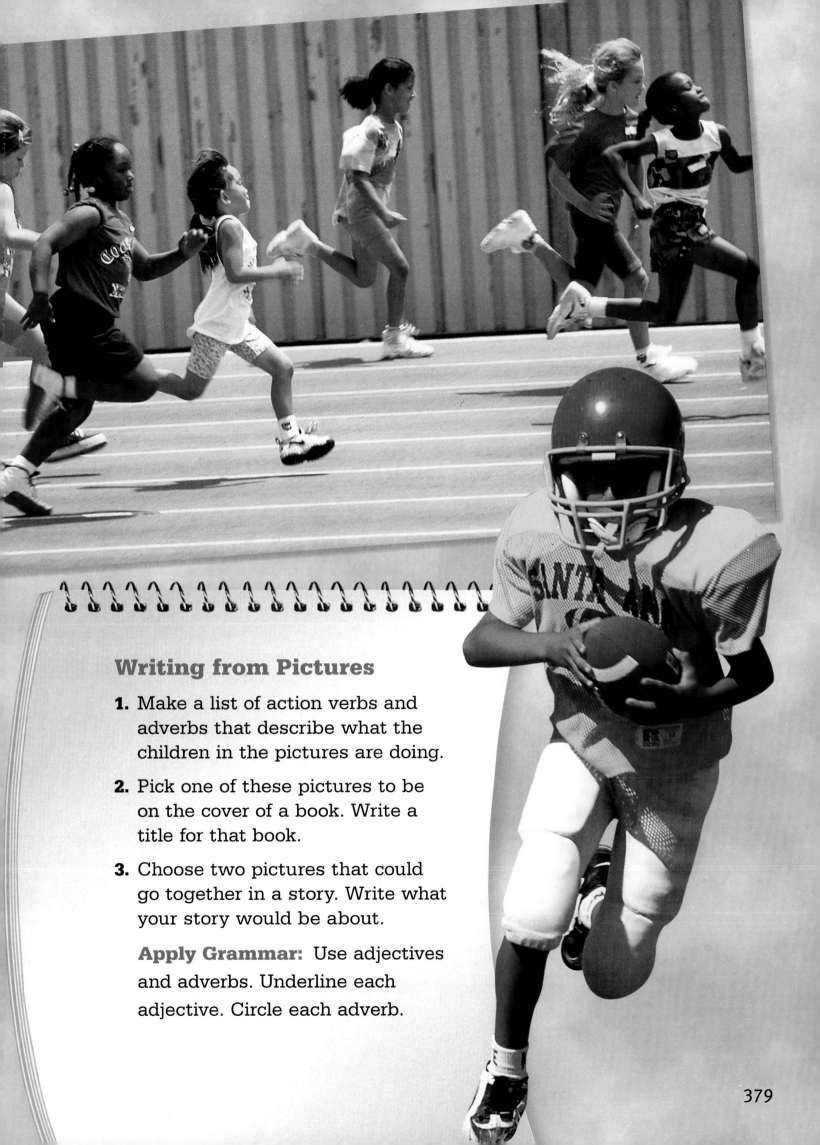

Writing from Pictures

1. Make a list of action verbs and adverbs that describe what the children in the pictures are doing.

2. Pick one of these pictures to be on the cover of a book. Write a title for that book.

3. Choose two pictures that could go together in a story. Write what your story would be about.

Apply Grammar: Use adjectives and adverbs. Underline each adjective. Circle each adverb.

A Story

A story tells about interesting characters and events. A story can also tell how characters solve their problems.

Learning from Writers

See how the author writes a clear beginning, middle, and end for his story.

THINK AND WRITE

Purpose
Write why you think people like to read or write stories.

Swimmy's Escape

A happy school of little fish lived in a corner of the sea somewhere. They were all red. Only one of them was as black as a mussel shell. He swam faster than his brothers and sisters. His name was Swimmy.

One bad day a tuna fish, swift, fierce and very hungry, came darting through the waves. In one gulp he swallowed all the little red fish.

Only Swimmy escaped. He swam away in the deep wet world. He was scared, lonely and very sad.

But the sea was full of wonderful creatures, and as he swam from marvel to marvel Swimmy was happy again.

— Leo Lionni from *Swimmy*

The Poor Dog

Long ago there was a little dog named Rover. He was a poor dog who had no home. People didn't care. Some children would stop to stare.

Then one day a little boy took Rover home in his arms. Rover's life was good now. He was no longer a poor dog. When he was three he was already famous. He could do many tricks, like flip, play dead, and roll over.

Even though he was famous and loved, he was still just a dog that didn't brag.

Rover loved his life.

— Laurie Bennis

PRACTICE and APPLY

Thinking Like a Reader

1. How did Swimmy feel after he escaped?

2. How did you picture Rover as you read "The Poor Dog"?

Thinking Like a Writer

3. How did the author show how Swimmy felt?

4. What describing words help you "see" Rover?

5. **Reading Across Texts** Tell why "Swimmy's Escape" and "The Poor Dog" are both fun to read.

Features of a Story

DEFINITIONS AND FEATURES

A **story** tells about made-up characters and what happens to them. A good story does these things:

► It **entertains** the reader.

► It has a clear **beginning, middle, and end.**

► Uses **describing words** to tell about its characters, setting, and plot.

► Entertains

Reread "Swimmy's Escape" by Leo Lionni on page 380. What makes this story fun to read?

> One bad day a tuna fish, swift, fierce and very hungry, came darting through the waves. In one gulp he swallowed all the little red fish.

The author makes the story exciting.

McGraw-Hill School Division

▶ **Beginning, Middle, End**

Each story should have a clear beginning, middle, and end. The beginning introduces the characters and the problem. The middle tells how the characters try to solve the problem. The ending shows how everything turns out.

> But the sea was full of wonderful creatures, and as he swam from marvel to marvel Swimmy was happy again.

How did the author show that Swimmy solved his problem?

▶ **Describing Words: Characters**

To help readers "see" the characters and what they are doing, an author will use adjectives and adverbs. Describing words tell the reader what kind, how many, how, when, and where.

> Only one of them was as black as a mussel shell.

What describing words did the author use?

Features	Examples

PRACTICE and APPLY

Create a Features Chart

1. List the features of descriptive writing.
2. Reread "The Poor Dog" by Laurie Bennis on page 381.
3. List the characters and problem in the story.

Prewrite

Writing PROCESS

A story tells about interesting characters and what happens to them as they try to solve their problems.

Purpose and Audience

The purpose of writing a story is to entertain the reader. Think about who will read your story. Create characters and events that readers will find fun or interesting.

Choose a Topic

Start by **brainstorming** a list of possible characters and events for your story. Then choose one your readers will like.

Explore your ideas and list.

THiNK AND WRITE

Audience
Write how an audience might tell the difference between a story and expository writing.

This will be a fun story.

Danny's Move
Danny will move to Texas.
Nothing to do there.
Tells friends at school.
Friends plan a surprise.
They make a book about Texas.
Look for facts.
Give Danny the book.

McGraw-Hill School Division

Organize • Beginning, Middle, End

A good story has a clear beginning, middle, and end. To plan your story, you can use a story map.

STORY MAP

Title
Danny's Move

Characters
Danny, Janie, Tim

Problem
Danny thinks there will be nothing to do in Texas.

Beginning
Danny will move to Texas.
There is nothing to do there.

Middle
Janie and Tim want to surprise Danny.
They will make a book about Texas.
The friends look for facts about Texas.

End
The two friends give him the book.

Checklist ✓
Prewriting

☐ Did you brainstorm story ideas?

☐ Did you think about your purpose and audience?

☐ Does your story have a clear beginning, middle, and end?

☐ Do you need to find out any more information?

PRACTICE and APPLY

Plan Your Own Story

1. Brainstorm story ideas.

2. Choose a character, or characters, and something that will happen.

3. Plan the story's beginning, middle, and end.

Writing PROCESS

Prewrite • Research and Inquiry

▶ Writer's Resources

To make your story seem real, you may need to do some research. Start with a list of questions. Then find resources to answer them.

What Else Do I Need to Know?	Where Can I Find the Information?
Are there interesting facts about Texas?	Look in the card catalog at the library for a book about Texas.
What fun things are there to do in Texas?	Look at chapter titles in books about Texas.

▶ Card Catalog

A card catalog lists all the books in a library. You can look up books by title, author, or subject. Some catalogs are online.

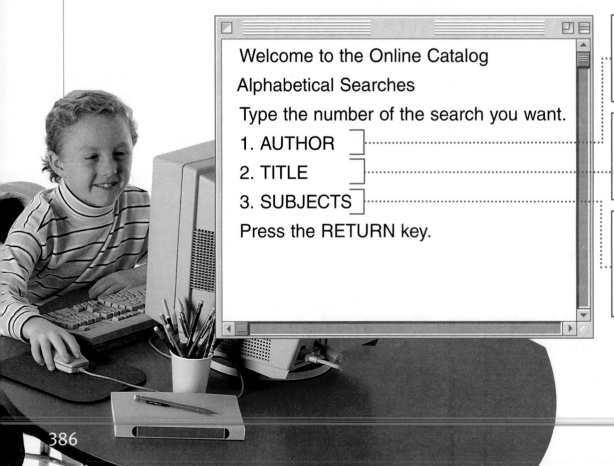

Welcome to the Online Catalog

Alphabetical Searches

Type the number of the search you want.

1. AUTHOR

2. TITLE

3. SUBJECTS

Press the RETURN key.

If you want to find books by one writer, use this search.

If you know the title or part of the title, use this search.

If you want to find books about Texas or other topics, use this search.

McGraw-Hill School Division

▶ Parts of a Book

You can find interesting details in books to add to your story. To find out the topics in a book, look at its Table of Contents. See if there is a chapter about the subject you want.

Use Your Research

Add what you learned in your research to your story map. This writer added interesting facts about Texas.

Handbook
pages 464–465

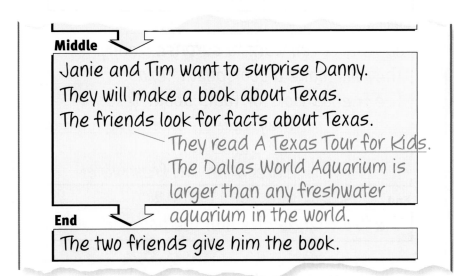

Middle

Janie and Tim want to surprise Danny.
They will make a book about Texas.
The friends look for facts about Texas.
　　They read A Texas Tour for Kids.
　　The Dallas World Aquarium is
　　larger than any freshwater
End　　aquarium in the world.
The two friends give him the book.

Checklist ✓

Research and Inquiry

☐ Did you list your questions?

☐ Did you find resources to answer your questions?

☐ Did you add the answers to your story map?

PRACTICE and APPLY

Review Your Plan

1. Reread your story map.

2. List questions you have.

3. Use resources to answer questions.

4. Add new information to the story map.

Writing PROCESS

Draft

Use your story map to plan how to break your story into paragraphs. Plan paragraphs for the beginning, middle, and end of the story.

STORY MAP

Title

Danny's Move

Characters

Danny, Janie, Tim

Problem

Danny thinks there will be nothing to do in Texas.

Beginning

Danny will move to Texas.
There is nothing to do there.

Middle

Janie and Tim want to surprise Danny.
They will make a book about Texas.
The friends look for facts about Texas.

They read A Texas Tour for Kids.
The Dallas World Aquarium is larger than any freshwater aquarium in the world.

End

The two friends give him the book.

Main idea for first paragraph: Danny will move to Texas.

Main idea for second paragraph: The friends make a book.

Supporting details: Facts the friends find

✓ Checklist

Drafting

☐ Did you think about your purpose and audience?

☐ Does your story have characters, setting, and plot?

☐ Does your story have a beginning, middle, and end?

☐ Will your story be fun to read?

You can see in the draft below how the writer added details about Texas to make his story more interesting.

DRAFT

This summer Danny will move to Texas.

Danny thinks there is nothing to do there.

Tim and Janie plan a surprise for

Danny. They will make a book about Texas.

The friends look in the library to learn more

about Texas. Janie and Tim read A Texas

tour for Kids. They read about the Dallas

World Aquarium. It is the larger freshwater

aquarium in the world.

The next week Danny's friends give him

the book they made. Danny hugs his book.

Main idea of paragraph

Main idea of second paragraph tells how they will solve the problem.

Details tell about the book.

Last paragraph tells more about the characters.

PRACTICE and APPLY

Draft Your Own Story

1. Look back at your list of ideas.

2. Write about the story events.

3. Write a clear beginning, middle, and end.

Revise

Elaborate

You can make your writing better by elaborating, or adding details when you revise.

> fun things to do in
> They will make a book about ⌃Texas.

DESCRIBING WORDS

pretty	quickly
caring	short
funny	sleepy
happy	small
kind	sweet
lucky	tall

Word Choice

Describing words tell the reader more about the characters or setting. What adjectives did this writer add to tell more about the characters or setting?

> kind
> The next week Danny's ⌃friends give him
> the book they made.

TiP!

Conferencing for the Reader

■ Read your partner's writing. Check to see if it has:
  • a story that is fun to read
  • a clear beginning, middle, and end
  • describing words

Better Sentences

Listen to the way your sentences sound when you read them out loud. Do they sound choppy? See how this writer revised his story.

REVISE

₍A surprise for Danny
This summer Danny will move to Texas.

Danny thinks there is nothing to do there.
                    special
Tim and Janie plan a surprise for
                    fun things to do in
Danny. They will make a book about Texas.

The friends look in the library to learn more

about Texas. Janie and Tim read <u>A Texas</u>

<u>tour for Kids</u>. They read about the Dallas

World Aquarium. It is the larger freshwater
   Danny has always wanted to visit a aquarium.
aquarium in the world.
                    kind
The next week Danny's friends give him
                       and smiles
the book they made. Danny hugs his book.

Checklist ✓
Revising

☐ **Did you think about your purpose and audience?**

☐ **Do you need to add more details?**

☐ **Do the sentences sound right when you read the story out loud?**

☐ **Does the story have a clear beginning, middle, and end?**

☐ **Did you use words to describe the characters and setting?**

PRACTICE and APPLY

Revise Your Own Story

1. Read your draft to yourself.

2. Share your draft with a partner.

3. Elaborate to make your writing better.

4. **Grammar** Can you combine sentences?

Proofread

After you revise your story, go back and read it again and again. Each time look for a different kind of mistake.

STRATEGIES FOR PROOFREADING

- Look for words that need capital letters.

- Find all the contractions and possessives. Make sure they have apostrophes.

- Check your spelling. Start at the end of the story and check one word at a time.

TECHNOLOGY

Sometimes it's hard to see your mistakes on the computer screen. Try printing out your story. Mark changes on the paper. Then make the changes on the computer.

REVIEW THE RULES

GRAMMAR

- The articles *a* and *an* are easy to mix up. Use *an* only if the next word starts with a vowel sound. Use *a* the rest of the time.

- Add *-er* to an adjective that compares two nouns. Add *-est* to compare three or more nouns.

MECHANICS

- Use capital letters in a book title. Begin the first word and each important word with a capital letter.

McGraw-Hill School Division

Look at the proofreading corrections made on the draft below. What does ≡ mean? Why change?

PROOFREAD

∧A surprise for Danny
This summer Danny will move to Texas.

Danny thinks there is nothing to do there.
                    special
Tim and Janie plan a surprise for
                    ∧
                        fun things to do in
Danny. They will make a book about Texas.
                                    ∧

The friends look in the library to learn more

about Texas. Janie and Tim read A Texas

tour for kids. They read about the Dallas
    ≡
                        largest
World Aquarium. It is the larger freshwater
                            ∧   an
Danny has always wanted to visit a aquarium.
aquarium in the world.   ∧
                    ∧
                    kind
The next week Danny's friends give him
                            ∧
                            and smiles
the book they made. Danny hugs his book.
                                        ∧

Checklist ✓

Proofreading

☐ **Did you fix spelling mistakes?**

☐ **Did you use *a* and *an* correctly?**

☐ **Did you indent each paragraph?**

☐ **Did you use capital letters correctly?**

PROOFREADING MARKS

⌗ new paragraph

∧ add

ℒ take out

≡ Make a capital letter.

/ Make a small letter.

ⓈⓅ Check the spelling.

⊙ Add a period.

PRACTICE AND APPLY

Proofread Your Own Story

1. Fix any spelling mistakes.

2. Check capital letters in titles.

3. Check to see if describing words that end in -er or -est are correct.

393

Publish

Read your story again before you publish it. Use a checklist as you look at your writing.

✓ **Self-Check** **A Story**

- ☐ Did I keep my purpose and audience in mind?
- ☐ Will my story be fun to read?
- ☐ Did I write a good beginning, middle, and end?
- ☐ Did I combine short, choppy sentences?
- ☐ Did I use describing words?
- ☐ Did I proofread and fix my mistakes?
- ☐ Did I add a title?

Read "A Surprise for Danny" again. Do you think it is ready to be published?

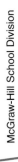

A Surprise for Danny

by James Clay

This summer Danny will move to Texas. Danny thinks there is nothing to do there.

Tim and Janie plan a special surprise for Danny. They will make a book about fun things to do in Texas. The friends look in the library to learn more about Texas. Janie and Tim read <u>A Texas Tour for Kids</u>. They read about the Dallas World Aquarium. It is the largest freshwater aquarium in the world. Danny has always wanted to visit an aquarium.

The next week Danny's kind friends give him the book they made. Danny hugs his book and smiles.

PREWRITE

DRAFT

REVISE

PROOFREAD

PUBLISH

TiP!

Handwriting

Take your time and write your story neatly. Try leaving a little extra space between each line. That will help to make your writing easy to read.

PRACTICE and APPLY

Publish Your Own Story

1. Read your story again.

2. Copy your story neatly.

3. Make drawings or pictures.

4. Put your story in a class book of stories.

Present Your Story

Planning ahead will make your presentation better.

McGraw-Hill School Division

Listening Strategies

- Think about why you are listening. Will you learn something new? Is it just for fun?

- Try to picture the characters and events.

- Look at the speaker. Show that you are enjoying the story.

- Listen to the speaker's voice. See if it changes at different parts of the story.

STEP 1

How to Tell Your Original Story

Strategies for Speaking When you tell a story, you are like an actor. Be a storyteller and have fun.

- Highlight important words on note cards.
- Look your audience in the eye.
- If the story is exciting, make your voice sound excited. If a character in the story is happy, smile as you speak.
- Speak loud and clearly

Multimedia Ideas

You might want to tape-record music to play with your story while you tell it. Ask a librarian to help you find the music.

STEP 2

How to Show Your Original Story

Suggestions for Illustrations Show pictures to get your audience interested.

- Draw the characters or events.
- Cut out pictures of people from magazines who could be your characters and paste them on poster board.
- Label your pictures.

STEP 3

How to Share Your Original Story

Strategies for Rehearsing Be sure to practice your story ahead of time.

- Tell your story to a partner.
- Tell your story to family members.
- If you make a mistake, just keep going.

PRACTICE and APPLY

Rehearse Your Own Story

1. Write note cards to help you remember.

2. Collect the things you will show.

3. Practice telling the story so you know it well.

4. Ask a friend to listen to you practice.

TiP!

Viewing Strategies

- Look at the drawings or objects the speaker shows.

- Read the labels.

- Use the drawings to learn more about the characters or events than the speaker tells you.

Writing Tests

Remember to read the prompt on a writing test carefully. Look for key words and phrases that tell you what to write about and how to do your writing.

Sometimes a prompt does not tell who the audience is.

Look for words that tell the purpose of the writing.

Look for words that tell you the kind of writing to do.

Prompt

One day two friends were looking in a toy chest. What they saw surprised them.

<u>Write a story</u> telling all about <u>what the two friends saw</u> and <u>what happened</u>.

How to Read a Prompt

Purpose Look at the prompt again. Find the words that tell you the purpose of the writing. The words "write a story" tell you that the purpose will be to entertain.

Audience If the prompt does not name the audience, you can think of your teacher as your audience.

Writing a Story When you write a story, you tell about characters and how they solve a problem. The words "what they saw surprised them" lets you know something unusual is about to happen. The words "what the two friends saw" and "what happened" tell you that the story should have a beginning, middle, and end.

Test Tip

Remember to plan your writing before you begin doing it.

How to Write to a Prompt

Remember these tips when you are given a writing prompt.

Before Writing **Content/Ideas**	• Think about your writing purpose. • Remember who your audience is. • Plan the beginning, middle, and ending of your story.
During Writing **Organization/ Paragraph Structure**	• Start with a good opening sentence. • When writing a story, use describing words to tell about characters. • Tell what happens in the story. • Give the story a good ending.
After Writing **Grammar/Usage**	• Proofread your work. • Begin each sentence with a capital letter. • Spell each word correctly. • Make sure adjectives and adverbs are used correctly.

Apply What You Learned

Find words that tell what the writing will be about. Think about the purpose and audience. Plan your writing. Put the events in order.

> **Prompt**
>
> Imagine that you saw a dinosaur and wanted it for a pet.
> Write a story telling what happened when you took the dinosaur home.

Name _____

Grammar and Writing Review

pages 346–353 ## Adjectives and Articles

A. **Circle the correct word in ( ). Underline each adjective.**

1. Pip is (a, an) tiny pig.

2. Pip is the (smaller, smallest) pig on the farm.

3. Once (a, an) angry bee stung Pip's nose.

pages 356–361 ## Adverbs

B. **Underline each adverb. Circle the verb it describes. Write if the adverb tells *how*, *when*, or *where*.**

4. Amy quickly walks to the library. _____

5. Amy goes upstairs to the children's room. _____

6. Soon Amy finds a book about Mars. _____

Mechanics and Usage: Book Titles and Quotation Marks

pages 354, 362

C. **Add quotation marks where they belong. Underline each book title. Then write it correctly.**

7. My favorite book is lemonade for sale, I said.

_____

8. Jan asked, Have you read strega nona?

_____

9. The same author wrote the popcorn book, Jan said.

_____

pages
372–373

Vocabulary: Antonyms

D. **Circle the antonym in ( ) for the underlined word.**

10. The gray kitten is <u>cute</u>. (ugly, pretty)

11. <u>Little</u> kittens are a lot of fun. (small, big)

12. The kittens are <u>rough</u> with each other. (gentle, playful)

pages
374–375

Composition: Beginning, Middle, End

E. **Write 1, 2, and 3. Put the sentences in an order that makes sense. They should tell a story that has a beginning, a middle, and an end.**

13. As soon as I fell asleep, I was a robot! _____

14. I went to bed after watching a movie about robots. _____

15. I heard my mother say, "Wake up, Eric," and I knew

it had all been a dream. _____

pages
392–393

Proofreading a Story

F. **16.–20. Use proofreading marks to correct the 5 mistakes. Then write the story correctly on a piece of paper.**

Kayla's Big Adventure

At bedtime, Kayla and her mother red a

story called <u>Where the Wild things Are</u> .

Soon Kayla fell asleep Then a amazing thing

happened. She became part of the story.

The next morning, Kayla woke up and

said, What a great adventure that was!"

**Save this page until
you finish Unit 6.**

Project File

A Poem

A **poem** paints a picture with words.

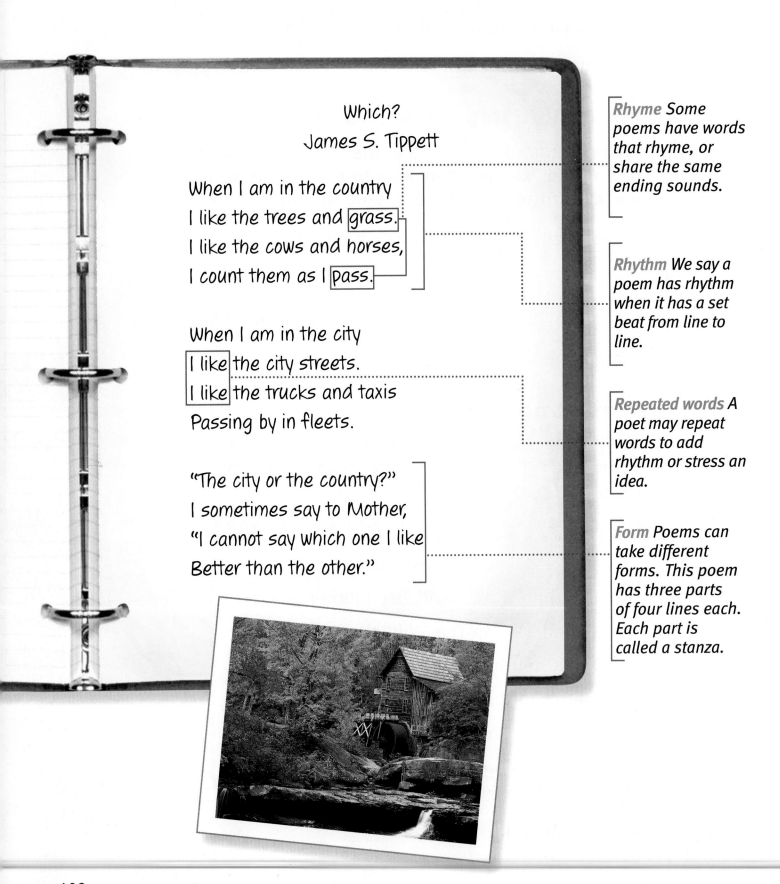

Which?
James S. Tippett

When I am in the country
I like the trees and grass.
I like the cows and horses,
I count them as I pass.

When I am in the city
I like the city streets.
I like the trucks and taxis
Passing by in fleets.

"The city or the country?"
I sometimes say to Mother,
"I cannot say which one I like
Better than the other."

Rhyme *Some poems have words that rhyme, or share the same ending sounds.*

Rhythm *We say a poem has rhythm when it has a set beat from line to line.*

Repeated words *A poet may repeat words to add rhythm or stress an idea.*

Form *Poems can take different forms. This poem has three parts of four lines each. Each part is called a stanza.*

Make up a poem about clouds. Look out the window. Are there any clouds in the sky? What shapes are they? What do the clouds look like to you? Choose a cloud and draw an outline of it. If you don't see a cloud, imagine one.

Write a poem. Will your poem rhyme? Will your poem have rhythm? What describing words will you choose? Write your poem inside the cloud shape you drew.

PROJECT 2

A Point of View

How would you like to stay in an underwater hotel like the one in Florida? What must the fish think as they look at you through the round windows?

A Fish-Eye View Write an imaginary conversation between two fish. What are they saying about the people in the underwater hotel?

403

Adjectives

A. Circle the adjective that describes each underlined noun.

1. This year we had a different <u>Thanksgiving</u>.

2. After dinner, Dad took me to the funny <u>parade</u> in town.

3. We stood on a crowded <u>curb</u>.

4. The bands played loud <u>marches</u>.

5. Marchers wore colorful <u>costumes</u>.

6. A silly <u>clown</u> shook my hand.

7. Riders on white <u>horses</u> waved.

8. I liked the big <u>floats</u>.

9. Dad bought me hot <u>cocoa</u>.

10. Instead of walking home, we decided to take the new <u>bus</u>.

B. Circle the adjective or adjectives in each sentence.

11. We had a great dinner.

12. Dad carved the golden turkey.

13. Mom made tasty stuffing and hot gravy.

14. We also had green beans and red beets.

15. Grandma made creamy pies for dessert.

Save this page until you finish Unit 6.

Adjectives That Tell *How Many*

A. Circle the adjective that tells *how many*.

1. I bought one watermelon.

2. It weighed nine pounds.

3. It cost three dollars.

4. I gave the clerk five dollars.

5. The clerk gave me two dollars back.

6. Dad cut the melon into four parts.

7. Each part had many seeds.

8. I counted fifty seeds in my part.

9. I planted ten seeds.

10. I soon had ten plants.

B. Fill in the blank with an adjective that tells *how many*.

11. Mom bought _____ tomatoes.

12. Dad wanted _____ grapes and peaches.

13. My sister didn't want _____ melon.

14. We spent _____ dollars at the market.

15. We grew _____ vegetables.

Grammar

Articles: *a, an*

A. Circle the correct article in ( ).

1. My sister is writing (a, an) story.

2. Her story is about (a, an) ox.

3. The ox lives on (a, an) island.

4. The island is in (a, an) ocean.

5. The ox goes on (a, an) adventure.

6. The ox meets (a, an) butterfly on the way.

7. The two friends follow (a, an) path.

8. The path leads to (a, an) forest.

9. The ox and the butterfly meet (a, an) owl.

10. The story doesn't have (a, an) ending yet.

B. Fill in the blank with the correct article.

11. I have _____ book of animal stories.

12. My favorite story is about _____ eagle.

13. The eagle has never seen _____ airplane.

14. One day _____ jet flies over the eagle's nest.

15. "What kind of _____ bird are you?" he asks.

Adjectives That Compare

A. **Circle the correct adjective in ( ) to complete each sentence.**

1. My seeds grew the (faster, fastest) of all.

2. Now your plants are (taller, tallest) than mine.

3. Pedro's plants are (smaller, smallest) than Hillary's.

4. Hillary's plants are the (taller, tallest) so far.

5. Her plants have the (thicker, thickest) stems.

6. Those roots are the (longer, longest) of all.

7. My plants are the (smaller, smallest) here.

8. Your soil feels (damper, dampest) than mine.

9. Hillary's soil is the (damper, dampest) in the room.

10. These leaves are (greener, greenest) than the others.

B. **Add -er or -est to each word in ( ). Write the new word.**

11. Our garden is the (small) one around. _____

12. The cucumbers are the (long) ever. _____

13. Some peppers are (green) than others. _____

14. The corn is (tall) than the tomato plants.

_____

15. Our spinach grew the (fast) of all.

_____

Writing Book Titles

A. Write each book title using capital letters where they belong.

1. digging up dinosaurs _____

2. johnny appleseed _____

3. fire! fire! _____

4. the post office book _____

5. koko's kitten _____

6. the maple tree _____

7. see through the forest _____

8. a duckling is born _____

9. dancing masks of africa _____

10. song of the swallows _____

B. Draw a line under each book title. Then write it correctly using capital letters where they belong.

11. My favorite book is henry and mudge.

_____

12. The last book I read was wagon wheels.

_____

13. I want to read sam the minuteman.

_____

14. My cousin just read hill of fire.

_____

15. Did you enjoy reading a very young rider?

_____

Adverbs

A. Write *how*, *when*, or *where* for the underlined adverb in each sentence.

1. <u>Yesterday</u> I saw a baby rabbit. _____

2. I was <u>outside</u> in the yard. _____

3. I tiptoed <u>quietly</u> to look. _____

4. I kneeled <u>down</u>. _____

5. <u>Then</u>, I called for my mom. _____

6. She was <u>upstairs</u>. _____

7. Mom <u>quickly</u> found a carrot. _____

8. We walked <u>softly</u> across the yard. _____

9. Mom put the carrot <u>down</u>. _____

10. We went back <u>inside</u> the house. _____

B. Underline the adverb. Then write *how*, *when*, or *where* to tell about the adverb.

11. The rabbit hopped slowly to the carrot. _____

12. The rabbit smelled the carrot carefully. _____

13. Then the rabbit took a bite! _____

14. It crunched the carrot loudly. _____

15. Mom and I watched happily. _____

Grammar

Adverbs That Tell *How*

A. Circle the adverb that tells *how* the underlined action is done.

1. Dad and I <u>walk</u> slowly to the tank.

2. We <u>watch</u> the fish quietly.

3. One fish <u>watches</u> us closely.

4. It <u>clings</u> tightly to the tank glass.

5. The fish suddenly <u>moves</u>.

6. It <u>swims</u> quickly to a rock.

7. Another fish <u>glides</u> by smoothly.

8. Seaweed <u>sways</u> gently in the tank.

9. Some pretty stones <u>shine</u> brightly there.

10. The whole tank really <u>interests</u> me!

B. Underline each verb. Circle each adverb that tells *how*.

11. Dad and I happily watch the dolphin show.

12. Two dolphins swim playfully.

13. The trainer whistles loudly.

14. How swiftly the dolphins come!

15. The dolphins jump easily.

McGraw-Hill School Division

Adverbs That Tell *When* or *Where*

A. Circle the adverb that tells about the underlined verb. Then write *when* or *where* for each adverb.

1. Yesterday we <u>started</u> our vacation. _____

2. Our car <u>pulled</u> away at six o'clock. _____

3. We <u>stopped</u> nearby for gas. _____

4. Afterward Dad <u>drove</u> to the highway. _____

5. Then the car <u>got</u> a flat tire. _____

6. Our family <u>didn't drive</u> far! _____

7. Dad soon <u>changed</u> the tire. _____

8. We <u>stopped</u> later for lunch. _____

9. Mom, Dad, and I <u>sat</u> outside. _____

10. Mom and I <u>walked</u> around. _____

B. Draw a line under each verb. Circle each adverb and write *when* or *where*.

11. Today we hiked in the mountains. _____

12. We walked up. _____

13. Dad and I walked ahead. _____

14. Mom stopped often to take photos. _____

15. We returned to camp early. _____

411

Quotation Marks

A. Underline each sentence that has quotation marks. Circle the words that a person says.

1. "Are you ready?" asked Mom.

2. I asked, "Where are we going?"

3. "Did you forget?" asked Mia.

4. Mia said she was going to the dentist.

5. Dad told Mia to brush her teeth.

6. "Don't forget to floss," Dad added.

7. Mom called, "We'll be in the car."

8. Mia asked us to hurry up.

9. "We can't be late," she said.

10. "I'm coming now," I answered.

B. Add quotation marks where they belong in each sentence.

11. Who's next? the nurse said.

12. I'm next, answered Kristen.

13. The nurse said, Come with me.

14. Okay, Kristen said to the nurse.

15. Have a seat, said Dr. Soo.

16. Have you been brushing? asked Dr. Soo.

17. Yes, answered Kristen.

18. Your teeth look very nice, said Dr. Soo.

19. Thank you, said Kristen.

20. You should be proud, said Dr. Soo.

Save this page until you finish Unit 6.

Grammar

Unit 1 Sentences

A. Write each sentence correctly.

1. my mom, dad, and I visited friends

_____

2. what a great time we had

_____

3. tell us all about it _____

4. what did you do _____

5. we went to the beach _____

B. Combine each pair of sentences with *and*. Write the new sentence on a piece of paper. Underline the subject in the new sentence.

6. Al joined the team. Tina joined the team.

7. Ann ran quickly. Ted ran quickly.

8. My sister raced ahead. I raced ahead.

9. Dad watched. Our coach watched.

10. Mom cheered for us. Grandma cheered for us.

Unit 2 Nouns

A. Circle each noun.

11. The family goes to the park.

12. The children are happy.

13. The baby sits in the swing.

14. The girls go down the slide.

15. The dog barks at the squirrels.

B. Write the proper nouns correctly.

16. Today is tuesday, october 4.

_____

17. The elm street children's club meets today.

_____

18. My friends amy and jeff are coming.

_____

19. We are in the columbus day parade.

_____

20. We have practice on saturday. _____

Unit 3 Verbs

A. Circle the correct verb in ( ).

21. Jon T. Dean, Jr., (write, writes) books.

22. My friends and I (like, likes) his books.

23. I (have, has) his last two books.

24. Amy (wish, wishes) for the latest book.

25. Mr. Dean's books (make, makes) us laugh.

B. Use *and* to combine the underlined predicates. Write the new sentence on a piece of paper.

26. Connie <u>loves birds</u>. Connie <u>reads about robins</u>.

27. Robins <u>like people</u>. Robins <u>live in open places</u>.

28. The female <u>builds the nest</u>. The female <u>lays blue eggs</u>.

29. Robins <u>like fruit</u>. Robins <u>eat insects, too</u>.

30. Their songs <u>fill the air</u>. Their songs <u>sound cheerful</u>.

Cumulative Review

Unit 4 **Verbs and Punctuation**

A. Circle the correct verb in ( ). Write *L* if it is a linking verb. Write *H* if it is a helping verb.

31. We (are, have) worked hard all day. _____

32. Now I (am, was) very hungry. _____

33. Mom and Dad (are, have) fixing dinner. _____

34. I'll do homework after I (am, have) eaten. _____

35. Dinner (is, were) ready at last! _____

B. Write the past tense of each underlined verb.

36. I see Amanda and run to meet her.

_____

37. Amanda says, "Let's do something." _____

38. We go home and do homework first.

_____

39. Dad comes home and gives us a new CD.

_____

40. Amanda and I sing along. _____

C. Add apostrophes and commas where they belong.

41. Moms new job is in Dallas Texas.

42. My sister and I arent very happy.

43. We dont want to leave Tulsa Oklahoma.

44. The Lee twins grandmother lives there.

45. They say that Dallas isnt so far.

Unit 5 Pronouns

A. Write the correct pronoun to replace the underlined words. Circle the correct verb.

46. Ann and Jim Smith (live, lives) in a small town. _____

47. Ann's and Jim's mom (work, works) in an office. _____

48. Mrs. Smith's job (is, are) in the city. _____

49. Mrs. Smith (take, takes) the train. _____

50. The train (come, comes) every half hour. _____

B. Write the contraction for the underlined words.

51. I am very lucky! _____

52. We are going to a nice place. _____

53. It is called Bryce Canyon. _____

54. We are meeting with Mr. and Mrs. Berg. _____

55. They are park rangers there. _____

C. Circle the correct pronoun in ( ).

56. My brother and (I, me) don't like to go to bed early.

57. We always ask Dad to read (we, us) a story.

58. (We, Us) have many favorite books.

59. After the story, Dad tells Patrick and (I, me) to close our eyes.

60. (I, Me) often start to giggle.

Grammar

Unit 6 Adjectives, Adverbs, and Quotation Marks

A. Underline the adjective. Circle the adverb. Write if it tells *how*, *when*, or *where*.

61. Tonight Dad read a new story. _____

62. He sat down in the old rocker. _____

63. Dad slowly opened the big book. _____

64. The two boys listened eagerly. _____

65. Soon the sleepy children began yawning. _____

B. Circle the correct article or adjective in ( ). Add quotation marks where needed. Write the two underlined book titles correctly.

66. Lori said, Here's (a, an) interesting book called <u>elephants of africa</u>.

_____

67. Are elephants the (larger, largest) land animals? Juan asked.

68. Cal said, My book called <u>big trunks</u> says that (a, an) African elephant is very large.

_____

69. Lori added, It is (larger, largest) than the Asian elephant.

70. Juan said to himself, What (a, an) beautiful animal it is!

Troubleshooter

Contents

Incomplete Sentences

- A sentence is a group of words that tells a complete thought.

- An incomplete sentence does not tell a complete thought.

Problem 1

An incomplete sentence that does not have a predicate

Incomplete Sentence: *My best friend.*

> What about my best friend?

Solution 1

What is or what happens is called the predicate of the sentence. You must add a predicate to this incomplete sentence to make it a complete sentence.

Complete Sentence: *My best friend plays on my team.*

Problem 2

An incomplete sentence that does not have a subject

Incomplete Sentence: *Warm up first.*

> Who warms up first?

Solution 2

Who or what is called the subject of the sentence. You must add a subject to this incomplete sentence to make it a complete sentence.

Complete Sentence: *We warm up first.*

McGraw-Hill School Division

Problem 3

An incomplete sentence that does not have a subject or a predicate

Incomplete Sentence: *At ten o'clock.*

Who is this about? What happened?

Solution 3

You must add a subject and a predicate to this incomplete sentence to make it a complete sentence.

Complete Sentence: *Our soccer game starts at ten o'clock.*

Practice Write the incomplete sentences correctly. Add a subject, a predicate, or a subject and a predicate.

1. The game is over. Wins the first match.

2. The coaches smile. Proud of us.

3. Both teams line up. All the players.

4. I run to Mom and Dad. A big hug.

5. I like soccer. A great sport.

For more help, see Subjects in Sentences on pages 10–11, Predicates in Sentences on pages 12–13, and Handbook page 433.

Confusing Plurals and Possessives

- A plural noun names more than one person, place, or thing.

- A possessive noun shows who or what owns or has something. A possessive noun needs an apostrophe.

Problem 1

Using an apostrophe in a plural noun

Incorrect: *The kitten's are so cute.*

> Is more than one kitten cute?

Solution 1

A plural noun does not need an apostrophe (').

Correct: *The kittens are so cute.*

Problem 2

Leaving out the apostrophe in a singular possessive noun

Incorrect: *The dogs name is Spike.*

> How do you show that the name belongs to one dog?

Solution 2

You need to add an apostrophe (') and *s* to a singular noun to make it possessive.

Correct: *The dog's name is Spike.*

Problem 3

Leaving out the apostrophe in a plural possessive noun

Incorrect: *The horses names are Rocket and Jet.*

How do you show that the names belong to two horses?

Solution 3

A plural possessive noun shows what more than one person, place, or thing has. You need to add an apostrophe (') to most plural nouns to make them possessive.

Correct: *The horses' names are Rocket and Jet.*

Practice Write the sentences correctly. Add apostrophes that are needed. Take out apostrophes that are not needed.

1. Birds make good pets. My two sister's have pet birds.

2. My sisters' birds are small. The birds cages are big.

3. Parakeets are cute. Both bird's are parakeets.

4. Ann's bird has blue feathers. Amys bird is green.

5. Some birds talk. Both girls' have birds that talk.

Need More Help? For more help, see Plural Nouns on pages 78–79, Singular Possessive Nouns on pages 82–83, Plural Possessive Nouns on pages 84–85, and Handbook pages 436–437.

Lack of Subject-Verb Agreement

- In a sentence, a present-tense verb must be singular if the subject is singular.

- Do not add -s or -es to a present-tense verb that tells about more than one person or thing.

Problem 1

Using a plural verb with a singular subject

Incorrect: *Jack take notes.*

> Is the subject one or more than one?

Solution 1

You need to add -s or -es to the present-tense verb to make the verb and the subject agree.

Correct: *Jack takes notes.*

Problem 2

Using a singular verb with a plural subject or *I* or *you*

Incorrect: *The girls adds trees and grass.*

> How do you make the verb agree with its subject?

Solution 2

When the subject of a sentence is more than one person or thing or *I* or *you*, do not add -s or -es to a present-tense verb.

Correct: *The girls add trees and grass.*

Problem 3

Using a singular verb when a subject has two nouns joined by *and*

Incorrect: *Sam and Lisa draws cars.*

How many nouns are in the subject?

Solution 3

When the subject of a sentence has two nouns joined by *and*, you do not add *-s* or *-es* to a present-tense verb. Take out *-s* or *-es* to make the subject and verb agree.

Correct: *Sam and Lisa draw cars.*

Practice Write the sentences correctly. Make the subject and verb agree.

1. Everyone cleans up. Miss Jones help us.

2. Jen and Tina gather the brushes. Ted and Al washes them.

3. I put away the scissors. You closes the jar of paste.

4. The boys study the mural. The girls looks, too.

5. You say, "What a great mural!" I likes it a lot.

Need More Help? For more help, see Present-Tense Verbs on pages 142–143, Subject-Verb Agreement on pages 144–145, and Handbook pages 438–439.

Incorrect Verb Forms

- The verbs *have* and *be* have special forms in the present tense and in the past tense.

- Some verbs do not add *-ed* in the past tense.

- An apostrophe (') takes the place of the letters that are left out when two words are combined.

Problem 1

Using the incorrect form of *be* or *have*

Incorrect Form of *be*: **We is going to the pond today.**

> What present-tense form of *be* goes with *We*?

Solution 1

You need to use the form of *have* or *be* that agrees with the subject of the sentence and helps show the action.

Correct Form of *be*: **We are going to the pond today.**

Problem 2

Forming the past tense of irregular verbs incorrectly

Incorrect Form of Irregular Verb:
I runned all the way home.

> What is the past form of *run* — *runned* or *ran*?

Solution 2

You need to use the special forms of the irregular verbs.

Correct Form of Irregular Verb: *I ran all the way home.*

McGraw-Hill School Division

Problem 3

Leaving out the apostrophe in a contraction

Incorrect Contraction:

Our town doesnt have an ice rink.

What takes the place of the left-out letter in *doesnt*?

Solution 3

A contraction is a short form of two words.
You need to add an apostrophe (') to take the place of the letters that are left out.

Correct Contraction: *Our town doesn't have an ice rink.*

Practice Write the sentences. Be sure to write each verb correctly.

1. Mom is coming to the pond. We were leaving now.

2. I have skated for two years. Mom have helped me a lot.

3. Mom did a spin for me. I gived it a try.

4. The spin isn't so easy. I didnt get dizzy.

5. My friends saw me. They sayed, "Good for you!"

Need More Help? For more help, see Helping Verbs on pages 212–213, Irregular Verbs on pages 218–223, Contractions with *not* on pages 224–225, and Handbook pages 440–441.

Incorrect Use of Pronouns

- Use *I* and *me* to tell about yourself.

- Use *we* and *us* to tell about yourself and another person.

- Some contractions and possessive pronouns sound alike.

Problem 1

Using *me* or *us* as the subject

Incorrect: *Dad, Ben, and me fix breakfast.*

> Which sounds right: "I fix" or "me fix"?

Solution 1

Do not use *me* or *us* as the subject of a sentence. Use the pronouns *I* or *we* instead.

Correct: *Dad, Ben, and I fix breakfast.*

Problem 2

Using *I* or *we* in the predicate

Incorrect: *Officer Lee helps we cross the street.*

> Where does *we* come—before the verb or after it?

Solution 2

Use the pronouns *me* or *us* after an action verb.

Correct: *Officer Lee helps us cross the street.*

Problem 3

Confusing contractions and possessive pronouns

Using a Contraction for a Possessive
Pronoun: *Please take you're seat.*

Can you say
"You are seat"?

Solution 3

A possessive pronoun shows who or what owns
something. A pronoun-verb contraction is a shortened
form of a pronoun and a verb. It has an apostrophe.

Using a Possessive Pronoun Correctly:
Please take your seat.

Practice Write the sentences. Be sure to write all
pronouns, contractions, or possessive pronouns
correctly.

1. Ben and I study. Tomorrow he and me have
   a test.

2. Mom helps Ben and me. She gives him and I
   a problem.

3. It's not so hard. Its really easy.

4. Mom said, "You're ready. You're brother is
   ready, too."

For more help, see *I* and *Me* on
pages 282–283, *We* and *Us* on
pages 284–285, Possessive
Pronouns on pages 290–291,
Contractions—Pronoun and Verb on
pages 292–293, and Handbook
pages 442–443.

Incorrect Use of Adjectives

- You can use **adjectives** to compare people, places, and things.

- Add *-er* to an adjective when you compare two nouns.

- Add *-est* to an adjective to compare more than two nouns.

Problem 1

Using *-er* or *-est* incorrectly

Incorrect: *Our pine tree is tallest than our oak tree.*

> Are you comparing two or more than two?

Solution 1

Count how many people, places, or things you are comparing. Then add *-er* or *-est*.

Correct: *Our pine tree is taller than our oak tree.*

Practice Write each sentence. Be sure to write adjectives that compare correctly.

1. Toads have shorter back legs than frogs. Frogs have smoothest skin than toads.

2. What is the world's longest fish? The whale shark is the longer fish of all.

3. Lions are faster than zebras. Are zebras fastest than rabbits?

4. The ostrich is the largest bird of all. The hummingbird is the smaller bird of all.

Handbook

Contents

Grammar

Mechanics and Usage

Build Skills

Writing

Handbook

RULE 1
pages 2–3

Sentences

- A **sentence** tells a complete thought. Words that do not tell a complete thought are not a sentence.

Practice **Write each complete sentence.**

1. Blackie is a gerbil.

2. He runs on his wheel.

3. Is very small and furry.

4. Our teacher and the students.

5. Dina touches his fur.

RULE 2
pages 4–5, 6–7

Kinds of Sentences

- Every sentence begins with a capital letter.

Kind of Sentence	Example
A **statement** tells something. It ends with a period.	*Firefighters put out fires.*
A **question** asks something. It ends with a question mark.	*Why do firefighters wear boots?*
A **command** tells someone to do something. It ends with a period.	*Watch the firefighters climb the ladder.*
An **exclamation** shows strong feeling. It ends with an exclamation mark.	*At last, the fire is out!*

Practice **Tell what kind of sentence you see.**

1. Firefighters work together.

2. Would you like to be a firefighter?

3. What a great job it is!

McGraw-Hill School Division

RULE 3
pages 10–13

Subjects and Predicates in Sentences

- Every sentence has two parts.
  The subject tells who or what does something.
  The predicate tells what the subject does or is.

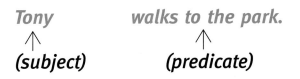

Tony   *walks to the park.*

(subject)   (predicate)

Practice Write each sentence. Draw one line under the subject. Circle the predicate.

1. The children go to the pond.
2. Tony and Nancy catch fish.
3. Nancy watches the frogs.

RULE 4
pages 14–15

Combining Sentences

- Use the word and to join two sentences that have the same subjects or the same predicates.

Margo went to the zoo.   *Margo and Sam*
Sam went to the zoo.   *went to the zoo.*

Practice Use *and* to put together each pair of sentences. Write the new sentence.

1. Monkeys jumped. Kangaroos jumped.
2. Lions roared. Tigers roared.
3. Bears splashed. Bears played.

 QUICK WRITE Imagine you are at a zoo. Write an example of each type of sentence.

Handbook

RULE 1
pages 68–69

Nouns

- A noun is a word that names a person, place, or thing.

  The boy makes a sandwich in the kitchen.

  (person)   (thing)   (place)

Practice **Write the sentences. Draw a line under each noun.**

1. The family lives in the city.

2. The children play ball in the park.

3. A woman walks to the beach.

4. A man gets on the bus.

5. A boy sells newspapers.

RULE 2
pages 72–73

Proper Nouns

- A proper noun is a word that names special people, pets, and places.

- A proper noun begins with a capital letter.

  Roberto Brown walks Buddy down Main Street.

  special person   special pet   special place

McGraw-Hill School Division

Practice Write each sentence. Begin each proper noun with a capital letter.

1. I have a friend named peter.

2. He has a dog named simon.

3. Peter lives on maple street.

4. We both go to davis school.

5. Rick and julie are in our class.

Days, Months, and Holidays

• **Some proper nouns** name days of the week, months, and holidays.

Is Flag Day on a Monday in June?

⤊ ⤊ ⤊

(holiday)   (day of week) (month)

Practice Write each sentence. Begin each proper noun with a capital letter.

1. On new year's day, we always have a party.

2. Tomorrow is valentine's day.

3. What holiday is in may?

4. School begins in september.

5. My birthday is next friday.

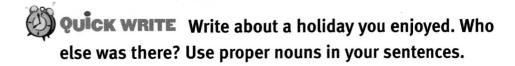 **QUICK WRITE** Write about a holiday you enjoyed. Who else was there? Use proper nouns in your sentences.

435

RULE 1
pages 78–79

Plural Nouns

- A noun can name more than one. Add *-s* to form the plural of most nouns.

    bird, birds   song, songs   street, streets

- Add *-es* to form the plural of nouns that end in *s*, *sh*, *ch*, or *x*.

    dish, dishes   box, boxes   ranch, ranches

Practice Write the sentences. Make the noun in ( ) name more than one.

1. We have (box) of books.

2. The books are about (bird).

3. Do you know any bird (song)?

RULE 2
pages 80–81

More Plural Nouns

- If a word ends in a consonant plus *y*, change the *y* to *i* and add *-es* to form the plural.

    bunny, bunnies   pony, ponies   cherry, cherries

- Some nouns change their spelling to name more than one.

Singular	Plural
man	men
woman	women
child	children
tooth	teeth
mouse	mice
foot	feet

Practice Make the noun in ( ) name more than one. Write the new sentence.

1. Three (child) came to our farm.

2. There are ten (bunny) on our farm.

3. All the rabbits have big (foot).

RULE 3
pages
82–85

Singular and Plural Possessive Nouns

- A possessive noun is a noun that shows who or what owns something. Add an apostrophe (') and an *s* to a singular noun to make it possessive.

  Rita's sisters wear red boots in the winter.

- Add just an apostrophe (') to most plural nouns to make them possessive.

  The sisters' boots are all alike.

- Add an apostrophe (') and an *s* to form the possessive of plural nouns that do not end in *s*.

  The children's boots are lined up in the closet.

Singular Possessive	Plural Possessive
boy's lunch	boys' lunches

Practice Write each sentence. Use the possessive form of the noun in ( ).

1. (Trina) dog is called Sparky.

2. (Sparky) food is in his dish.

3. Where are the (pets) bowls?

4. The (kittens) mother feeds them.

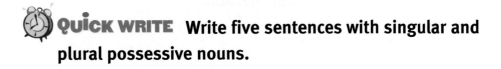 **QUICK WRITE** Write five sentences with singular and plural possessive nouns.

Handbook

RULE 1
pages 140, 214

Action Verbs and Linking Verbs

- An action verb is a word that shows action.

  Kim plays the piano.

- A linking verb does not show action. The verb *be* is a linking verb.

  Mr. Lee is her teacher.

Practice Write the sentences. Draw a line under each action verb. Circle each linking verb.

1. The yard is messy.

2. The children clean the yard.

3. Sara mows the grass.

4. Kevin rakes the leaves.

5. The children are very busy.

RULE 2
pages 142, 148

Present- and Past-Tense Verbs

- Present-tense verbs tell what is happening now. Add -*s* or -*es* to tell what one person or thing is doing.

  Frank drives to work. Rita fixes her car.

- Past-tense verbs tell about actions in the past. Most past-tense verbs end with -*ed*.

  Chuck spilled the grape juice.

- For verbs like stop, double the final consonant before adding -*ed*.

  Ben stopped at the red light.

- For verbs like race, drop the *e* before adding -*ed*.

  Laura raced home after school.

McGraw-Hill School Division

Handbook

Practice Write each sentence in present or past tense as shown in ( ).

1. (present) We (like) farms.

2. (present) We (collect) pictures of animals.

3. (past) Last week, our class (plan) a trip to a farm.

4. (past) Everyone (like) the trip.

5. (past) The class (thank) the teacher.

RULE 3
pages
144–145

Subject-Verb Agreement

• A subject and verb must agree. Add *-s* or *-es* only if the subject tells about one person or thing.

One	More Than One
Martha sings **a song.**	*Martha and Tim sing* **a song.**

Practice Choose the correct verb in ( ). Then write each sentence correctly.

1. Mr. Chin (teach, teaches) math.

2. Tony and Ron (read, reads) their math books.

3. Molly (write, writes) in her notebook.

4. The teacher (help, helps) the students.

5. We (learn, learns) about numbers.

QUICK WRITE Describe a game you like to play. Circle the action verbs.

Handbook

RULE 1
pages
150–151

The Verb *Have*

- The verb *have* has three forms:

    have   *has*   *had*

- Use *have* and *has* for the present tense. Use *had* for the past tense.

    Present tense → *Today I have fun in school.*
    Past tense ——→ *Yesterday, I had fun, too.*

Practice Choose the correct verb in ( ). Write the sentence.

1. Yesterday, we (had, has) company.

2. Today, we (have, had) more company.

3. My sister (have, has) a friend at our house.

RULE 2
pages
210–211

The Verb *Be*

- The verb *be* has special forms in the present tense and in the past tense.

Subject	Present	Past
I	am	was
she, he, it	is	was
you, we, they	are	were

Practice Choose the correct verb in ( ). Write the sentence.

1. Yesterday, it (is, was) hot and sunny.

2. We (was, were) at the beach.

3. Now, the sky (is, was) cloudy.

4. We (is, are) at the park.

McGraw-Hill School Division

RULE 3
pages
212–213

Helping Verbs

- A helping verb helps another verb show action.

- *Am*, *is*, and *are* can help tell about action that is happening now.

- *Has* and *have* can help tell about past actions.

Practice Write each sentence. Underline the helping verb.

1. We are eating lunch.

2. We have asked for pizza.

RULE 4
pages
218–223

Irregular Verbs

- Irregular verbs do not add *-ed* in the past tense. They have a different spelling in the past tense.

Verb	Now	Past
go	go, goes	went
say	say, says	said
see	see, sees	saw
come	come, comes	came
give	give, gives	gave

Practice Write the sentences. Use the past tense of the verb in ( ).

1. I (go) home after school.

2. Mom (give) me a hug.

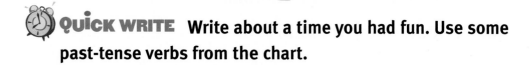

QUICK WRITE Write about a time you had fun. Use some past-tense verbs from the chart.

Handbook

RULE 1
pages 280–281

Pronouns

- A **pronoun** takes the place of a noun or nouns. Pronouns match the noun or nouns they replace.

  Tina plays ball. She plays ball.

- Use *I* and *we* to tell about yourself and others in the subject of a sentence. Use *me* and *us* after an action verb.

  Lil and I play outside. Bob gives us the ball.

Practice Write each sentence. Replace the underlined words with the correct pronoun in ( ).

1. <u>The children</u> kick the ball. (They, We)

2. <u>The ball</u> rolls to Kim. (She, It)

3. <u>Kim</u> scores a goal. (He, She)

4. <u>Lucy and I</u> give a cheer. (She, We)

5. The coach helps <u>Lucy and me</u>. (us, we)

RULE 2
pages 288–289

Pronoun-Verb Agreement

- A **present tense verb** must agree with a pronoun in the subject of a sentence.

- If the pronoun is *he, she,* or *it,* add *-s* to the action verb. If it is *I, you, we,* or *they,* do not add *-s.*

  He eats pizza.   We eat popcorn.

Practice Write each sentence. Choose the correct verb in ( ).

1. We (walk, walks) to the store.

2. I (buy, buys) some bananas.

3. He (get, gets) some bread.

McGraw-Hill School Division

RULE 3
pages
290–291

Possessive Pronouns

- A **possessive pronoun** takes the place of a possessive noun. It shows who or what owns something.

Susan's friends are fun. Her friends are fun.

One Person or Thing	More Than One
my	our
your	your
her, his, its	their

Practice Write the sentences. Replace the underlined words with a possessive pronoun.

1. <u>Eric's</u> dad goes by train.

2. <u>Jane's</u> mom goes by car.

3. <u>The children's</u> friend rides a bike.

RULE 4
pages
292–293

Contractions

- A **contraction** is a short form of two words.

- An **apostrophe** (') takes the place of the letters that are left out of the contraction.

Practice Write the sentences. Replace the underlined words with the correct word in ( ).

1. <u>I am</u> writing a story. (It's, I'm)

2. <u>It is</u> about two bear cubs. (He's, It's)

3. <u>They are</u> a brother and sister. (We're, They're)

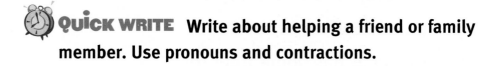

QUICK WRITE Write about helping a friend or family member. Use pronouns and contractions.

Handbook

443

Handbook

RULE 1
pages 346–349 — **Adjectives**

- An **adjective** is a word that describes a noun. Some adjectives tell *what kind* and *how many*.

  happy children   *two children*
  ↑   ↑
  what kind   *how many*

Practice **Write the sentences. Draw one line under each adjective.**

1. We had a great party.

2. We played two games.

3. Some clowns showed up.

4. The clowns had big noses.

5. They carried red balloons.

RULE 2
pages 350–351 — **Articles**

- The words *a* and *an* are special adjectives called **articles**. Use *a* before a word that begins with a consonant sound. Use *an* before vowel sounds.

  a turtle   *an otter*
  ↑   ↑
  consonant   *vowel*

Practice **Write each sentence. Use the correct article in ( ).**

1. I have (a, an) toy train.

2. Sally gave me (a, an) elephant.

3. (A, An) octopus is in the toy chest.

4. I put (a, an) doll on my bed.

5. (A, An) friend has some new toys.

RULE 3
pages
352–353

Adjectives That Compare

- Add *-er* to an adjective to compare two nouns.

- Add *-est* to compare more than two nouns.

    A horse is faster than a rabbit.
    A cheetah is the fastest animal of all.

Practice Write the sentences. Add *-er* or *-est* to the adjective in ( ).

1. Ducks are (small) than swans.

2. A turkey is (great) than a goose.

3. Whales have the (long) body of all.

4. Kangaroos leap (high) than rabbits.

5. A snail is the (slow) animal I know.

RULE 4
pages
356–361

Adverbs

- An adverb is a word that tells more about a verb. Adverbs tell *how, when,* or *where.*

    Yesterday, the band played loudly.

Practice Write *how, when,* or *where* to show what each underlined adverb tells about the verb.

1. Drums banged <u>loudly</u>.

2. <u>Soon</u> a horn sounded.

3. I sat <u>there</u>.

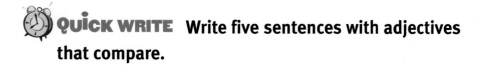 **QUICK WRITE** Write five sentences with adjectives that compare.

Handbook

Handbook

Abbreviations

- An abbreviation is a short form of a word.

Titles

- The abbreviation of a title before a name begins with a capital letter and ends with a period.

  Mr. John Carpenter   *Ms.* Barbara Clarke

  Mrs. Bruce Murdock   *Dr.* Harold Natola

Practice Write each abbreviation correctly.

1. mr Dwight Collins   **3.** dr Sarah Romer

2. ms Dara Atkinson   **4.** mrs Amanda Ling

Days of the Week/Months of the Year

- When you abbreviate the days of the week or the months of the year, begin with a capital letter and end with a period.

  Sun. Mon. Tues. Wed. Thurs. Fri. Sat.

  Jan. Feb. Mar. Apr. Aug. Sept. Oct. Nov. Dec.

- Do not abbreviate the following words.

  May   June   July

Practice Write each abbreviation correctly.

1. mar   **4.** aug

2. sat   **5.** oct

3. fri

Handbook

States

- When you write the address on an envelope you may use United States Postal Service Abbreviations for the names of the states. The abbreviations are two capital letters with no periods.

Alabama	AL	Kentucky	KY	North Carolina	NC
Alaska	AK	Louisiana	LA	North Dakota	ND
Arizona	AZ	Maine	ME	Ohio	OH
Arkansas	AR	Maryland	MD	Oklahoma	OK
California	CA	Massachusetts	MA	Oregon	OR
Colorado	CO	Michigan	MI	Pennsylvania	PA
Connecticut	CT	Minnesota	MN	Rhode Island	RI
Delaware	DE	Mississippi	MS	South Carolina	SC
District of Columbia	DC	Missouri	MO	South Dakota	SD
		Montana	MT	Tennessee	TN
Florida	FL	Nebraska	NE	Texas	TX
Georgia	GA	Nevada	NV	Utah	UT
Hawaii	HI	New Hampshire	NH	Vermont	VT
Idaho	ID			Virginia	VA
Illinois	IL	New Jersey	NJ	Washington	WA
Indiana	IN	New Mexico	NM	West Virginia	WV
Iowa	IA	New York	NY	Wisconsin	WI
Kansas	KS			Wyoming	WY

Practice Write the U.S. Postal Service abbreviation for each of the following states.

1. Oregon
2. Rhode Island
3. Texas
4. Vermont
5. West Virginia

Handbook

┌─ **First Word in a Sentence** ──────────────────┐

- The first word in a sentence begins with a capital letter.

  It is raining today.
  We are staying in the house.

- The first word in a quotation begins with a capital letter. A quotation is the exact words of a person speaking.

  My brother said, "Our dog is getting wet."
  "Let's put him in the basement," I said.

└───┘

┌─ **Letters** ───────────────────────────────────┐

- All of the words in a letter's greeting begin with a capital letter.

  Dear Mrs. Drake,

- Only the first word in the closing of a letter begins with a capital letter.

  Yours truly,

└───┘

Practice Write each item. Use capital letters correctly.

1. dear uncle jerry,

2. our dog Gabby got wet in the rain.

3. Mom said, "let's give Gabby a bath."

4. gabby is clean and dry now.

5. yours truly,

┌─── **Names and Titles of People** ───────────────┐

- The names of people begin with a capital letter.

    Martha Bates   Jason S. Golov

- Titles begin with a capital letter.

    Senator Hunter   Aunt Terri   Mr. Wasserman

- Always make the pronoun *I* a capital letter.

    My sister Natalie and I went apple picking.

└──┘

Practice **Write the sentences. Use capital letters correctly.**

1. We visited mr. cook's apple orchard.

2. Natalie and i picked lots of apples.

3. We watched mrs. cook make apple cider.

┌─── **Names of Places** ───────────────────────────┐

- The names of cities, states, countries, and continents begin with a capital letter.

    Chicago   Nevada   Canada   Africa

- The names of streets, buildings, and planets begin with a capital letter.

    Longwood Street   Lincoln Memorial   Earth

└──┘

Practice **Write the sentences. Use capital letters correctly.**

1. Erica visited her best friend Katie in england.

2. Katie lives on dexter street in london.

3. They saw a famous clock called big ben.

More Proper Nouns and Adjectives

- The names of schools, clubs, and businesses begin with a capital letter.

    Ambrose School   Drama Club   Randal Company

- The days of the week, months of the year, and holidays begin with a capital letter. Do not begin the names of the seasons with a capital letter.

    Sunday   June   Columbus Day   winter

- Most abbreviations have capital letters.

    Dr.   Ms.   Street   Mt.

- The first, last, and all important words in the title of a book, poem, song, story, play, movie, magazine, and newspaper begin with a capital letter.

    The Owl and the Pussycat
    The Wizard of Oz
    The Los Angeles Times

Practice Write the sentences. Use capital letters correctly.

1. Julie's class at rockville school is having a science show.

2. Julie is in the young inventors club.

3. The science show is this spring in may.

4. It's on memorial day at the b & k arena.

5. The is *rockville news* is printing a story about the science show.

McGraw-Hill School Division

— **End Marks** —

- A statement is a sentence that tells something. It ends with a period (.).

  We have a birdfeeder in our backyard.

- A command is a sentence that tells or asks someone to do something. It ends with a period (.).

  Buy some seeds for the birds.

- A question is a sentence that asks something. It ends with a question mark (?).

  Do they like sunflower seeds?

- An exclamation is a sentence that shows strong feeling. It ends with an exclamation mark (!).

  That bag of seeds is too big!

— **Periods** —

- Use a period to show the end of an abbreviation. An abbreviation is the short form for a word.

  Mr.   Dr.   Ave.

- Use a period with initials. Initials are capital letters that stand for a person's name.

  J. P. Morgan   C. S. Lewis

Practice **Write the sentences. Add end marks.**

1. Lots of sparrows come to our birdfeeder

2. Don't make loud noises near the birdfeeder

3. How many birds do you count

4. There are so many birds

Handbook

Commas

- Use a comma (,) between the names of cities and states.

  Seattle, Washington   Detroit, Michigan

- Use a comma between the day and the year in dates.

  December 25, 2001   July 4, 1776

- Use a comma after the greeting and closing in a letter.

  Dear Grandpa,   Sincerely,

Practice **Write the items. Add commas.**

1. Orlando Florida

2. April 1 2002

3. Your best friend

4. Dear Aunt Betty

Commas

- Use a comma to separate words in a series.

  Jeremy plays soccer, t-ball, and hockey.

- Use a comma after the words *yes* or *no* or the name of a person being spoken to.

  Yes, he likes soccer. Jim, do you play tennis?

Practice **Write the sentences. Add commas.**

1. Marcia do you have a snack for the game?

2. Yes I have oranges apples and juice.

3. Reynaldo do you want to come to the game?

4. No I'm going to my cousin's house.

Handbook

Diagrams

DEFINITIONS AND **FEATURES**

- A diagram is a special kind of drawing. It can show how something is put together or how it works.

- The title tells what the diagram shows.

- Labels name the different parts of the diagram.

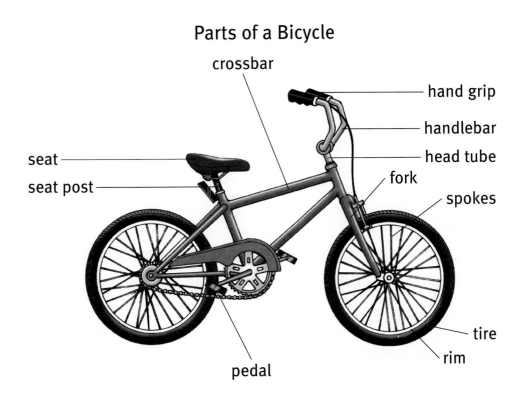

Parts of a Bicycle

Practice Use the diagram to answer these questions.

1. What is the title of the diagram?

2. What parts make up the wheel of the bike?

3. What parts are on the ends of the handlebar?

4. What part is between the seat post and the head tube?

5. What is the part that holds the front wheel called?

461

Handbook

Alphabetical Order

DEFINITIONS AND FEATURES

- You can put words in ABC order by their first letter.

- When words begin with the same letter, use the second letter to put them in ABC order.

- When words begin with the same two letters, use the third letter to put them in ABC order.

ABC Order by Second Letter	ABC Order by Third Letter
bank	milk
bird	mine
black	miss

Practice Write each group of words in ABC order. Use the first, second, or third letter as needed.

1. yellow, blue, orange

2. balloon, butterfly, beaver

3. home, holly, hoe

4. giant, garden, geese

5. milk, music, moon

6. farm, fast, fall

7. jacket, juice, jelly

8. troop, train, truck

9. tomato, thick, tulip

10. write, wing, worm

McGraw-Hill School Division

Index

DEFINITIONS AND **FEATURES**

- An index lists all the subjects in a book.

- The subjects are listed in ABC order.

- Each main subject may have one or more subtopics.

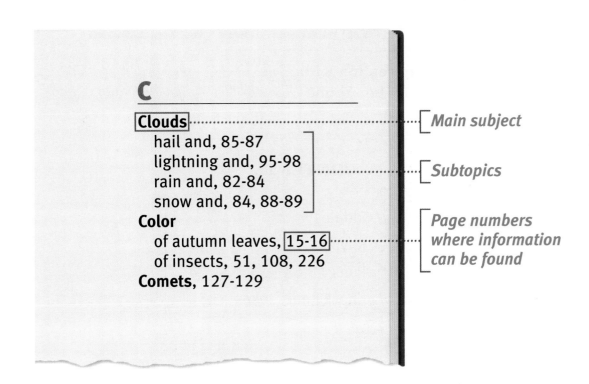

C

Clouds .... Main subject
    hail and, 85-87
    lightning and, 95-98 .... Subtopics
    rain and, 82-84
    snow and, 84, 88-89
Color
    of autumn leaves, 15-16 .... Page numbers where information can be found
    of insects, 51, 108, 226
Comets, 127-129

Practice Use the index above to answer these questions.

1. What is the first main subject under the letter C?

2. What are the subtopics under Color?

3. How many pages tell about the color of insects?

4. What pages have information on lightning and clouds?

5. On what pages would you find out about comets?

Handbook

Parts of a Book

DEFINITIONS AND **FEATURES**

- The first page in every book is the title page. It tells the name of the book and the author.

- The table of contents follows the title page. It lists the name and page number of each chapter in the book.

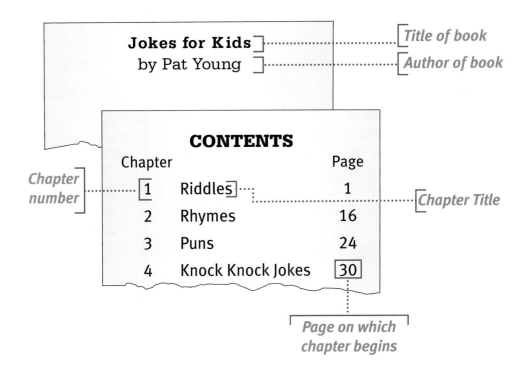

Jokes for Kids ⌐············· ⌐Title of book
by Pat Young ⌐············· ⌐Author of book

CONTENTS

Chapter number ······⌐1 Riddles⌐···   Chapter Title

Chapter		Page
1	Riddles	1
2	Rhymes	16
3	Puns	24
4	Knock Knock Jokes	30

Page on which chapter begins

Practice Use the title page and table of contents to answer these questions.

1. What is the title of the book?

2. What is the author's name?

3. What is the title of Chapter 1?

4. On what page does Chapter 2 begin?

5. What is the number of the chapter on Knock Knock Jokes?

Handbook

Card Catalog

— **DEFINITIONS** AND **FEATURES** —

- The card catalog contains information about all of the books in the library.

- Each book has a title card, an author card, and a subject card.

- The call number helps you find the book.

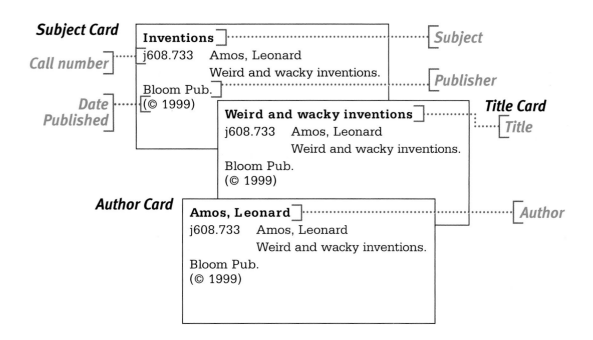

Practice Use the catalog cards above to help you answer these questions.

1. If you wanted to find a book on inventions, what card would you use?

2. If you were looking for a book by Leonard Amos, what card would you use?

3. If you knew the book's title but not its author, what card would you use?

4. What is the title of Leonard Amos's book?

5. What is the call number of the book?

RULE 1
pages 26–27

Time-Order Words

- Time-order words **show the order** in which things happen.

- Time-order words help you **tell about events in order.**

Time-Order Words and Phrases

first	after	a long time ago
next	before	last of all
then	later	now
last	yesterday	next month

RULE 2
pages 96–97

Compound Words

- A compound word is a word that is made from two smaller words.

- Knowing the meaning of the two smaller words can help you figure out the meaning of the compound word.

Two Words	Compound Word	Meaning
note + book	notebook	a book you take notes in
blue + berry	blueberry	a berry that is blue
dog + house	doghouse	a house for a dog
bed + room	bedroom	a room with a bed in it

Handbook

RULE 3
pages
164–165

Prefixes

- A prefix is a word part that is added to the beginning of a word.

- A prefix changes the meaning of a word.

- You can use prefixes to **say things in a shorter way.**

Prefix	Meaning	Example
un-	not, do the opposite of	unlock
re-	again, back	refill
dis-	not, the opposite of	disappear
pre-	before	preschool

RULE 4
pages
236–237

Suffixes

- A suffix is a word part that is added to the end of a word.

- A suffix changes the meaning of the word.

Suffix	Meaning	Example
-less	without	careless
-ful	full of	careful
-er	person who	catcher
-ly	in a certain way	carefully

Handbook

RULE 5
pages
304–305

Synonyms

- A synonym is a word that has the same or almost the same meaning as another word.

- A synonym **can be used instead** of another word.

Word	Synonyms	
fast	quick	rapid
end	finish	complete
little	tiny	small
big	huge	giant
glad	happy	joyful
laugh	chuckle	giggle
say	speak	tell
see	watch	view
cure	heal	fix
clean	pure	clear
grab	grip	hold
true	real	right

Handbook

RULE 6
pages
372–373

Antonyms

• **Antonyms** are words with opposite meanings.

Word	Antonyms	
young	old	aged
tall	short	low
old	new	fresh
large	small	tiny
quiet	noisy	loud
happy	sad	unhappy
hot	cold	icy
dry	wet	damp
slow	fast	quick
go	stop	halt
fly	fall	sink
break	fix	repair

Problem Words

Some words in the English language are confusing. Sometimes these words are not used correctly. The following charts will help you see how to use these words in the correct way.

Words	Correct Usage	Correct Usage
can/may	*Can* means "to be able to." *My dog can run very fast.*	*May* means "to be allowed." *May we go to the movies this afternoon?*
good/well	*Good* is an adjective that describes a noun. *I am having a good day.*	*Well* is often an adverb. *Well* describes a verb by telling "how." *Rena did very well on the math test.*
in/into	*In* means "inside of." *The bird is in the cage.*	*Into* means "move to the inside of." *I stepped into the car.*
its/it's	*Its* is a possessive pronoun. *Its* has no apostrophe. *The cat likes its new toy.*	*It's* is a contraction. It is the shortened form of "it is." *It's hot outside!*
lay/lie	*Lay* means "to put something down." *I will lay my coat on the chair.*	*Lie* means "to rest on something" *I like to lie on my bed and read a book.*

McGraw-Hill School Division

Words	Correct Usage	Correct Usage
sit/set	*Sit* means "to be seated." *The teacher asked us to sit in a circle.*	*Set* means to "put something in a certain place." *I set the cup on the saucer.*
their/they're	*Their* is a possessive pronoun. It means "belonging to them." *That is their house.*	*They're* is a contraction. It is the shortened form of "they are." *They're going on a field trip tomorrow.*
then/than	*Then* means "next." *I walked home from school and then I ate a snack.*	*Than* means "to compare something." *Your dog is bigger than my dog.*
to/too	*To* means "in the direction of." *She walked to the door and opened it.*	*Too* is an adverb. It means "also." *I want a pizza, too.*
your/you're	*Your* is a possessive pronoun. It means "belonging to you." *Is that your backpack?*	*You're* is a contraction. It is the shortened form of "you are." *I think you're a great friend.*

QUICK WRITE Create your own chart of problem words. Include words from this chart or other words you sometimes get confused. Write sentences to help you remember how to use the words correctly.

Difficult Words to Spell

For many writers, some words are difficult to spell. You can use this list to check your spelling. You can also practice spelling these words correctly.

again	been	early	money	said	tired
along	before	family	myself	school	together
also	buy	finally	o'clock	soon	until
always	charge	first	off	started	upon
another	clothes	friend	once	sure	were
any	color	heard	our	than	when
anything	could	hurt	please	their	which
around	dear	know	pretty	they	while
balloon	decide	little	really	third	would
because	does	might	right	through	write

Homophones

Homophones are words that sound the same. But they are spelled differently, and they have different meanings. *See* and *sea* are examples of homophones.

ant	buy	hear	know	sea	whole
aunt	by	here	no	see	hole
bare	dear	hour	meat	some	wood
bear	deer	our	meet	sum	would
be	eye	knew	one	their	to
bee	I	new	won	there	too
blew	flour	knot	road	threw	two
blue	flower	not	rode	through	

Handbook

Words You Often Use

Here is a list of words that writers often use in their writing. Test yourself and see how many of these words you can spell correctly.

a	came	have	me	saw	upon
about	can	he	men	say	us
after	color	her	morning	school	very
all	could	him	mother	see	want
am	day	his	my	she	was
an	did	home	night	so	we
and	didn't	house	no	some	well
are	do	I	not	soon	went
around	don't	if	now	stand	were
as	down	in	of	that	what
at	eat	into	on	the	when
away	find	is	one	them	where
back	first	it	or	then	white
ball	for	just	our	there	who
be	found	know	out	they	will
because	four	last	over	things	wish
big	friend	left	people	think	with
black	from	like	play	this	woman
book	get	little	pretty	time	women
box	girl	live	put	to	would
bring	go	look	red	too	year
but	got	made	run	two	you
by	had	man	said	up	your

Spelling Rules and Strategies

Learning these spelling rules can help you spell many words.

1. When words end in silent *e,* drop the *e* when adding an ending that begins with a vowel. *(save + ed = saved)*

2. When a base word ends with a consonant followed by *y,* change the *y* to *i* when adding the ending. *(story + es = stories)*

3. When a base word ends with a vowel followed by *y,* do not change the ending when adding suffixes or endings. *(day = days)*

4. When a one-syllable word ends in one vowel followed by one consonant, double the consonant before adding an ending that begins with a vowel. *(run + ing = running; drop + ed = dropped)*

5. The letter *q* is always followed by *u. (quick)*

6. No English words end in *j, q,* or *v.*

7. Add *-s* to most words to form plurals or to change the tense of verbs. Add *-es* to words ending in *x, z, s, sh,* or *ch. (map = maps; bus = buses; wish = wishes; fox = foxes)*

Use these tips to help you become a better speller.

1. Learn about sound-alike words such as *hear* and *here.* Be sure you use the right one.

2. Use spell-check on a computer. Spell-checkers are not perfect! If you write a word that sounds like the word you need, spell-check will not catch the mistake.

3. Think of a word that rhymes with the new word. Rhyming words often have the same spelling pattern. *(b + and = band; h + and = hand)*

4. Use words you know how to spell to help spell new words. Word beginnings and endings can help. (<u>st</u>ar + <u>b</u>one = <u>stone</u>)

5. Make up clues to help you remember the spelling. *("What you <u>k</u>now is O<u>K</u>." <u>K</u> begins <u>k</u>now.)*

6. Break the word into word parts or syllables. *(be cause)*

7. Look for a smaller word in a new word to help you write the new word. *(<u>heard</u> has <u>hear</u> in it)*

8. Word families have words with the same endings. Use word families to help you spell new words. *(pen, ten)*

9. Use the dictionary to look up spellings of words.

10. Study each letter in words that do not match spelling patterns or rules. Say and write the words carefully.

11. Think of when you have seen the word before. Think of how it looked. Write the word in different ways to see which one looks correct. *(~~fal~~, ~~faul~~, fall)*

12. Keep a Personal Word List in your Spelling Journal. Write words you have trouble spelling.

Play

A **play** is a story that is written to be acted out. Characters use actions and words, called dialogue, to tell the story.

A play has a title .... **Jack and the Beanstalk**

Characters: JACK
MOTHER
A play has a TESSY THE COW
cast of .... OLD MAN
characters GIANT

The setting **Setting:** Long ago in a small village
tells where and
when the play **Act I**
takes place. ....
Scene I: The play begins in Jack's house. Jack
An act is one and his mother are sitting near an empty fireplace.
part of a play .... Tessy is chewing Mother's straw hat.

MOTHER (grabbing her hat away from Tessy)
You must sell the cow, Jack, so we can buy
something to eat.

A character's **JACK** No, Mother, Tessy is the only friend I have.
words are
written after .... **TESSY** (nodding her head) Moo.
his or her
name. **JACK** But, Mother…

MOTHER Don't you "but, Mother" me. The cow goes
or I go.

Stage
directions in () **TESSY** (pushing Mother out of the door) Moooo!
tell how the ....
characters **MOTHER** Get this cow away from me!
move and act.

Practice Think of characters from a story you like. Think about what they do and say. Then write the beginning of the story as a play.

Handbook

Poem

In a **poem**, words are used in special ways to help you imagine an idea or a subject. A poem is different from other writing. It has a special sound and form.

Repeated words help stress an important idea in this poem.

The way that lines of this poem are written helps show that an action takes place over a period of time.

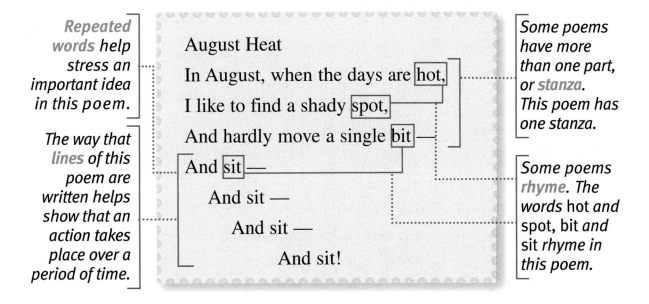

August Heat

In August, when the days are hot,
I like to find a shady spot,
And hardly move a single bit —
And sit —
  And sit —
    And sit —
      And sit!

Some poems have more than one part, or stanza. This poem has one stanza.

Some poems rhyme. The words hot *and* spot, bit *and* sit *rhyme in this poem.*

GUIDELINES FOR WRITING A POEM

- Choose a fun or interesting object or idea.

- Write words that make a picture of the object or idea.

- Do you want your poem to rhyme? Do you want an idea to repeat? Use rhyming words or repeated words in your poem.

- How many stanzas will your poem have? Write as many stanzas and lines as you want.

- Give your poem a title.

Practice Look around your classroom or outside. Choose an object or an idea to write a poem about. Then write the poem and draw a picture to go with it.

Handbook

Business Letter

A **business letter** is a special kind of letter. It is more formal than a friendly letter. You can write a business letter to a company or to a person.

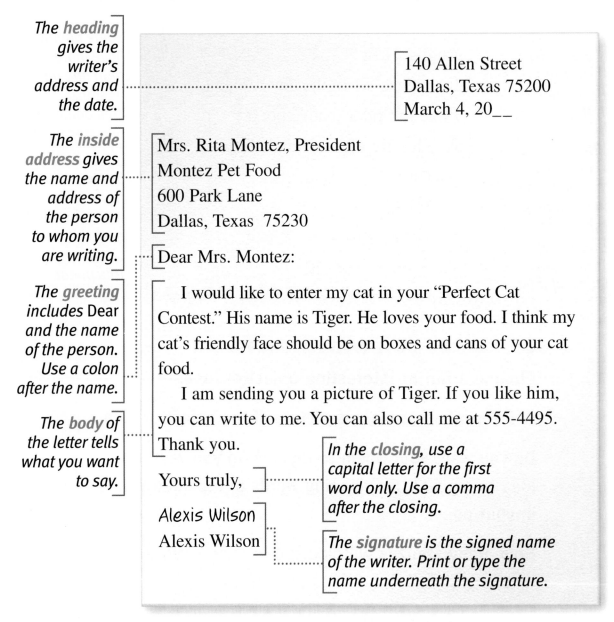

The *heading* gives the writer's address and the date.

> 140 Allen Street
> Dallas, Texas 75200
> March 4, 20__

The *inside address* gives the name and address of the person to whom you are writing.

> Mrs. Rita Montez, President
> Montez Pet Food
> 600 Park Lane
> Dallas, Texas 75230

The *greeting* includes Dear and the name of the person. Use a colon after the name.

> Dear Mrs. Montez:

The *body* of the letter tells what you want to say.

>   I would like to enter my cat in your "Perfect Cat Contest." His name is Tiger. He loves your food. I think my cat's friendly face should be on boxes and cans of your cat food.
>   I am sending you a picture of Tiger. If you like him, you can write to me. You can also call me at 555-4495. Thank you.

> Yours truly,

> Alexis Wilson
> Alexis Wilson

In the *closing*, use a capital letter for the first word only. Use a comma after the closing.

The *signature* is the signed name of the writer. Print or type the name underneath the signature.

Practice Think of something you like about your school. Write a business letter to your principal.

Research Report

A **research report** gives information about a subject. You find facts for the report from sources such as encyclopedias, books, magazines, and the Internet.

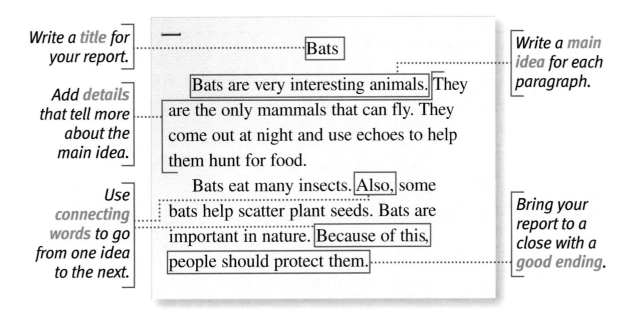

Write a title for your report.

Add details that tell more about the main idea.

Use connecting words to go from one idea to the next.

Bats

Bats are very interesting animals. They are the only mammals that can fly. They come out at night and use echoes to help them hunt for food.

Bats eat many insects. Also, some bats help scatter plant seeds. Bats are important in nature. Because of this, people should protect them.

Write a main idea for each paragraph.

Bring your report to a close with a good ending.

GUIDELINES FOR WRITING A REPORT

- Choose a topic that you find interesting.

- List questions you have about the topic.

- Do research. Use different sources. You may need to go to the library.

- Take notes on index cards.

- List your sources at the end of your report.

Practice What topic do you want to learn more about? Write a research report about that topic. Share your report with the class.

Using the Dictionary

A dictionary is an alphabetical list of words with their meanings and information about how to use them. Look at this entry for *little*.

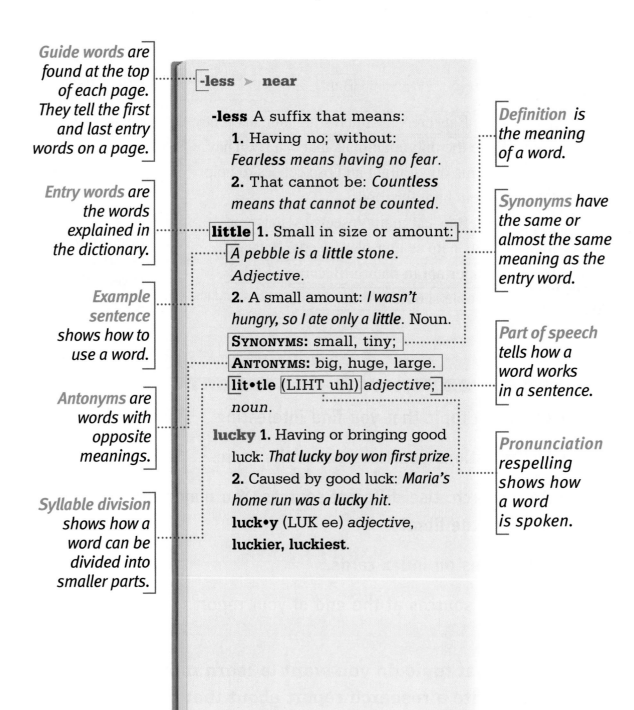

Guide words are found at the top of each page. They tell the first and last entry words on a page.

Entry words are the words explained in the dictionary.

Example sentence shows how to use a word.

Antonyms are words with opposite meanings.

Syllable division shows how a word can be divided into smaller parts.

-less ▷ near

-less A suffix that means:
1. Having no; without: *Fearless means having no fear.*
2. That cannot be: *Countless means that cannot be counted.*

little **1.** Small in size or amount: *A pebble is a little stone.* Adjective.
2. A small amount: *I wasn't hungry, so I ate only a little.* Noun.
SYNONYMS: small, tiny;
ANTONYMS: big, huge, large.
lit•tle (LIHT uhl) *adjective; noun.*

lucky **1.** Having or bringing good luck: *That lucky boy won first prize.*
2. Caused by good luck: *Maria's home run was a lucky hit.*
luck•y (LUK ee) *adjective,* **luckier, luckiest.**

Definition is the meaning of a word.

Synonyms have the same or almost the same meaning as the entry word.

Part of speech tells how a word works in a sentence.

Pronunciation respelling shows how a word is spoken.

Practice: Use the example on page 480 to answer these questions.

1. What are the guide words?

2. What is the first meaning given for *little*?

3. What is the example sentence for the second definition of *little*?

4. What are the synonyms for *little*?

5. Which of these words would come on the same page with the guide words *happy/late*?
   hard, lucky, kind, hot, little

Practice: Use the dictionary to answer the questions below.

6. What antonyms are given for *cold*?

7. What synonyms are given for *happy*?

8. Is *quiet* an antonym or a synonym for *noisy*?

9. What two synonyms are listed for *wet*?

10. What are two antonyms for *begin*?

11. How many word parts, or syllables, does *sunflower* have?

12. What is the definition of *blueberry*?

13. What part of speech is the word *lucky*?

14. Does the *a* in *tall* stand for the same sound as in *father* or in *saw*?

15. Which two parts of speech are shown for the word *first*?

When you write a poem, choose words that will paint a clear picture for the reader.

Practice: Read the poem below. Use the dictionary to answer the questions.

Frog on a Log in the Fog

Once I saw a small, sleepy frog

Sitting on a crisp, narrow log.

The frog croaked loudly.

The log went "Crack!"

And all I saw was the cold, dull fog.

1. What are the guide words for *small* and *sleepy*?

2. What is the definition for *crisp*?

3. How many word parts, or syllables, are in *narrow*?

4. Which definition of *dull* tells how it is used here?

5. What part of speech is the word *narrow*?

Pronunciation Key

The **Pronunciation Key** has examples for the sound spellings in the **pronunciation** of each dictionary entry. Use the key when you look up how to say a word.

Sound Spellings	Examples	Sound Spellings	Examples
a	cat	oh	go, home
ah	father	oo	too, do
air	there, hair	or	more, four
ay	late, day	ow	out, cow
aw	saw, fall	oy	toy
b	bit, rabbit	p	pig
ch	chin	r	run, carry
d	dog	s	song, mess
e	met	sh	shout, fish
ee	he, see	t	ten, better
f	fine, off	th	thin
g	go, bag, bigger	thh	them
h	hat	u	sun
hw	wheel	û	look, should
ih	sit	uh	about, happen, lemon
i	fine, tiger, my		
ihr	near, deer, here	ur	turn, learn
		v	very, of
j	jump, page	w	we
k	cat, back	y	yes
l	line, hill	yoo	music, new
m	mine, hammer	z	has, zoo
n	nice, funny	zh	treasure, division
ng	sing		
o	top		

A

after Following in place; behind: *My dog followed after*. Adverb.
▲ Following in time; later: *She got there after you left*. Preposition.
af•ter (AF tuhr) *adverb; preposition*.

B

backyard A yard behind a building: *We planted flowers in our backyard*.

spoiled: *The milk went bad*.
ᴀɴᴛᴏɴʏᴍ: good.
bad (BAD) *adjective*,
worse, worst.

beautiful Pleasing to look at, hear, or think about: *The sunset last night was beautiful*.
beau•ti•ful (BYOO tuh fuhl) *adjective*.

bedroom A room for sleeping: *My brother and I share a bedroom*.
bed•room (BED room) *noun, plural* **bedrooms**.

back•yard (bak YAHRD) *noun, plural* **backyards**.

bad 1. Not good; *a bad movie*. **2.** Having a harmful effect: *Candy is bad for your teeth*. **3.** Severe or violent: *a bad storm*. **4.** Rotten or

before In front of; ahead of: *We came home before dark*. Preposition.
▲ At an earlier time: *I've read this book before*. Adverb.
be•fore (bih FOR) *preposition; adverb*.

McGraw-Hill School Division

begin **1.** To do the first part of something; make a start: *Begin writing now.* **2.** To come into being; start: *The race will begin in five minutes.* SYNONYM: start; ANTONYMS: end, finish **be•gin** (bih GIHN) *verb,* **began, begun, beginning.**

behind **1.** At the back of: *Jorge stood behind me in line.* **2.** Later than; after: *Our bus was five minutes behind the first bus.* **be•hind** (bih HIND) *preposition.*

below In or to a lower place: *From the plane we could see the mountains far below. Adverb.*
▲ In a lower place than; beneath: *My friend's apartment is below mine. Preposition.*
be•low (bih LOH) *adverb; preposition.*

beside At the side of; next to: *A spider sat down beside Miss Muffet.* **be•side** (bih SID) *preposition.*

big Great in size; large: *We live in a big city.*

SYNONYMS: huge, large; ANTONYMS: little, small, tiny **big** (BIHG) *adjective,* **bigger, biggest.**

birthday The date a person was born: *We played games on my birthday.* **birth•day** (BURTH day) *noun, plural* **birthdays.**

bitter Having a biting, harsh, bad taste: *The coffee had a bitter taste.* **bit•ter** (BIHT uhr) *adjective.*

blueberry A small, dark blue, sweet berry with tiny seeds: *Blueberries grow on a shrub.* **blue•ber•ry** (BLOO ber ee) *noun, plural* **blueberries.**

bright 1. Giving much light; filled with light: *The sun's light is bright.* **2.** Clear; strong: *The rose was bright red.* **3.** Smart; clever: *Sandy is a bright child.* **ANTONYM:** dull. **bright** (BRIT) *adjective,* **brighter, brightest.**

butterfly An insect with a thin body and four large, often brightly colored wings: *I saw a yellow butterfly on a flower.* **but•ter•fly** (BUT uhr fli) *noun, plural* **butterflies.**

careful Paying close attention; watchful:

Be careful when you cross the street. **ANTONYM:** careless. **care•ful** (KAIR fuhl) *adjective.*

clean Free from dirt: *Put the clean dishes away.* **ANTONYM:** dirty. **clean** (KLEEN) *adjective,* **cleaner, cleanest.**

cold 1. Having a low temperature; not warm: *The weather is cold today.* **2.** Feeling a lack of warmth; chilly: *I was cold after playing in the snow.* **SYNONYMS:** chilly, freezing; **ANTONYMS:** hot, warm. **cold** (KOHLD) *adjective,* **colder, coldest.**

crisp Hard or firm but breaking easily into pieces: *Fresh celery should be crisp.* **crisp** (KRIHSP) *adjective,* **crisper, crispest.**

crunch To chew or crush with a noisy, crackling sound: *The cracker crunched when I bit into it.* **crunch** (KRUNCH) *verb,* **crunched, crunching.**

McGraw-Hill School Division

D

delicious Pleasing or delightful to the taste or smell: *The freshly picked apples were delicious.* **de•li•cious** (dih LISH uhs) *adjective.*

dry Not wet or damp; with very little or no water or other liquid: *A desert is a dry place.* **ANTONYM:** wet. **dry** (DRI) *adjective,* **drier, driest.**

dull 1. Not sharp or pointed: *The knife was so dull it would not cut.* **2.** Not interesting; boring: *The book was so dull I fell asleep.* **SYNONYMS:** blunt, boring; **ANTONYMS:** interesting, sharp. **dull** (DUL) *adjective,* **duller, dullest.**

F

few Not many: *I have only a few pages left to read.* **ANTONYM:** many. **few** (FYOO) *adjective,* **fewer, fewest.**

finally At the end; at last: *Baseball season is finally here!* **fi•nal•ly** (FI nuh lee) *adverb.*

finish To bring to an end; complete: *Finish your homework before you watch TV.* **SYNONYM:** end; **ANTONYMS:** begin, start. **fin•ish** (FIHN ihsh) *verb,* **finished, finishing.**

first 1. Coming before all others: *John was in the first race. Adjective.* ▲ Before anything else: *First, I do my homework, and then I play. Adverb.* **ANTONYM:** last. **first** (FURST) *adjective; adverb.*

flashlight An electric light powered by batteries and small enough to be carried. **flash•light** (FLASH lit) *noun, plural* **flashlights**.

football **1.** A game played by two teams of eleven players each on a big field with goals at each end: *Football is a popular sport*. **2.** The oval ball used in this game: *The player carried the football across the goal line*. **foot•ball** (FÛT bawl) *noun, plural* **footballs**.

-ful A suffix that means: **1.** Full of: *Fearful means full of fear*. **2.** Able to; likely to: *If you are forgetful, you are likely to forget things*. **3.** The amount that will fill something: *Cupful means the amount that will fill a cup*.

goldfish A fish that is usually orange-gold in color, often kept in home fish tanks: *Jan has three goldfish in a tank*. **gold•fish** (GOHLD fish) *noun, plural* **goldfish**.

good **1.** Of high quality; not bad or poor: *Kit is reading a good book*. **2.** Nice or pleasant: *Eric got good news about his uncle*. **3.** Acting properly: *My dog is good and doesn't jump on the sofa*. **ANTONYM:** bad. **good** (GÛD) *adjective*, **better, best**.

grasshopper A flying insect with long, powerful legs for jumping: *A grasshopper can make a chirping sound with its leg*. **grass•hop•per** (GRAS hop uhr) *noun, plural* **grasshoppers**.

H

happy Feeling or showing pleasure or gladness: *Margie was happy with her good grades.* **Synonyms:** glad, joyful; **Antonym:** sad. **hap•py** (HAP ee) *adjective*, **happier, happiest.**

hard 1. Solid and firm; not soft: *Loni fell and landed on the hard floor.* **2.** Difficult; not easy: *The math test was hard.* **Antonyms:** easy, soft. **hard** (HAHRD) *adjective*, **harder, hardest.**

hot Having a high temperature: *Don't touch the hot stove.* **Antonym:** cold. **hot** (HOT) *adjective*, **hotter, hottest.**

I

inside 1. On, in, or into the inner side or part of: *I went inside the house.* **2.** Indoors: *We played inside because it was raining.* **Antonym:** outside. **in•side** (IHN SID *or* ihn SID *or* IHN sid) *adverb*.

K

kind Gentle, generous, and friendly: *Luz is kind to animals.* **Antonym:** mean. **kind** (KIND) *adjective*, **kinder, kindest.**

L

last 1. Coming after all others: *December is the last month of the year. Adjective.* ▲ After all others: *Ron came in last. Adverb.* **Antonym:** first. **last** (LAST) *adjective; adverb*.

late 1. After the usual time: *Kevin was late for dinner. Adverb.* ▲ Coming near the end: *The game started in the late afternoon. Adjective.* **Antonym:** early. **late** (LAT) *adverb, adjective*, **later, latest.**

489

Dictionary

-less A suffix that means:
1. Having no; without:
*Fearless means having no
fear.* **2.** That cannot be:
*Countless means that
cannot be counted.*

little 1. Small in size or
amount: *A pebble is a
little stone. Adjective.*
2. A small amount: *I
wasn't hungry, so I ate
only a little. Noun.*
SYNONYMS: small, tiny;
ANTONYMS: big, huge,
large.
lit•tle (LIHT uhl)
adjective; noun.

lucky 1. Having or bringing
good luck: *That lucky girl
won first prize.* **2.** Caused
by good luck: *Maria's
home run was a lucky hit.*
luck•y (LUK ee)
adjective, **luckier,
luckiest.**

many 1. Made up of a large
number: *A library has many
books. Adjective.* **2.** A
large number: *Many of my
friends came to my party.
Noun.* **ANTONYM:** few.
man•y (MEN ee)
adjective, **more, most;**
noun.

mean Cruel; not kind or
nice: *It is mean to tease
a dog.* **ANTONYM:** kind.
mean (MEEN) *adjective,*
meaner, meanest.

narrow Not wide or
broad: *Andy jumped
across the narrow stream.*
nar•row (NAR oh)
adjective, **narrower,
narrowest.**

near 1. Not far or distant:
*The holiday season is
drawing near. Adverb.*
2. Close to or by: *My
grandparents live near the
beach. Preposition.*
near (NIHR) *adverb,*
nearer, nearest;
preposition.

new 1. Recently grown or made: *In spring the trees have new leaves*. **2.** Not yet used or worn: *My new sneakers are so white!* **ANTONYM:** old. **new** (NOO) *adjective*, **newer, newest**.

next 1. Following in time or order: *It rained Monday, but the next day was sunny*. **2.** Nearest: *The next street is mine*. *Adjective*. ▲ Immediately after: *Read this book next*. *Adverb*. **next** (NEKST) *adjective; adverb*.

noisy Making much noise: *The noisy children had to leave the library*. **ANTONYM:** quiet. **nois•y** (NOY zee) *adjective*, **noisier, noisiest**.

now 1. At this time: *I am sitting at my desk now*. **2.** Immediately: *Do your homework now*. **now** (NOW) *adverb*.

──────○──────

old 1. Having existed for a long time: *That castle is very old*.

2. Of a certain age: *Enrique is seven years old*. **ANTONYMS:** new, young. **old** (OHLD) *adjective*, **older, oldest**.

opposite 1. On the other side of or across from: *Leon lives on the opposite side of the street from me*. **2.** Turned or moving the other way: *We passed a car going in the opposite direction*. *Adjective*. ▲ Something that is completely different from another: *Hot is the opposite of cold*. *Noun*. **op•po•site** (OP uh ziht) *adjective; noun, plural* **opposites**.

outside The outer side, surface, or part: *The outside of the house needs painting.* Noun. ▲ Outdoors: *We played outside all day.* Adverb. **ANTONYM:** inside.
out•side (OWT SID *or* owt SID *or* OWT sid) *noun; adverb.*

Ⓟ

pale Not bright in color: *The rose was a pale pink.*
pale (PAYL) *adjective,* **paler, palest.**

Ⓠ

quarter 1. One of four equal parts: *Fifteen minutes is a quarter of an hour.* **2.** A coin worth 25 cents: *There are four quarters in a dollar.*
quar•ter (KWAWR tuhr) *noun, plural* **quarters.**

quiet Making little or no noise: *It is always quiet in the library.* **ANTONYMS:** loud, noisy.
qui•et (KWI it) *adjective,* **quieter, quietest.**

Ⓡ

rainbow A curve of colored light seen in the sky: *A rainbow is caused by the sun's shining through drops of water in the air.*
rain•bow (RAYN boh) *noun, plural* **rainbows.**

re- A prefix that means: **1.** Again: *Refill means to fill again.* **2.** Back: *Recall means to call back.*

Dictionary

S

sad Unhappy: *Fern was sad when her best friend moved away.* ANTONYMS: glad, happy. **sad** (SAD) *adjective,* **sadder, saddest**.

sailboat A boat that is moved by the wind blowing against its sail or sails: *The sailboat flew across the water.* **sail•boat** (SAYL boht) *noun, plural* **sailboats**.

seashell The shell of a clam or other sea animal: *Ella found a pretty seashell on the beach.* **sea•shell** (SEE shel) *noun, plural* **seashells**.

shiny Shining; bright: *The new penny was shiny.* ANTONYM: dull. **shin•y** (SHI nee) *adjective,* **shinier, shiniest**.

short Not long or tall: *Ken got a very short haircut.* ANTONYM: tall. **short** (SHORT) *adjective,* **shorter, shortest**.

sleepy Ready for or needing sleep: *I take a nap when I feel sleepy.*
SYNONYM: tired. **sleep•y** (SLEE pee) *adjective,* **sleepier, sleepiest**.

small Not large; little: *A mouse is a small animal.* SYNONYMS: little, tiny; ANTONYMS: big, huge, large. **small** (SMAWL) *adjective,* **smaller, smallest**.

soft 1. Easy to shape; not hard: *Pete rolled the soft clay into a ball.* 2. Smooth to the touch: *A baby has soft skin.* 3. Gentle or light; not harsh: *Lia has a soft voice.* ANTONYM: hard. **soft** (SOFT) *adjective,* **softer, softest**.

Dictionary

soon 1. In a short time: *Come see us again* **soon**. **2.** Early: *Our guests came too* **soon**. **3.** Quickly: *I'll be there as* **soon** *as I can*. **soon** (SOON) *adverb*.

start 1. To begin to act, move, or happen: *Let's* **start** *the game now*. **2.** To make something act, move, or happen: *You turn the key to* **start** *the car*. **ANTONYMS:** end, finish. **start** (STAHRT) *verb*, **started, starting**.

sunflower A large flower that grows on a tall plant: *A* **sunflower** *has a brown center and yellow petals*. **sun•flow•er** (SUN flow uhr) *noun*, *plural* **sunflowers**.

sunlight The light of the sun: *The* **sunlight** *warmed our faces*. **sun•light** (SUN lit) *noun*.

tall 1. Higher than average; not short or low: *Chicago has many* **tall** *buildings*. **2.** Having a certain height: *Jack is four feet* **tall**. **ANTONYM:** short. **tall** (TAWL) *adjective*, **taller, tallest**.

tame 1. Taken from the wild state and made gentle or obedient: *Tame elephants walked in the circus parade*. **2.** Not fearful or shy: *The birds were* **tame** *enough to eat out of my hand*. **ANTONYM:** wild. **tame** (TAYM) *adjective*, **tamer, tamest**.

today 1. The present day or time: *Is* **today** *a school day? Noun.* **2.** On or during the present day: *Do you want to go bike riding* **today**? *Adverb*. **to•day** (tuh DAY) *noun; adverb*.

tomorrow The day after today: *Today is Friday, so tomorrow will be Saturday.* Noun.

▲ On the day after today: *We're going to the beach tomorrow. Adverb.*
to•mor•row (tuh MOR oh) *noun; adverb.*

un- A prefix that means: **1.** Not: *Uncooked means not cooked.* **2.** To do the opposite of: *Unlock means to do the opposite of lock.*

waterfall A stream of water falling from a high place: *Take a picture of the lovely waterfall.*
wa•ter•fall (WAW tuhr fawl) *noun, plural* **waterfalls**.

wet Covered, soaked, or damp with water or other liquid: *My hair was wet from the rain.*
Synonyms: damp, moist; **Antonym:** dry.
wet (WET) *adjective,* **wetter, wettest.**

wild Not controlled by people; living or growing in nature: *A raccoon is a wild animal.*
Antonym: tame.
wild (WILD) *adjective,* **wilder, wildest.**

yesterday **1.** The day before today: *Yesterday was a holiday.* **2.** On the day before today: *I just started this book yesterday.*
yes•ter•day (YES tuhr day) *noun; adverb.*

young In the early part of life or growth; not old: *A lamb is a young sheep.*
Antonym: old.
young (YUNG) *adjective,* **younger, youngest.**

Index

499

Index

ACKNOWLEDGMENTS

The publisher gratefully acknowledges permission to reprint the following copyrighted material:

"Apt. 3" from *Apt.3* by Ezra Jack Keats. Copyright © 1971 by Ezra Jack Keats. Reprinted by permission of Aladdin Books.

"August Heat" from *Read-Aloud Rhymes for the Very Young* selected by Jack Prelutsky. Copyright ©1986 by Alfred A. Knopf, Inc.

"Fossils Tell of Long Ago" from *Fossils Tell of Long Ago* by Aliki. Copyright © 1972, 1990 by Aliki Brandenberg. Reprinted by permission of Harper Trophy, a division of HarperCollins Publishers.

"Higher on the Door" from *Higher on the Door* by James Stevenson. Copyright © 1987 by James Stevenson. Reprinted by permission of Greenwillow Books.

"Jamaica Tag-Along" from *Jamaica Tag-Along* by Juanita Havill. Illustrations copyright © 1989 by Anne Sibley O'Brien. Text copyright © 1989 by Juanita Havill. Reprinted by permission of Houghton Mifflin Company. All rights reserved.

"Night Animal, Day Animal" by Judith Lechner. Copyright © McGraw-Hill School Division.

"The Relatives Came" from *The Relatives Came* by Cynthia Rylant. Text copyright © 1985 Cynthia Rylant. Reprinted with the permission of Simon & Schuster Books for Young Readers, an imprint of Simon & Schuster Children's Publishing Division.

"Swimmy" from *Swimmy* by Leo Lionni. Copyright © 1963 by Leo Lionni. Reprinted by permission of Pantheon Books, a division of Random House, Inc.

"Tomás and the Library Lady" from *Tomás and the Library Lady* by Pat Mora. Illustrations copyright © 1997 by Raul Colón. Text copyright © 1997 by Pat Mora. Reprinted by permission of Alfred A. Knopf, Inc.

"When I Was Young in the Mountains" from *When I Was Young in the Mountains* by Cynthia Rylant, copyright © 1982 by Cynthia Rylant. Used by permission of Dutton Children's Books, a division of Penguin Putnam Inc.

"Which?" by James S. Tippett from *Crickety Cricket! The Best-Loved Poems of James S. Tippett*. Text copyright © 1973 by Martha K. Tippett. Reprinted by permission of HarperCollins Publishers.

"Zipping, Zapping, Zooming Bats" from *Zipping, Zapping, Zooming Bats* by Ann Earle. Illustrations copyright © 1995 by Henry Cole. Text copyright © 1995 by Ann Earle. Reprinted by permission of HarperCollins Children's Books, a division of HarperCollins Publishers.

Cover Design and Illustration: Robert Brook Allen
Cover Photo: Gary Buss/FPG International

ILLUSTRATION CREDITS: Daniel DelValle, 49, 49, 51, 119, 189, 261, 397. Lou Pappas 329, 395.

PHOTO CREDITS: All Stock-Picture Quest: Charles Krebs 343. Animals Animals: Joe McDonald 258. Art Resource: Werner Forman 399. Beaura Ringrose: 224, 399. Bob Daemmerich: 219, 220, 339. Bruce Coleman Inc.: James Blank 43; Jane Burton 142; Bob and Clara Calhoun 273; Robert Carr 156; D. Donadoni 137; Wendell Metzen 259; Jack Montgomery 268; M. Timothy O'Keefe 7; Hans Reinhard 409; Lee Rentz 487. Corbis: 320, 356, 357; Bruce Burkhardt 148, Joseph-Siffred Duplessis 324. David R. Frazier Photolibrary: 275, 286, 486; Aaron Haupt 9. DRK Photo: John Cancalosi 314; Steve Kaufman 46; Stephen J. Kraseman 246; Pat O'Hara 112; Barbara Cushman Rowell 94; Larry Ulrich 1, 131; Don and Pat Valenti 272. Earth Scenes: Patti Murray 119. EyeWire Inc.: Digital Vision 259. FPG International: 288; Paul Avis 137; Jose Luis Banus-March 225; Ken Chernus 373; Jim Cummins 186, 267, 488; Tony Miller 375. H. Armstrong Roberts, Inc.: Richard Fukuhara 197. Hutchings Photography: T2, T4, T6, T10, T13, T14, T17, 12, 38, 40, 44, 48, 49, 50, 81, 108, 110, 114, 118, 120, 129, 141, 143, 148, 154, 176, 178, 182, 186, 188, 248, 250, 254, 258, 260, 289, 316, 318, 322, 326, 328, 337, 344, 384, 386, 390, 398, 400, 407. Image Bank 221. Impact Visuals 341. Index Stock Imagery: Scott Shapiro 130. Index Stock Photography Inc.: 201, 343, 482. Lawrence Migdale 78, 163, 381. MMSD 355; Ken Cavanagh 149; Ken Karp 135; Bob Randall 196; Francis Westfield 5. Monkmeyer: Pat Farley 347. Panoramic Images: Paul Chandris 410, Jeff Lepore 402, Bruce McNitt 12, James Schwabel 290. Peter Arnold Inc.: C & M Denis-Huot 26; John Kieffer 271; Gerard Lacz 358; NASA 354. Photo Edit: 296; Bill Bachmann 212; Gary A. Conner 14, 346; Myrleen Ferguson 2, 59, 65, 99, 103, 171, 175, 245, 280; Tony Freeman 33, 35, 60, 72, 153, 327, 379; Robert Ginn 313; Spencer Grant 326; Will Hart 277; Richard Hutchings 283; John Neubauer 27; Michael Newman 15, 56, 105, 243, 266, 361, 489; Alan Oddie 491; D.A. Ramey 74; David Young-Wolff 57, 69, 73, 186, 194, 199, 216, 226, 284, 379, 412, 494. Photo Researchers, Inc.: 171; Ron Church 282; Ray Coleman 406; Gregory G. Dimijian 208; Richard Hutchings 70, 144, 281; Tom and Pat Leeson 258; Renee Lynn 285; Maslowski 128; Susan McCartney 404; Tom McHugh 239; Lawrence Migdale 222; Rod Planck 270; J. H. Robinson 406; Gregory K. Scott 224; Lee F. Snyder 276; Jim Steinberg 495; Jerry Wachter 152; Jim Weiner 340; F. Stuart Westmorland 382. Photodisc: 18, 58, 68, 132, 134, 184, 200, 202, 252, 256, 275, 336, 348. Picture Quest 6, 292. Rainbow: Coco McCoy 36, B. & J. McGrath 307. Stock • Boston: 11; J. Cancalosi 234; Bob Daemmerich 11, 33; Frank Siteman 29. Stock • Boston-Picture Quest: Eric Neurath 218. SuperStock: 3, 25, 61, 75, 77, 80, 121, 126, 129, 142, 164, 187, 243, 327, 350, 353, 370, 371, 405, 408, 484, 493; A.K.G., Berlin 326; Leslie Braddock 310; Collection of Gregory Erwin/Jane Wooster Scott 32; Christian Pierre 242; Lance Richbourg 378. The Bridgeman Art Library: Patricia Espir 170; Dora Holzhandler 102. The Granger Collection Rembrandt Peale 291. The Image Works: Bill Bachmann 213; Tom Brakefield 303; Bob Daemmerich 33, 71, 218; Townsend P. Dickinson 24; Jacksonville Journal Courier 152; James Marshall 88; Yva Momatiuk and John Eastcott 492; Okoniewski 145; Tim Reese 311. The Stock Market: 311; Roger Ball 138; Paul Barton 490; Ed Bock 294; Tom Brakefield 302; Anthony Edgeworth 360; Joe Feingersh 150; Charles Gupton 83; John Henley 165; Henley and Savage 278; Ted Horowitz 147; John Madere 304; Rob Matheson 210; Jeffrey Myers 127; Robert Ono 96; Jose L. Pelaez 151, 203, 398; Zefa Reinhard 118; Norbert Schäfer 348, 352; George Schiavone 362; Ariel Skelley 82, 167, 214, 485; William Waterfall 293. Tony Stone Images: 195; 215; Amwell 28; Dan Bosler 140; Rick Burton 48; Laurie Campbell 119; Cosmo Condina 63; Kate Connell 64; Daniel J. Cox 116, 351, 359; Bob Daemmerich 236; Tim Davis 305, 364; Philipp Engelhorn 173; Ken Fisher 372; David Hanover 64; Alan Hicks 106; Klaus Lahnstein 10; Vito Palmisano 235; Peter Pearson 4; Lori Adamski Peek 103; Greg Probst 403; John Riley 413; Hugh Sitton 84; Karen Su 359; Mike Timo 211; Keith Wood 85.